Sparks Amidst the Ashes

Sparks Amidst the Ashes

The Spiritual Legacy of Polish Jewry

Byron L. Sherwin

New York   Oxford
OXFORD UNIVERSITY PRESS
1997

Oxford University Press

Oxford New York

Athens Auckland Bangkok Bogota Bombay Buenos Aires
Calcutta Cape Town Dar es Salaam Delhi Florence Hong Kong
Istanbul Karachi Kuala Lumpur Madras Madrid Melbourne
Mexico City Nairobi Paris Singapore Taipei Tokyo Toronto

and associated companies in
Berlin Ibadan

Published by Oxford University Press, Inc.
198 Madison Avenue, New York, New York 10016

Oxford is a registered trademark of Oxford University Press

Library of Congress Cataloging-in-Publication Data
Sherwin, Byron L.
Sparks amidst the ashes : the spiritual legacy of Polish Jewry /
Byron L. Sherwin.
p. cm.
Includes bibliographical references and index.
ISBN 0-19-510685-7
1. Judaism—Poland—History.   2. Jews—Poland—Intellectual life.
3. Poland—Intellectual life.   4. Spiritual life—Judaism.
5. Rabbis—Poland.   6. Holocaust, Jewish (1939–1945)—Poland—
Influence.   I. Sherwin, Byron L. Duchowe dziedzictwo Żydów
polskich. II. Title.
BM337.S54   1997
296'.09438—dc20   96-22761

Permission has been granted to use extended quotations from the following copyrighted works:

Alfred Döblin, *Journey to Poland*, trans. Joachim Neugroschel, permission granted by Paragon House Publishers; Arnošt Lustig, *A Prayer for Katerina Horovitzova*, permission granted by the author; Hayyim Hazaz, "The Sermon," in *Israeli Stories*, ed. Joel Blocker, permission granted by Schocken Books, published by Pantheon Books, a division of Random House, Inc.; Yitzhak Katzenelson's "Song of the Murdered Jewish People," permission granted by Beit Lohamei Haghetaot (Ghetto Fighters' House, Israel), and for the English translation by N. Rosenbloom permission granted by Ha-Kibbutz Hameuchad Publishing House (in Israel). To Mrs. Ilya (Resha) Schor for permission to reproduce a facsimile of a woodcut by Ilya Schor for the book cover. This woodcut is one of a series of sixteen woodcuts designed to illustrate *The Earth Is the Lord's* by Abraham Joshua Heschel.

1 3 5 7 9 8 6 4 2

Printed in the United States of America
on acid-free paper

In Memory of My Grandparents
Faige Rivke (Fanny) Yashanofsky Rabinowitz
(Born in Warsaw in 1896; died in New York in 1968)
and
Sholom (Samuel) Rabinowitz
(Born in Berditchev in 1894; died in New York in 1963)
My Links with the Lost Atlantis of East European Jewish Life

Preface

Although I did not know it at the time, I began my research for this book when I was a very young child. It was then that my grandmother first told me about the land of her birth, the dwelling place of our ancestors, a realm far away in space and time: pre–World War I Poland. It was a domain populated by saints, scholars, and wonder-working rabbis, and marked by poverty and deprivation. It had once been the epicenter of Jewish life and learning.

In the 1950s, the New York City I knew as a child was a very "Jewish" city. Yet it was not as Jewish as had been the Warsaw of my grandmother's childhood, where one of each three inhabitants were Jews. In the years immediately preceding my birth, the Holocaust had occurred. Poland was transformed into the largest Jewish ghost town in history. A fire-spewing dragon had invaded that land, engulfing its enormous Jewish community in a flood of fire. Polish Jewry became a lost Atlantis. Yet many people who populated the world of my childhood had escaped from that place, both before and after the great conflagration. For reasons unbeknownst to me at that time, I sought out such people, eager to listen and to learn of a world that was no more.

Before I started school, I was taught how to read. My grandmother encouraged me to make books my friends, for they would never desert me; they could accompany me wherever I might go and whenever I might want their company. From then until now, books have been my constant companions. Throughout the years, I searched for books that would tell me more about the lost kingdom that my grandmother and others had described in their tales. These included books filled with terror and horror that describe how, in the years just before I was born, millions of Jews were transformed from flesh and blood into ashes and their hopes and dreams into smoke. Reflecting upon the mystery of my own existence, I realized that had my grandmother not left that land, she would have been consumed by the fire-spewing dragon of the Nazi death camps and I never would have been born.

While my preoccupation with the Holocaust did not subside, my hunger to know more about that vanished world of Polish Jewry continued to grow. This quest catapulted me back through the centuries of Jewish life in Poland. The more I became aware of the riches of the spirit created and cultivated there, the deeper grew my understanding of not only who but what was destroyed by the "Final Solution."

In my late teens I began to prepare for rabbinical studies and in my early twenties I undertook such studies. It was at this time that I met mentors who embodied the extraordinary breadth and depth that characterized the best of Jewish learning in pre–World War II Poland. Coupled with their mastery of the scope of Jewish knowledge was their astounding erudition in various areas of Western culture, including law, literature, and philosophy. Then a dying breed and now a memory, such scholars will perhaps never be seen again. They guided me through the maze of the biblical text and its large corpus of commentaries, the vast labyrinth of Talmudic literature, the complexities of Jewish philosophy, the perplexities of Jewish mysticism, the detailed analysis of Jewish law, and the limitless alleyways of Jewish literature of the ancient, medieval, and modern periods. Simultaneously I also studied the history of ideas, philosophy, and culture at some of the best American universities.

At that time, American Jews were engaged in an exercise in amnesia, trying hard to forget their largely east European roots. As they passionately pursued acculturation, social acceptance, and material success in America, their memories of life and learning in eastern Europe were quickly fading. Even in the world of Jewish learning, the Sefardic Jews of the Spanish golden age, the German Jews of the Enlightenment, and the masters of philosophy and belles lettres of both medieval and modern times were the focus of scholarly study, research, and writing. The vast legacy of piety and learning created by the lost Atlantis of Polish Jewry was largely ignored, except as a nostalgic reminiscence. The east European experience was spurned and rejected as having little to contribute to the re-creation of Jewish life in the New World.

Even among those of my teachers who had come from that lost world, there was little interest in conveying the shattered fragments of that realm to their American students. Instead, they taught us how ancient Babylonian inscriptions could elucidate the Bible, how ancient Greek literature could be utilized to uncover new meanings of Talmudic texts, how Roman law compared to Jewish law, how Arabic philosophy influenced medieval Jewish philosophy, and how Russian literature inspired a preoccupation with certain motifs in the development of early modern Hebrew literature. Only one of my mentors, who became my master, helped me to continue my search for the lost Atlantis of east European Jewish life and thought. This was Abraham Joshua Heschel, the preeminent Jewish theologian of our times, whose name will appear frequently in the pages that follow. He introduced me to many of the spiritual luminaries who populated the landscape of Jewish life and thought in Poland in centuries past. When he would discuss them, he demonstrated a familiarity with their lives and works that made one believe he had just concluded an intimate conversation with them. Many of these scholars and masters of piety had been his forebears. When he taught their writings, told their tales, and discussed their ideas, it was like being part of a family reunion.

At a seemingly arbitrary juncture in my studies, I received a variety of degrees and certificates informing me that somehow I had made the transition from a pupil to a teacher, from a reader to a potential author, from a student to a scholar. I began to teach and to write. Yet my childhood preoccupation with the spiritual legacy of Polish Jewry stayed with me. I continued to learn more and to understand less about the Holocaust. I continued my research and writing about east European Jewish life and thought.

In the meantime, my daily personal and professional encounters with Jewish communal life convinced me that American Jewry was committing spiritual suicide. Materially robust, socially self-assertive, and enormously effective in sociopolitical activities, American Jewry nonetheless seemed to be suffering from an advanced stage of spiritual atrophy of which it appeared to be unaware. Jewish life had become a spiritual wasteland; it had formulated and predicated its communal existence upon a set of dogmas that had coalesced in a "civil religion" for American Jews that bore little resemblance to the ideas and values that constituted the spiritual heritage of Judaism, and that both neglected and negated the spiritual legacy of Polish Jewry. In effect, American Jewry had become a *non sequitur* in relation to the spiritual inheritance bequeathed by its forebears. It had become discontinuous with the past. The chain of tradition had been broken. A precious bequest was being squandered. In Heschel's view, it was like a "second Holocaust," an exercise in spiritual suicide disguised as a success story in social dynamics, political activism, and communal organization.

In the early 1990s I became involved in groundbreaking though highly controversial work in the area of Polish-Jewish/Catholic-Jewish relations both in Poland and the United States. Numerous visits to Poland introduced me to the actual places where the spiritual heritage of Polish Jewry had developed down through the centuries, as well as to the locations in which the mass murder of much of European Jewry had taken place. Being in Poland stimulated my desire to retrace my ancestors' steps, to engage in intensive genealogical research in order to discover who my forebears were and how their story merged into the historical experience of Polish Jewry I had studied for so many years. The proximity in time and space, during my multiple visits to Poland, of seeing both the remains of the Nazi ghettos and death camps and those of the cities and towns where the Polish masters of Jewish piety, learning, and spirituality once lived led me to a number of conclusions based upon premises and discussions that are detailed in the various chapters of this book.

First, any forthright and authentic response to the Holocaust must include an intimate encounter with the spiritual legacy of Polish Jewry.

Second, the spiritual heritage of Polish Jewry, not the "civil religion" of contemporary Jewry, offers the most viable foundation for Jewish continuity and for the re-creation of Jewish life and thought in the present and future.

Third, for the majority of North American Jews who are of east European origin, east European Jewish life and thought holds the key to their physical and spiritual identity.

Fourth, the treasure trove of spiritual insight created by Polish Jewry can effectively address and inform the spiritual malaise, disorientation, and alienation increasingly characteristic of the contemporary human condition.

On a more prosaic but necessary note, it is important for me to mention that throughout this book Polish and Hebrew transliterations are given without diacritical marks. Readers of these languages should nonetheless be able to decode the terms noted. Most Polish terms are names of places where the spiritual masters of Polish Jewry lived. While these places are known in Hebrew and Yiddish sources by their designations in those languages, I also wanted to include their Polish names for two reasons. First, the proper geographical names of these places are usually their designations in Polish. And, second, I wish to demonstrate that Jewish life flourished for many centuries in almost every corner of the historical lands of Poland. Polish names of towns and cities are usually given only the first time they are mentioned in the text. For any errors in this book, I apologize in advance.

Chicago, Ill.   B. L. S.
February 18, 1996

Acknowledgments

During my visits to Poland, I had occasion to deliver lectures and to participate in conferences at a variety of academic, religious, and professional institutions. These included the University of Warsaw, the Jewish Historical Institute, the Academy of Catholic Theology, the Academy of Christian Theology, and the Metropolitan Children's Hospital (all in Warsaw); the Jagiellonian University, the Pontifical Theological Academy, and the Jesuit College (all in Cracow); diocesan seminaries in Lublin, Wloclawek, Gniezno, Bialystok, and Poznan; and the Auschwitz-Birkenau State Museum. Some of these places involved multiple visits. Many of these lectures were published in various journals in Poland in Polish translation, including *Collectanea Theologica* and *Przeglad Powszechny*. In 1995 these lectures were collected and published in book form by Vocatio Publishing Company of Warsaw under the title *Duchowe Dziedzietwo Zydow Polskich* (*The Spiritual Heritage of Polish Jews*). Soon after the publication of that volume, I decided to completely recast, rewrite, and expand its contents into a book for an English-speaking public. This work is the result of that effort.

My participation in an ongoing Polish-Jewish dialogue that led to the publication of my Polish book and subsequently to this English-language volume would not have been possible without the help, support, and encouragement of many individuals, both in Poland and the United States. To them goes my deepest gratitude. These include Joseph Cardinal Bernardin, archbishop of Chicago; Joseph Cardinal Glemp, primate of Poland; Franciscus Cardinal Macharski, archbishop of Cracow; Henryk Muszynski, archbishop of Gniezno; Dr. Howard A. Sulkin, president of the Spertus Institute of Jewish Studies; Alfred Abramowicz, bishop of Chicago; Father Joseph Mytych of Chicago; Michal Grocholski and the late Dr. Hubert Romanowski, consuls general of the Republic of Poland in Chicago; and Andrzej Jaroszynski, consul at the Polish Consulate in Chicago and, more recently, of the Polish Embassy in Washington, D.C. I am also especially grateful to Tadeusz Debski and Elizabeth Slosarski of Chicago, who selflessly gave much-needed assistance, advice, and help whenever it was requested. My secretary, Pamela Spitzner, utilized her considerable technical skills in the preparation of the many drafts of this book; to her go my deep thanks. I am also grateful to the Polish Council of Christians and Jews for bestowing upon me the first Man of Reconciliation Award in 1992 for my work in fostering a Polish-Jewish dialogue. And I am thankful to the former president of the Republic of Poland, Lech Walesa, for awarding me the Officer's Medal of Merit in recognition of my efforts. Without the dedicated and tireless help and support of my friend and colleague Father Dr. Waldemar Chrostowski of the Academy of Catholic Theology of Warsaw, little of what I was able to accomplish in Poland would have been attained. To him I owe abiding gratitude.

To Cynthia Read, executive editor at Oxford University Press, I wish to express my profound thanks for agreeing to undertake the publication of this volume. Because of the deep personal meaning this book has for me, I am especially grateful that it is being published by such a venerable and prestigious publisher as Oxford University Press. I am also grateful to my friend and colleague Howard Schwartz for encouraging me to submit the proposal for this book to Oxford University Press. Also, I am grateful to my friend and colleague Harold Kasimow for his confidence in my work in this area of research and writing. To Rosaline Cohn and the Cohn Scholars' Fund, I am grateful for financial support that helped to defray some expenses related to the preparation of this book.

Though my work in furthering Polish-Jewish dialogue through my writing and research has not proceeded without problems and frustrations, these have been offset by the patience and support of my precious friend and cherished colleague Krystyna Zielinski-Zambrzycki, European-American consultant of the Catholic Archdiocese of Chicago. Her wisdom and encouragement served both as a gyroscope and a rudder as I tried to sort out the mass of information, the diverse experiences, and the turbulent emotions that inevitably characterized my encounter with Poland, past and present. She enabled me to extract profound personal meaning and an unexpected depth of self-understanding and spiritual transformation from an emotional and intellectual roller-coaster ride that shuttled me between the present and the past.

This book is dedicated to my beloved grandparents of blessed memory. My grandfather, Samuel Rabinowitz, who was born in Berditchev, taught me many things; most important, I learned from him how to express unconditional love and how to act in accordance with deep personal commitment. My grandmother, Fanny Yashanofsky Rabinowitz, was born in Warsaw. Her forebears came to Poland in the mid-fifteenth century and dwelled there until they left for America in the first years of the twentieth century. Among the many things I learned from her was the need to perpetuate the story of our Polish ancestors. I hope that this heritage will be preserved and transmitted by my son, Jason, and by other members of my family. To Jason and to my ever-patient wife, Judith, my gratitude for their forbearance whenever I travel to Poland, whether across the sea by airplane or across the centuries while secluded in my study.

Contents

Sparks Amidst the Ashes

To rekindle the flame,
search for sparks
amidst the ashes.

Dov Baer of Mezeritch

To Reclaim a Legacy

An ancient Jewish legend tells that when the Holy Temple in Jerusalem had been set ablaze by the enemy and its destruction was imminent, a group of priests climbed up to the roof and held the keys to the Temple aloft. Thereupon, a hand reached down from heaven to reclaim the keys for safekeeping.[1] Centuries later, another conflagration began that ultimately would decimate the countless temples of stone, wood, and flesh that constituted the Jewish community of Poland. This time, however, no angelic hand reached down to reclaim the keys. They remained in the hands of the citizens of the lost Atlantis of the Polish-Jewish community that was consumed by a flood of fire. What was once the greatest Jewish community in the world is now little more than a memory, a fastly fading photo in the family album of the Jewish people.

In 1939, on the eve of the Holocaust, more than 80 percent of all the Jews in the world were either living in the historic Polish lands or were descended from Jews who had lived there.[2] Now, little remains in Poland of what once was. There are synagogues without worshipers, homes without their inhabitants, tombstones without graves, graves without tombstones, and memories that have faded into oblivion. Gone is the Polish Jew, a vital organ of Jewish life, an integral part of Polish historical experience.

Gone are the candles, flickering on a Friday night to welcome the Sabbath Queen in thousands upon thousands of Jewish homes throughout Poland. Gone are the Hanukkah candelabras burning brightly with the memory and the hope of freedom. Gone is the sound of the blast from the shofar (ram's horn) announcing a Jewish New Year.

Gone is the taste of matzot, the bread of affliction and of liberation, eaten at the Passover meal and gone, too, are the aromatic spices inhaled to bid adieu to the Sabbath each week. Gone is the hum of study in the rabbinic academies, and men who enveloped their bodies in prayer shawls to pray to God. Gone are the Yiddish poets who argued passionately with God about the way the world is run, and gone are the Hasidic Jews who danced through the night hoping that, in losing themselves in God, they would find God.

Gone are the families of the great Jewish novelists and poets who immeasurably enriched the literature of Poland and the world. The Krochmalna Street in today's Warsaw bears little resemblance to the Krochmalna Street of which Isaac Bashevis Singer wrote. Gone too is the family of the "Dr. Seuss of Poland," Julian Tuwim, who when asked why he was a Jew said, "I am a Jew because I like it."

In 1945 the sage known as the Preacher of Helm arrived at the Israeli port of Haifa from Poland. In his hand was a large cage filled with birds. The customs agent asked him, "Why have you brought these birds all the way from Europe? Are there no birds in the Land of Israel?" "Yes, there are birds here," the sage replied, "but in Poland there are now no Jewish children left to feed them."[3]

In his classic poem "The Song of the Murdered Jewish People" the Yiddish poet Yitzhak Katzenelson, who witnessed the destruction of the Warsaw Ghetto, writes of the end of the Polish-Jewish community. Katzenelson saw his wife and his two youngest sons deported from the ghetto, never to return. On April 30, 1944, Katzenelson arrived in Auschwitz, where he and his oldest son, Zvi, were gassed to death on the same day. Katzenelson was murdered, but his lament for a world destroyed lives on. He wrote:

Ten a day, then a thousand Jews a day.
Soon they took fifteen thousand.
Warsaw! The city of Jews—the fenced-in, walled-in city
Dwindled, expired, melted like snow before my eyes. . . .
They suffered more and greater pains, each one.
The little, simple ordinary Jew from Poland of today—
Compared with him, what are the great men of a past bygone?
A wailing Jeremiah, Job afflicted, Kings despairing, all in one—it's they. . . .
Show yourself, my people. Emerge, reach out
From the miles-long, dense, deep ditches
Covered with lime and burned, layer upon layer,
Rise up! up! from the deepest, bottomless layer!

Come from Treblinka, Sobibor, Auschwitz,
Come from Belzec, Ponari, from all the other camps,
With wide open eyes, frozen cries, and soundless screams. . . .

Come, you dried, ground, crushed Jewish bones.
Come, form a big circle around me, one great ring—
Grandfathers, grandmothers, fathers, mothers, carrying babies. . . .
Come Jewish bones, made into powder and soap.

Emerge, reveal yourselves to me. Come, all of you, come.
I want to see you. I want to look at you. I want
Silently and mutely to behold my murdered people. . . .

Never will the voice of Torah be heard from yeshivot, synagogues and pale
    students . . .
Masters of Talmud and Codes . . . all gone.

Never will a Jewish mother cradle a baby . . .
Never will plaintive songs of Jewish poets be sung.
All's gone, gone.
No Jewish theater where men will laugh or silently shed a tear.
No Jewish musicians or painters to create and innovate in joy and sorrow. . . .

Woe is unto me, nobody is left.
There was a people, and it is no more.
There was a people and it is—Gone.[4]

It is a Jewish custom to place small stones on a grave one visits to show that someone has been there, that someone remembers the person buried there. But most Jewish
graves in Poland have no tombstones on which to place small stones. Instead, millions who died during the Nazi horror dug their graves in the sky. These graves hover
over the gray landscape of the Nazi death camps. And of those Jews who have both
graves and tombstones, few have small stones upon them. No one remembers them.

Stones are symbols of memory. Perhaps only the stones know what people have
forgotten. Perhaps only the stones remember the Jews of Poland: in 1931, 32 percent
of the population of Lodz, 26 percent of the population of Cracow, 35 percent of the
population of Lublin, 43 percent of the population of Bialystok—10 percent of the
population of all of Poland.[5] There are too many to remember, too many to forget.
Are there enough stones in all of Poland to remember the lost Atlantis of Polish Jewry?

For Jews, amnesia is an especially deadly disease. Without memory, the Jew is a
conclusion without a premise, a fallacy. In Judaism, faith is rooted in the memory of
significant events; to believe is to remember. As the eminent twentieth-century Jewish theologian Abraham Joshua Heschel wrote, "The riches of a soul are stored up in
its memory. This is the test of character—not whether a person follows the daily fashion, but whether the past is alive in his present. When we want to understand ourselves, to find out what is most precious in our lives, we search our memory. . . .
Remembrance is the touchstone of all actions."[6]

Abraham Joshua Heschel bore the name of his ancestor, Abraham Joshua
Heschel, the rabbi of Apt (Polish: Opatow). The rabbi of Apt believed in the kabbalistic
doctrine of transmigration of souls. This belief articulates a profound insight: to know
who we *are*, we must know who we *were*. For many of today's Jews, knowing who
they are means knowing who they were when they dwelled in Poland. While the Jews
no longer dwell in Poland, Poland still dwells in the Jews. By encountering the Jewish past in Poland, a Jew can recover past memories, nearly surrendered legacies, a
rapidly fading identity, a quickly evaporating continuity. Through discovering his or
her past in Poland, the Jew of today can remember who he was, who she is.

Losing one's memory means losing one's mind. Bereft of memory, a person
becomes *dis*membered from his or her own self. Life without memory is no life at all.
Memory is the custodian of that which we consider meaningful; it is the novelist of the
soul, providing a plot and forging coherency from seemingly unrelated facts and events.
Memory differs from nostalgia, for while nostalgia idealizes a frozen past, memory links
the past with a living present and with an anticipated future. Rooted in the past, memory
is a key to identity, continuity, and creativity, while nostalgia is sterile, stillborn.[7]

A generation of Jewish immigrants and their children, anxious to cut the cord with Europe and to embrace Americanization, summarily surrendered the rich spiritual heritage that was their birthright. The past was reviled, discarded, rejected. Now these sacred sparks are trapped in the shards of commercialized souvenirs and trivialized nostalgia.

Memories of the spiritual legacy of Polish Jewry are fading into oblivion. The arias of ideas, the symphonies of the soul created by a millennium of Jewish life in Poland are being supplanted by nostalgic reminiscences that have little relation to what once was. Precious memories are being eclipsed by the virtual reality of "cybershtetl." The holy has been exchanged for the grotesque. For example, in elegant restaurants in Warsaw catering to American Jewish tourists and to the Polish chic, non-Jewish waiters dress in Hasidic garb—yarmulkes, caftans, fringes (tzitzit)—to serve Polish sausage (kielbasa) to a nostalgia-hungry clientele while violinists play serenades from *Fiddler on the Roof*.[8] Cherished memories have been replaced by cheap commercial gimmicks. A tradition of spiritual elegance has been reduced to an exercise in uninformed bad taste. Meanwhile, authentic memories fade into the shadows of a forgotten past.

It was the nineteenth-century Hasidic master called the Seer of Lublin who taught that each person should be like a baby, for a baby can laugh and cry at the same time.[9] Jews visiting Poland today must laugh and cry, be happy and sad, simultaneously. They must rejoice in the enormous educational, cultural, and spiritual accomplishments of the Jews during their thousand-year-long residence on Polish soil. But at the same time one must cry because it was in Poland that millions of Jews were murdered by the Nazis during World War II. In the mausoleum at Majdanek, where the remains of many of victims are kept, there is this inscription: "I see my relatives in each handful of ashes." Being aware of the vital Jewish presence and creativity in Poland before 1939 makes realizing what was done there all the more difficult to bear.

Only when what existed in Poland before the Holocaust is understood can one truly discern the dimensions of the loss. From this perspective, it is important for Jews today to see Poland not only as a huge Jewish cemetery, but also as a country where Jews created unprecedented works of the spirit, as a land where Judaism flourished freely and developed beyond what it previously had been, as a landscape dotted with Jewish spiritual monuments. To understand the Holocaust in terms of what was lost, to understand Judaism in terms of what it is, Jews must become more aware of what treasures of the spirit Jews produced in Poland. An authentic response to the Holocaust aimed at re-creating Jewish life after death must first appreciate *what* as well as *who* was destroyed. For Jews to abandon their religious and spiritual traditions—to allow these spiritual monuments to be cast into oblivion—would in effect give the Nazis a posthumous victory by completing the process of the destruction of Judaism. A refocusing of Jewish attention upon the spiritual treasures and monuments of Polish Jewry represents a desirable shift from an obsession with Jewish survival, and from a preoccupation with sterile nostalgia, to a heightened awareness of the need for Jewish continuity and spiritual revival.

There are two components to being a Jew: Jewish religion and the Jewish people. The two are inseparable. One cannot be a part of the faith-community of Judaism without being a part of the Jewish people. Yet throughout Jewish history theologians have posed the question: Do the people of Israel exist by virtue of Judaism; or does Judaism exist because of the Jewish people? In medieval Jewish philosophy, both views are represented. Saadya Gaon, who lived in the tenth century, claimed that Jews are a people only by virtue of Judaism.[10] On the other hand, the twelfth-century poet and philosopher Judah Halevi reminds us that "if there were no Jews, there would be no Judaism."[11]

For centuries, the view expressed by Saadya was the dominant one. The preservation and the continuity of Jewish faith took precedence. Since Jewish faith was assumed to be the raison d'être for the existence of the Jewish people, the primacy of the religion of the Jews over the Jewish people was affirmed both in theological teachings and in communal actions. But with the Holocaust this changed. The priority became the physical survival of the Jewish people. It is now becoming increasingly clear, however, that Jewish religious faith provides the basis for the meaning of Jewish survival; that spiritual meaning is the premise on which physical survival is based. Jewish survival for the sake of survival is logically a tautology and sociologically a self-defeating strategy. Preoccupation with Jewish survival has deflected attention from the fundamental question: Survival for what? Without identifying a source of meaning, sheer survival becomes meaningless. Viktor Frankl, reflecting on his survival at Auschwitz, quoted Nietzsche: "A person with a *why* to live can bear with almost any *how*."[12]

Contrary to popular assumptions, quantity does not necessarily ensure either the survival or the continuity of Judaism. As Salo Baron, the most significant Jewish historian of the twentieth century, commented, "In a sense, Judaism is independent of the number of those who profess it."[13] Reflecting on the future of Jewish life in America, he continued:

> When we speak about the future of the Jews in the United States quality is certainly at least as important as quantity. . . . If I were assured today that a generation hence we shall have 100 first-rate Jewish scholars, 100 first-rate rabbis, 100 first-rate teachers, 100 first-rate communal leaders and 100 first-rate writers, publicists and artists—their total number would amount to only 500, which in a population of some five million would be just one-hundredth of one percent—I should feel assured nevertheless of a great future for the Jews in this country. For I would feel confident that that 500 would detect the necessary paths to guide their people through the perplexities of life under the conditions of modern existence in the Western Hemisphere.[14]

For the majority of American Jews who have their roots in the historic lands of Poland, what was taught and lived by Polish Jewry can provide a key to Jewish meaning, to Jewish identity, to the re-creation of the shattered Jewish soul. Roots offer a foundation both for meaning and identity. Twenty-three centuries ago Oedipus cried out, "I must find out who I am and where I came from!" More recently, Alex Haley wrote in his book *Roots*, "I had to find out who I was. . . . I needed to find meaning in my life."[15]

A few months after World War II ended and the devastation of Polish Jewry sank into the consciousness of the Polish-Jewish diaspora in America, a memorial meeting was held in New York. At that occasion, Abraham Joshua Heschel said:

A world has vanished. All that remains is a sanctuary hidden in the realm of spirit. We of this generation are still holding the key. Unless we remember, unless we unlock it, the holiness of ages will remain a secret of God. We of this generation are still holding the key—the key to the sanctuary which is also the shelter of our own deserted souls. If we mislay the key, we shall elude ourselves.

In this hour we, the living, are "the people of Israel." The tasks, begun by the patriarchs and prophets and continued by their descendants, are now entrusted to us. We are either the last Jews or those who will hand over the entire past to generations to come. We will either forfeit or enrich the legacy of ages.[16]

Later in his life, reflecting on American Jewry's neglect of its spiritual heritage, Heschel observed, "Hitler destroyed our people. Now we let their spirit die." For Heschel, this was a "second Holocaust"—one perpetrated by Jews upon their own legacy, an exercise in spiritual suicide.[17]

Polish Jewry is no more, but its spiritual bequest survives. In Poland today the absence of Jews is their presence, because the reality of that absence can be felt in Polish cities and towns. For this reason, when in Poland a Jew is never alone. The souls of his ancestors welcome him, embrace him. Countless Jewish souls inhabit Poland. They do not want Jews who come to Poland to feel lonely in a land where so few Jews now reside. Or, perhaps, it is they who are lonely, and it is we who can comfort them in their loneliness—they are parents whose children have gone away, grandparents whose grandchildren departed long ago. Some of their descendants settled in far-off places—North America, Argentina, Israel. Others were sent to their deaths by the Nazis: almost three million Polish Jews were turned into smoke and ashes simply because they were Jews. Jews can journey to Poland to let their ancestors know that they have not been forgotten, that they are not abandoned. By confronting the dissolving inheritance of the past, descendants of Polish Jews can recapture an otherwise lost legacy, an otherwise obliterated identity.

Whether a journey through time or through space, or both, an encounter with the spiritual and historical dimensions of the Jewish past in Poland can become an adventure in self-understanding. For the Jewish person, Poland cannot be a realm for voyeuristic tourism, but it can readily become a spot where the Jewish soul may recover its own lost possessions.

There is a Hasidic tradition that one's soul is like a flame consisting of many sparks. Some of these sacred sparks dwell within the self; others live in exile, scattered throughout the world. To reunite these dislocated sparks with the soul-root, a person must journey to the place where the sparks reside. Once there, the individual is obliged to perform a sacred deed whereby the abandoned sparks may be redeemed and restored to their spiritual home, allowing the person to go from a state of spiritual alienation to spiritual wholeness. People can become whole by relocating, elevating, and integrating these hitherto lost elements of their spiritual identity into their soul. According to this teaching, each person has a unique mission that no one else can accomplish. The sparks of each of our souls wait for us to free them from the places of their indeterminable exile.[18] Each of us has a mission to merge the sparks already within us with those that await us. In the words of the nineteenth-century Hasidic master Levi Yitzhak of Berditchev (Polish: Berdyczow), "It is a great principle that to each place a person may journey, that person goes toward his or her source, for undoubtedly the source of his or her being is in that place. Once there, the individual needs to elevate the sparks found there so that they may become [reintegrated] with it [i.e., with the other sparks of the individual's soul-root]."[19] Through a rendezvous with one's Polish past, a Jew has the opportunity to recover the exiled sparks that are destined to be reunited with his or her own soul. In this way, one may discover who he or she is; one may become spiritually whole.

The Ba'al Shem Tov, the founder of Hasidism, taught that even a business trip can be a disguised opportunity for a spiritual reunion. "Sometimes," said the Ba'al Shem Tov, "a person must travel a long distance and he thinks he is traveling for business, but the intended purpose [of the journey] is that there is a spark that he must elevate . . . and every holy spark must be uplifted by that very person, for it is a portion of his soul that cannot be uplifted by anyone else."[20]

In May 1990 I took my first business trip to Poland. The "business" was interfaith dialogue. Yet what I discovered was that the Ba'al Shem Tov was right. What follows is the story of a journey that was to carry me across the ocean to Poland, across the centuries to the distant past. It is also the journal of an inward journey during which the life I seemingly had chosen began to look as if it had been scripted long ago by people I never knew—people who happened to be my ancestors. Unbeknownst to me, when I first visited Poland in 1990 a séance with my ancestors, an encounter with realities behind the pages of books I had studied for years, and an adventure of self-discovery was about to begin. My "business trip" soon became a portal not only to the past and the present, but to the future as well.

My point of departure at the time seemed to be O'Hare International Airport in Chicago, but, as I ultimately learned, my real points of departure were my childhood, my professional career, and a summons from my forebears. What I discovered not only shed light upon my own life and work, but illuminated a path to a mandated agenda for contemporary Jewry, an agenda rooted in the spiritual heritage of Polish Jewry.

Grandmother's Tales

The great psychotherapist Alfred Adler would always ask a patient in the beginning stages of therapy: "What are your earliest childhood memories?" He recognized that early memories often play a decisive role in shaping who we are and what we can become. Among my earliest memories are the Polish lullabies Grandma sang to me, the smell and taste of the kasha she fed me, the stories she told me. Long before I visited Poland for the first time, I was familiar with many things I would encounter there. Though I had studied for many years about Jewish life and thought in Poland, those memories of my grandmother seemed much more real and poignant than the information I was able to glean from books. Yet the key to relating my quest for knowledge to my search for self-understanding emerged in a quotation from the Hasidic master Rabbi Mendel of Kotzk (Polish: Kock): "What good is there in understanding a text if by so doing a person does not also understand his or her own self?"[1]

In Yiddish the term *bube-meises*, or "grandmother's tales," refers to stories not to be taken very seriously. This term is often translated as "tall stories" or "fairy-tales." But to the child I once was, as well as to the adult I became, these stories were of utmost significance. As Rabbi Nahman of Bratzlav put it, "Some say that the purpose of stories is to put people to sleep, but I say that stories are for waking people up." For the Hasidim, the goal of storytelling is to awaken one's spiritual potentialities, to allow the heart to surprise the mind. Through the act of hearing, words enter the body through the ear, thereby becoming incorporated into the self. The Hasidim taught that by repeating a tale, by reciting a text, one could become a participant in the event described, though the event itself might be far away both in time and in space. By responding to the tale, one could enter into a conversation with those from other times and from other places. For some of the Hasidic masters, travel through time and space by means of stories could bring a modicum of redemption to the world. It could redeem the exiled sparks of one's own soul.[2]

"When I was a little girl, about your age," Grandma would say as she began her favorite family saga, "my parents and I and my brothers and sisters lived in Warsaw, but before then our family lived in Makow." This was not a fairy-tale that she would read mechanically, but a memory that she would recall passionately—as if telling the tale would keep the past alive. This was not "once upon a time," but about a particular time in a specific place. This was not about strangers in some mythical land, but about "our family" and "our town." But for the little child I was, a hundred years before was still "once upon a time," and Makow was little different from Never-Never-Land.

"Where is Makow?" I would ask.

"Far, far away—in a land called Poland, the land where I was born."

"Farther than Florida, farther than California?"

"Yes, even farther away than that."

"Near where Snow White lives?"

"Maybe even farther away than that."

Like most Jewish stories, the primary purpose of the telling was not entertainment but the conveyance of a lesson. The message of her favorite story about her "famous" ancestor "the Makower Ruf" was to teach a simple rule of behavior: do not open empty bottles. ("*Ruf*" was how she pronounced "*Rav*"—Rabbi.)

Grandma began again, "When I was a very little girl about your age. . . ."

As usual I interrupted, "Did you live in the Bronx like now?"

"No, sweetheart, it was many, many years ago. Twelve years before I even came to America. Then I lived in Warsaw, in Poland—far, far away, across the ocean."

"Did your Mommy and Daddy come with you to America, and where are they now? I have never met them."

"Yes," she said. "They came with me to America. But they both died before you were born."

"Will you die too, Grandma? I don't want you to die. Why must people die?"

"One day I too will die. That is why I want to tell you this story. Remember this story and the others I tell you about who you are and about where we come from. If my stories remain with you, then I remain with you and the people in the stories remain with you—even after I'm gone. And when one day you will, God willing, be a daddy and a grandpa, you can tell these stories to your children, to your grandchildren."

I did not understand what she said or why she cried when she said it. She felt my mounting anxiety, and to assuage it she placed before me a glass of milk and a generous slice of her homemade sponge cake.

Patiently, she began once again, "When I was a little girl, just about your age, my mommy and daddy took me to visit my grandpa and grandma in the little town of Makow. We traveled by horse and wagon from the big city of Warsaw; it took half a day to get there. The next morning, I went looking around the house. On the wall in the house, there were shelves where my grandma kept the dishes and the glasses, and on the shelf way on top there was only one thing—an empty bottle. I wanted to see what was in the bottle. It stood alone on the top shelf as if it were waiting for me to come to open it.

"When no one was watching, I pushed one of my grandpa's big chairs next to the shelves, and I climbed onto the chair. I stretched until I could almost touch the bottle. Then I stood on my tiptoes and stretched again. The bottle tipped over and began to roll on the shelf and was about to fall when my grandma caught it and put it back. She then turned to me. Her eyes were filled not with anger but with fear. She lifted her hand as if she did not want to do what she felt she had to do, and she hit me on my behind. I began to cry. It was the only time she ever hit me. 'Grandma, why did you hit me? You never hit me before.' She gave me some milk and some sponge cake, and she told me why she hit me.

"'This bottle,' my grandma said to me, 'belonged to my father, the famous Makower Ruf—the chief rabbi of the town of Makow. Once a woman was brought to him, and there was a dybbuk inside this woman. The dybbuk made her do strange things. She would speak languages she could not possibly know. She would lift things that even three strong men could not lift. She would speak one minute with the voice of a man, the next with the voice of a woman, and the next with the voice of a child. She would move her body in strange ways. Sometimes she would whisper and other times she would scream and everyone in the town would hear her cries and become frightened. Somehow she knew secrets about everyone she could see, as if she could read people's deepest thoughts. Sometimes she would sit with her eyes open as if she were asleep, and sometime she would run with her eyes closed, somehow knowing where she was going. None of the doctors in the town knew what to do. None of their medicines helped. As days and weeks passed, she only got worse.

"'One day, her husband and her father decided that there was only one thing left to do, one thing left to try, one person left to see. And so they brought her—held by the strongest men in the town—to my father, the Makower Ruf.

"'When she saw him, she became wild. As if they were light as feathers, she pushed away the strongest men in the town. Her husband grabbed her, but she pushed him away, too. Everyone was frightened that she might kill someone. She started to throw the chairs and the tables around the house.

"'The Makower Ruf stood still, stroking his long white beard while he was concentrating on his prayers.

"'Suddenly, he looked at her and in a loud voice, he said,

"''Dybbuk, by the authority of the Rabbinic Court of the holy community of Makow, I command you to sit."

"'And the woman sat in a chair and was silent.

"''Dybbuk," he said, "who are you, and why have you entered the body of this pious woman?"

"'The woman looked at him. Her eyes were red with anger. Her face looked as if she had drunk sour milk. Suddenly, she spit at him. He wiped it off his coat, and he said again in a deep, strong voice,

"''Dybbuk, who are you, and why have you entered the body of this pious woman? By the authority of the Rabbinic Court of the holy community of Makow, I order you to answer me."

"''I am the soul of a great saint . . ." the woman began to say, but the Makower Ruf raised his right arm and said,

"''You lie, dybbuk. The soul of a great saint would not enter the body of this pious woman."

"'He opened a holy Hebrew book and he began to read what was printed there. Then he removed the shoe and stocking on her right foot. He quickly took the shofar, the ram's horn, and he blew on it many times. He read some more from the book and he put out the flames on the black candles that were lit in the room. And then, in a soft voice, almost a whisper, he said,

""'Dybbuk, in the name of the Rabbinic Court of the holy community of Makow, I command you to leave the body of this pious daughter of Israel."

""'No, I will not leave. I will not leave," said the dybbuk in a cackling voice.

"'In a louder, firmer, and deeper voice, the Makower Ruf said again,

""'Dybbuk, in the name of the Rabbinic Court of the holy community of Makow, I command you to leave the body of this woman—now. And I excommunicate your soul from the people of Israel."

"'The woman screamed, and her screams were heard throughout the town.

""'You do not have the power to make me leave!"

"'He read some more from the holy book. He blew again on the ram's horn, and in a deep and powerful voice, he said,

""'Dybbuk—I now command you—leave. Be gone. Depart."

"'The woman stretched her hands and legs and she looked like she was seven feet tall. She screamed like a wild beast caught in a trap from which there was no escape.

"'The Makower Ruf took a bottle from the shelf and placed it on the woman's big toe. The toe swelled until it was almost as big as her head. As she slumped in her chair as if she had fainted, a strange green gas was seen coming from her toe and entering the bottle. The Makower Ruf sealed the bottle with a cork.

"'The woman awoke, cheerful, as if from a long and restful sleep.

""'Rabbi," she said, "why am I here? Where is my husband? Where are my children?"

"'Not knowing why, she kissed the Makower Ruf's hand. She arose from the chair and said, "I must go home and cook dinner."

""'Remember to recite some of the Psalms every day and give thanks to the God of mercy and love," said the Makower Ruf.'"

"And so, you see," Grandma said, "what seems to be is not always what is. An empty bottle may not be an empty bottle. It may be a bottle in which a dybbuk lives, waiting to get out and hurt little boys and little girls—and even grandmas."

Years later, when I began to study kabbalah, the Jewish mystical tradition, I researched the traditions about the dybbuk.[3] But none of the texts I read, and none of the stories they told, seemed as real, as frightening, or as true as the tale of the Makower Ruf that Grandma told me as a child.

That night I found it hard to sleep. I was afraid that a dybbuk might enter my body. Yet the story of my great-great-great-grandfather's encounter with the dybbuk was far less terrifying than my reaction to seeing some of Grandma's old photographs from that distant realm of mystery called "Poland."

Grandma had a drawer in which she placed all of her photographs. There were photos of my mother when she was a girl, photos of my grandparents when they were young, of my aunts and uncles, and baby photos of me. A few photos were very old, tattered, and torn. One was a photograph of the portion of Grandma's family, of my family, that had not emigrated from Poland to America. Grandma told me the name of each of the more than thirty of her—of my—aunts, uncles, and cousins in the picture. There were old, young, and middle-aged men and women, and there were many, many little children. I told my grandmother that one day I would like to travel to Warsaw to meet them, to meet my family in Poland.

"You cannot meet them," Grandma said, her eyes filling with tears.

"Why, Grandma, why can I not meet them, and why, Grandma, are you crying? Do not cry, Grandma. I know they are far away, but one day you and I will go together to Warsaw and I will meet them and you will see them again. I know that you must miss them."

She sighed and said, "You will never meet them, and I can only see them again in this photograph. You see, they are all dead. They were killed by very bad people called Nazis during the world war."

"Why, Grandma? Why were they killed?" I asked, starting to cry myself.

She smiled and said, "When you get older, then you will understand."

I have gotten older, but still I do not understand. I have tried to understand. I have read many books about what happened, spoken to many people, including many survivors, about what happened, but still I do not understand. I know the major characters of the story, the facts of the story, and how it ends. Still, I do not understand why. Why people did what they did to other people; why people stood by and watched it happen; and why God allowed it to be done. Scholars have provided us with much information and with many theories. We know more and more, but we understand less and less. So the question a little boy asked his grandmother still remains.

It was with many questions in mind that I arrived in Warsaw in May 1990 for the first of many visits. Often over the years I had felt that a dybbuk had entered into me compelling me to confront the horror of the Holocaust, cajoling me to journey to Poland to vindicate the veracity of Grandma's tales; or, perhaps, to clarify my present by elucidating my past.

Sparks in Exile

My visit to Poland in 1990 was in response to an invitation from the Polish Episcopate's Commission on Dialogue with Judaism. The previous summer, at the invitation of the Catholic Archdiocese of Chicago, twenty-two Christian seminary professors from Poland had come to Chicago to study Judaica. Catholic priests from Poland studying Judaica at an institution of higher Jewish learning, at our institution, Spertus Institute of Jewish Studies, was something that never had been done before in the United States, or in Poland—especially in Poland, though Jews and Christians had lived there side-by-side for a millennium. I had been assigned not only to help design a curriculum and to serve as the chief instructor for this program, but to devise a way to try to overcome layers of prejudices and stereotypes that had developed between Poles and Jews.

A month before the Polish participants arrived, a roster of their names came by fax. I reviewed the list of seemingly unpronounceable names encumbered by clusters of consonants without the relief offered by vowels. I also reviewed the list of places throughout Poland from which they came. Since childhood I had studied, read, and heard about the life and thought of Jews in these towns and cities. Though the names of the seminar participants were strange, the names of the places from which they came—Warsaw, Cracow, Lublin, Lomza, Bialystok—were familiar. These were places of almost mythical proportions; places that had flourished in the lost Atlantis of Polish Jewry; places that I associated with a world that had passed into oblivion. The names of these cities and towns were like the names of holy books that one pores over in the quest for truth, beauty, and wisdom. While the names of the clergy were alien to me, the names of the great rabbis and pious Jewish sages who once had dwelt in the places in Poland from which they came were powerfully familiar. Through my studies, I had met giants of the spirit from those locales. Saintly Jewish scholars who had lived there in ages past had constituted a pantheon with few peers in the long history of Jewish spirituality. These were people for whom life was the highest form of art. These were geniuses, not only in learning but in building bridges from the heart to God.

Somehow seeing the names of the places our visitors were from made them less foreign, less inaccessible. I reviewed their dates of birth, only to discover that most were my contemporaries—roughly the same age, yet raised in an environment difficult for me to imagine. But of one thing I was sure: my grandmother and their grandmothers were born in Poland.

For two months they studied in Chicago. A few weeks after they left, a letter arrived thanking me for the hospitality afforded during their stay and offering to reciprocate with "the famous Polish hospitality." I accepted, wondering if the Poland that I would see is a place hospitable to Jews. Indeed, in the months between the arrival of the invitation and my departure for Poland, family, friends, and colleagues urged me not to go. "They are all anti-Semites," I was told on numerous occasions. "There will be a pogrom and you'll be killed." Poles I knew in Chicago offered a different portrait: "Poland is not an anti-Semitic country. Poles are not anti-Semites. Poland always has been hospitable to Jews."

As the weeks passed, two contradictory portraits began to take focus. Most American Jews viewed Poles as inherently anti-Semitic and Poland as a place that had *never* welcomed Jews. Polish anti-Semitism had made the millennium of Jewish life there a nightmare. Historically, deep-seated Polish anti-Semitism was not only responsible for the persecution of Jews in centuries past but was also brutally manifest in the twentieth century. Jews had left the Polish lands en masse to emigrate to North America and elsewhere precisely because Polish anti-Semitism was so intolerable. The Poles had collaborated with the Nazis in making the Holocaust possible. After World War II, Poles celebrated the decimation of Polish Jewry and eagerly appropriated Jewish property. The Nazi death camps had been placed in Poland because the Germans knew they could count on the support of the Polish people in carrying out the Final Solution. Pogroms and political actions against the remaining Polish Jews—survivors of the Holocaust—in postwar Poland and again in 1968, only demonstrated that Poles remained unrepentantly anti-Semitic. Even in contemporary Poland, there are virtually no Jews but there is still a pervasive anti-Semitism.

The perspective of Poles was altogether different. In their view, Poland always was and continues to be hospitable to Jews. Jews originally came to Poland to escape persecution elsewhere. In Poland, for most of its history, Jews flourished demographically, economically, and spiritually. Poles and Jews share a common history of oppression. Anti-Semitism is not indigenous to Poles or to Poland, but is a foreign import brought by occupying powers who partitioned Poland and used anti-Polish propaganda among Jews and anti-Jewish propaganda among Poles to drive a wedge between two fraternally and historically linked communities that had shared a tragic past. For centuries, Jews and Poles stood together in solidarity against invasion by Tatars, Cossacks, Swedes, and other occupying powers from the east and west. And Poles had suffered at least as much as Jews during the period of Nazi occupation. Pogroms in post–World War II Poland were not instigated by Poles, but by the Stalinists from the Soviet Union. If postwar Poles manifested any anti-Jewish feelings it was because Polish Jews allied themselves with the Russians. Polish Jews became atheistic communists, undermining Polish life and culture. Just as Poles resented Jewish alliances with the occupying powers in past centuries, and just as Jews agitated against the independence of Poland between the world wars, Jews during the communist era sought to sabotage legitimate Polish interests. If there is any anti-Semitism in Poland, it is because the Jews "sold out" Poland for their own advantage. Ultimately it's the Jews, throughout history, who are to blame for Poland's continuous misfortunes. Nevertheless, Poles always remained tolerant of the Jewish presence in their land. If Poland is viewed in a negative light today, it is because Jews throughout the world—especially in the United States—created and spread a negative image of Poles. Jewish film makers like Claude Lanzmann (*Shoah*), Jewish novelists like Leon Uris (*Mila 18*) and Jerzy Kosinski (*The Painted Bird*), and Jewish comedians with their "Polish jokes" maliciously disseminated anti-Polish propaganda.

The more deeply I investigated the matter, the more confusing things became. Hoping to encounter some objective analysis in the supposedly more sober and learned works by historians and sociologists, I instead discovered that many scholars simply reiterated—with stores of data and erudite documentation—the popular perspectives that I already had heard. Israel Gutman, professor of Holocaust studies at the Hebrew University, director of Holocaust studies at Yad Vashem, and a participant in the Warsaw Ghetto uprising, summarizes the situation as follows:

> This conspicuous confrontation might be interpreted by the generous spirit as a means of emotional release for people who have endured years of suffering, violence and humiliation. But no excuse can be made for historians and public figures, from whom we are entitled to expect a measure of dignified restraint and the ability to scrutinize events and complex problems in the spirit of scholarly detachment, for behaving in this manner. Regrettably, many books and publications dealing with the overall issue of Polish-Jewish relations or its specific aspects are marked by fixed a priori conceptions or have actually been written in the service of one or the other schools of thought in the public debate.[1]

Two visions of Polish-Jewish relations wrestle in my mind as the plane touches down in Warsaw. I am accompanied by a Polish-speaking priest from Chicago and the director of my college's library. I have not been able to sleep during the flight. We are greeted at the airport by one of the Polish priests who had been in Chicago the summer before, a point man in Polish-Jewish dialogue. Our housing is in the rectory of a church. Surrounded by crosses and pictures of Pope John Paul II, I fall into a blissful sleep. A few hours later, we wander through the streets of Warsaw. It's 1990. Communism is gone. But as I walk the crowded streets of a city where once one in every three people was a Jew, it becomes blatantly clear—the Jews are gone as well.

The streets of Warsaw bustle with movement. People are still bewildered by the collapse of communism only months before. Everything is in transition. The citizenry is both apprehensive and hopeful about the future. The stores, sprinkled with only a few goods not long before are now well-stocked. The lines of yesteryear are gone but not forgotten. People expect dysfunction as if it were the natural course of events. Criticism and complaining are the national pastime. A cautious movement toward a free market economy has begun. The silhouette of the city is gray. Few people smile. I walk the streets of Warsaw in a daze. Perhaps it is the jet lag; perhaps it's a time lag between what once was and what now is. It's like a mirage: Jewish life in Warsaw, in Poland, once vibrating, pulsating, effervescent, vigorous, dynamic—vitally alive—is dead, gone, vanished, leaving hardly a trace, a whisper, an echo, a memory.

The following morning is Saturday, Shabbat, the Jewish Sabbath. I walk to the only synagogue now functioning in Warsaw. The Catholic priest from Chicago accompanies me. He is my guide, my translator. As we walk, he talks constantly, commenting on everything we see. I remain oblivious to what he is saying. My only thought is: Warsaw is virtually *Judenrein*, free of Jews. I see no Jews walking to the synagogue on this Sabbath morning. No Jews at all.

We walk down a major thoroughfare crowded with people. It is called Jerusalem Avenue (Polish: Aleje Jerozolimskie). Jerusalem without Jews. Warsaw without Jews. A Jewish ghost town. We walk in the area that was once the Warsaw Ghetto. On Mila Street, once the site of an underground bunker that served as the headquarters of the 1943 Warsaw Ghetto uprising, a woman approaches us. "I live in a haunted house," she says. The Jewish population center of the Warsaw of today is the city's massive Jewish cemetery on Okopowa Street—over 200,000 graves, where tombstones stand leaning and fragile, like old people listening to the sounds of memories from a distant, evaporating past.

As I gaze down the street, a split-vision screen stands before me. It is as if I am viewing Poland through a trifocal lens. In one lens I see the present *Judenrein* landscape; in another, I imagine a pre-Holocaust Warsaw with thousands of Jews rushing to the synagogues on the Sabbath; and in the third lens I see huddled, hungry, diseased multitudes, gripped by fear and dismay, aware that at any moment they could be rounded up for deportation to Treblinka or Auschwitz.

We arrive at the synagogue. The service is chaotic. A few old Polish Jews sell newspapers and souvenirs, or beg for charity, despite Sabbath restrictions against handling money. Most of the worshippers are tourists. Many are Polish Jews from abroad returning for the first time since World War II. Some have their grown children with them. My companion speaks to them first in English, then in Polish. A young Orthodox Jew from New York interrupts my prayers, points to the priest, and admonishes me for bringing an "idol worshipper" into the synagogue. The service ends abruptly. I introduce myself to the rabbi. A Gerer Hasid from Israel, he was born in Poland. His tenure had begun only the year before. He had met his wife in a Nazi concentration camp. A genuinely warm and generous man, he officiates over a community largely populated by ghosts. We speak in Hebrew. He and the priest converse in Polish. Young Poles cast curious gazes at us as we walk to the rabbi's house for lunch. The rabbi wears traditional Hasidic garb. The priest says to me in English, "You see, there is no anti-Semitism in Poland." The rabbi says to me in Hebrew, "After everything that has happened to us here, you see how they still hate us. They are afraid that we might return."

Polish anti-Semitism, Jewish anti-Polonism—these topics accompany me wherever I go. Like everything else in Poland, few things are clear-cut. I try to make sense of things, but it is too early to reach any conclusions.

The priest and I return to the church rectory that is our "hotel" in Warsaw. The nuns have prepared our dinner. After dinner, the sun sets. Sabbath ends. My first full day in Poland concludes.

As I awaken very early the next morning, I hear the voices of children at play. From my window I see two girls playing in the cobblestone courtyard. I think of my grandmother. Perhaps some of the old cobblestones remember her playing nearby. Perhaps some of the trees remember her cries in the night. Perhaps the stars that twinkle in the Polish sky watched her when she left for America, never to return. And perhaps those same stars watched when her relatives, my relatives, were transformed into smoke in the chimneys of Treblinka and Auschwitz.

It's Sunday morning. Church bells ring. People flock to the church. As the mass is being recited yards away, I don my prayer shawl and tefillin and recite the morning prayers. I am sure that no one has done that before in my room at the rectory. But perhaps before the war a Hasidic *shteibel*, a small prayer house, had stood where the rectory or church now stands. Perhaps my ancestors lived on this spot. Perhaps Grandma played nearby. And, just perhaps, some exiled sparks of my soul had been reunited with their source because of my prayers.

One of the priests who had been a participant in the 1989 summer seminar in Chicago joins us at breakfast. We greet each other warmly. He has taken many risks to improve Catholic-Jewish relations in Poland. He is a one-man antidefamation league, defending Jews against anti-Semitism at the drop of a hat, a crusader. He will be at our disposal for the day.

"Where will we go today?" the American priest asks him in Polish.

"Perhaps to Treblinka."

The American priest concurs. I demur. After hearing for years about Warsaw, the most Jewish city in the world, and finding there a Jewish presence that could, contradictorily, be felt mainly in the starkness of its absence, I am too depressed to visit Treblinka just then. If my grandmother had not left for America, she and my mother would have lost their lives there and I never would have been born. In Treblinka, virtually all the inmates, all the victims, were Jews—unlike many camps, which witnessed a united nations of genocide. Over 800,000 Jews, mostly from Poland, were murdered in Treblinka. Going there then was too much, too soon.

"Where would you like to go?" the Polish priest asks.

"Perhaps to Gora Kalwaria," I respond.

"Why there?" the American priest asks. "It's a small town."

"Because that was the capital of Polish Hasidism."[2]

Only forty kilometers south of Warsaw, we are there within an hour.

Gora Kalwaria, Polish for "Mount Calvary." In Hebrew it is called *Ger*, "the place to dwell." Some Polish Jews called it "the new Jerusalem." No more than a village, it straddles a steep hill with the Vistula River below it. It could be somewhere in Iowa, except for the fact that it was the dwelling place of the most influential of all the later Polish Hasidic masters—the Gerer rebbe.[3]

A long line of men wait impatiently for noon, when the mass at the church will end and the tavern will open. The Polish priest approaches one of them and asks, "Where is the house of the tzaddik?"

A man gives directions. We walk down the block and turn left. Two brick buildings stand on a corner, overlooking the river. A metal frame of a Star of David can be seen on the former synagogue. Near the doorway is an indentation where the mezuzah once had been. Next door is the former home of the rabbi, where he held court. The synagogue is now a furniture warehouse. The rabbi's home is now the board of education for Gora Kalwaria.

A man suddenly appears, climbing out of a nearby basement apartment.

"You have come to see the place of the tzaddik," he says. "Who are you?"

I am introduced to him as an American rabbi. He looks surprised.

"The others who come here from America are differently dressed," he says, and then proceeds to describe Hasidic garb.

"This was the house of the tzaddik," he says, pointing to the board of education. Pointing to the building with the star, he says, "And this was the synagogue." He takes us behind the building and says, "and here is where they had the *sukkah*."

"Did you live here when the tzaddik was here?" I ask.

"I was a little boy then," he says. "But my father lived here then."

"Do you know of anything from those times?" I ask.

"On the Jewish holidays, a special train ran directly here from Warsaw bringing the tzaddik's followers. They came from all over Poland just to see him and to receive his blessing. There were too many to fit here. When they arrived at the station, they would stretch from here to the train. The tzaddik would come out of his house and would touch the hand of the first man he could reach standing nearby, and that man would touch the next man, until all of the men were thereby touched and blessed by the tzaddik."

"Do you remember when the Jews were taken away from here by the trains?" I ask.

The man blushes. "I know they were taken, but that's all I know." The man is agitated, nervous.

The Polish priest asks, "Where is the Jewish cemetery?"

The man replies, "Three miles down the road. Mr. Karpman has the key."

"Where can we find Mr. Karpman?" the Polish priest asks. The man gives directions. The American priest hands the man some money and we leave.

Felix Karpman is one of three elderly Jews left in Gora Kalwaria. Most of the other five thousand Jews of the town were murdered by the Nazis. The tzaddik escaped to Israel. Karpman lives in a spacious, well-kept house. He has just returned from church. It was his granddaughter's first communion. He offers us vodka to celebrate the occasion. On the way to the cemetery, he explains that he had been a childhood friend of the tzaddik, though he was not himself a Hasid. When the Germans entered the town, he fled to the forest. He was later sheltered by a Polish family. After the war, he found that the capital of Hasidic Poland no longer had Jewish residents. He married the daughter of the family that had sheltered him. Though he was never baptized, his wife and children were devout Catholics. He had spent many years and a great deal of his own money to rebuild the Jewish cemetery single-handedly. The Nazis had dismantled it, using the tombstones to pave nearby roads. He takes us there.

On the grave of the first Gerer rebbe there are mounds of *kvitlach*, or prayer notes, by Jews from all over the world asking the tzaddik to intercede in heaven for them and for their loved ones. Some notes are even photocopied. "Cure my dear wife." "Help my daughter to find a worthy husband." "Plead in heaven for success in my business transactions." Those who left these prayer notes also left donations to help pay for the upkeep of the cemetery. I recite a prayer, hoping once again to elevate sparks trapped in the shards of the tragedy and suffering that befell the Jews of Ger.

We return to Warsaw via Wilanow, the royal palace. After a tour we sit in the royal gardens. Tourists stroll by. I return to the car to retrieve a book, *Journey to Poland*. The author is Alfred Döblin, a German Jew, a physician, and a novelist. In the fall of 1924 he had visited Gora Kalwaria. I had read the book before coming to Poland. I open it again. My trifocal vision is projected against the explosion of blooming flowers in the king's gardens on a warm day in May. In one lens is the Ger I have just seen. Through a second lens I look at a photograph Karpman gave me. I see a long line of frightened Jews carrying bundles and knapsacks, taunted by German soldiers, on a road from which there is no return. Poles look on helplessly, passively. Some look sad. Others look impatient, waiting to loot the abandoned Jewish homes. In the third lens I read Döblin's description of the Ger he saw in the 1920s, when the father of Mr. Karpman's childhood friend led the Hasidim of Ger:

> Three Jews with sacks have been traveling for long days in passenger cars, all the way from northeastern Poland, on a pilgrimage to Gura Kalwarja. They are distressed. I see they have prayer books in their hand; they want help; the rebbe is a saint. He is, they say, more than the other rebbes, more than the rebbe of Chortkow, of Bels; he is the greatest, the greatest of them all.
>
> When the little train has swum along for two hours, it stops in Gura, emptying out completely. And, once again, we don't have to ask the way to the village. As we turn into the broad main street, a fantastic unsettling tableau heaves into view. This swarm of pilgrims in black—those who came with us and others—with bag and baggage, teeming along the lengthy street. These black skullcaps bobbing up and down. The yellow trees stand on either side, the sky above is pale gray, the soil tawny—between them, an almost frightening, bustling black throng moves along, hundreds of heads, shoulders serried together, an army of ants plods along, inches along. And from the other side, people trudge toward them, look down from the windows of the cottages, wave. . . .
>
> There is a table at the window. And at the table, with his back to the light, sits a stocky, pudgy man. He keeps rocking to and fro, incessantly, now less, now more. A round black skullcap perches on the crown of his head. His head is completely wreathed in a tremendous mass of curls, dark brown, with touches of gray. Thick sheaves of curls tumble over his ears, over his cheeks, along the sides of his face all the way down to the shoulders. A full fleshy face surges out from the curls. I can't see his eyes; he doesn't look at me, doesn't look at my companion, as we stand next to the plain wooden table. The rabbi's thick hands burrow through a heap of small papers lying in front of him; slips of paper with writing on them. He and my companion are conversing. The rabbi stops rocking, he keeps rummaging through the papers. His expression is ungracious, he never looks up for even an instant. He shakes his head. All at once, my companion says: "He says you can ask him something." I think to myself: Impossible, that's not what I'm after; I want to speak to him, not question him. But the rebbe is already speaking again, softly; I can't understand a single word of this very special Yiddish. Then, suddenly, I have his hand, a small slack fleshy hand, on mine. I am astonished. No pressure from his hand; it moves over to mine. I hear a quiet "*Sholem,*" my companion says: "We're leaving." And slowly, we leave. Someone else has already come in, he puts down a slip of paper, says a few words, goes out, backward, facing the small rocking figure at the window.
>
> What happened? My companion tells me that the elderly man at the door thanked my companion for our coming to speak to the saint. . . . He has nothing to ask me and I have nothing to answer. In conclusion, he was gracious, said "*Sholem,*" a blessing. . . .
>
> In the afternoon, they mob the tsadik's banquet. A big crowd, like the audience that morning, even bigger. A huge table is carried into the hall. Several men crawl under the table very early, to make sure they'll be near the saint. The tsadik

sits down with his sons and the important guests. Everyone else stands around. At the table, the tsadik speaks, provides exegeses on the Talmud and the Torah, new interpretations. The pious observe him and his guests, his movements, seize upon every word, elucidate it to one another. The biggest prize is eating *shirayim*, leftovers from the tsadik's plate. They fight over them. Occasionally, the tsadik himself hands someone a scrap from his plate.

The villagers pay scant attention to the tsadik and his followers; they earn money off them. The father of the present rebbe was a very pious man; this one is too worldly for them. He is very rich, by birth, through heavy contributions, shrewd investments. . . . He never takes a penny from the pious who consult him. Fantastic stories circulate about him. I find a printed pamphlet with a picture of him, this spiritual prince of the Jewish people. . . .

"The sages say: This world is merely a hallway or vestibule leading to the real house, the afterworld. But there is a verse that says: 'An hour of good deeds is better than the whole afterlife.' What does this mean, what is its sense?" That was what the rebbe asked. His Hasidim were unable to reply. Whereupon he continued: "In reality, this world too is the afterworld. But we do not realize it. . . ."[4]

We return to Warsaw. The Polish priest gives us an extensive tour of the area that was the Warsaw Ghetto. We come to Umschlagplatz, where the Jews of Warsaw were transported to a place from which there was no return. It is marked by somber white walls of stone. Again, the split vision: Warsaw before the war—the most Jewish city in the world. Warsaw now—a *Judenrein* city awakening from communism. World War II Warsaw—its Jews being sent away to be murdered. I can almost hear the wails of mothers holding starving children in their arms, the screams of young women being attacked by dogs, the grunts of men being truncheoned. I think of what one of the survivors of the Warsaw Ghetto uprising once said, "If you could lick my heart, the poison would kill you."[5]

A group of Jewish tourists stands nearby. Some look angry. Others cry. Most just stare in horror and disbelief. It is only then that the Polish priest says that he was glad that we had not gone to Treblinka. With his usual spontaneous sense of humor—somehow both inappropriate yet necessary there and then—he says, "Now we'll go to see America in Warsaw." Within minutes we are having dinner at the Warsaw Marriott Hotel. A Polish version of "authentic American apple pie" is placed in front of me. My stomach is in knots. I am unable to eat.

The following morning at 6 A.M. we set off for Lublin, a three-hour drive from Warsaw. As we approach Lublin, I see a sign indicating that we are near Kock (Kotzk), the home of the famous Kotzker rebbe. There is no time to divert our course, yet there are sparks in need of redemption. As we pass by Kotzk, a Talmudic adage comes to mind: "He who quotes the saying of a sage by name brings redemption to the world."[6] I recite to myself a story told about Rabbi Mendel of Kotzk:

A skeptic once came to see the rabbi of Kotzk. The skeptic asked the rabbi, "Is it true that you can perform miracles?"

"Yes," said the rabbi.

"Then show me how you can resurrect the dead," said the skeptic.

"I prefer to show you how I can resurrect the living," responded the rabbi.[7]

Life, Learning, and Luria in Lublin

We arrive in Lublin and are greeted by a participant of the 1989 seminar who teaches there. I am to lecture at the seminary later that afternoon—the first rabbi ever to do so, despite the long history of a Jewish presence in Lublin. In the meantime, an English-speaking seminarian is assigned to us as a guide. Our entourage sets out in search of the Jewish past of that city. I ask to be shown Szeroka (Broad) Street where the Council of Lands—the governing body of Polish Jewry—used to meet during the annual spring fairs.

Without parallel in the history of diasporan Jewry, the council epitomized Jewish self-government in Poland. Some historians consider the council as representative of the unique opportunity for Jewish religious and sociopolitical autonomy afforded by the comparatively tolerant Polish attitude toward the Jews. Other historians view the council as a foreshadowing of and as a precedent for Jewish self-government in the State of Israel. Still others interpret the establishment of the council as a self-serving Polish strategy for the centralized taxation and control of Polish Jewry. All three views have some credence.[1]

Though the tour guidebooks note that Szeroka Street was once the meeting place of the Council of Lands, most Lublinites, even the taxi drivers, do not know this. The center of the supreme court of Polish Jewry, the Sanhedrin of the Diaspora, is not known by the current inhabitants of Lublin. It's as if it were never there.

Before the Holocaust, about 45,000 of the 122,000 residents of Lublin were Jews. On July 23, 1944, when Lublin was liberated by the Red Army, only 594 Jews were found in the city and in the neighboring towns.[2] At the time of my first visit in 1990, only 17 remain. Our guide finds the caretaker of the old Jewish cemetery that dates back to the sixteenth century. He lets us in to see all that is left of a glorious past.

The cemetery is enclosed behind a brick wall, adjacent to a Catholic cemetery that adjoins a large church. Huge weeping willow trees, swaying like men at prayer, shelter the Jewish graves. Like many cemeteries in Poland, the Jewish and Catholic cemeteries abut one another. In death, as in life, Jewish and Christian Poles dwell in close proximity, but always with a boundary between them.

Anxious for American currency, the caretaker ushers us in. He shows us the graves of prominent rabbis, reciting their names by rote while pointing to their dilapidated tombstones. The names evoke no recognition from my companions. When asked who they were, the caretaker simply repeats their names. He seems not to grasp the significance of the eminent rabbis of the past whose physical remains he tends. But to me the names are familiar. That the men who answered to them lived, studied, taught, and died here—in Lublin, not in some mythical realm—suddenly becomes crisply clear.

The tombstones in this cemetery are in two small clusters, with smaller clusters scattered throughout. They are relatively few in number. Before the Holocaust, however, closely packed tombstones covered much of the hilly ground. Most of the tombstones were taken by the Germans for construction purposes. On the empty space that remained, Jews were executed by the Nazis. Ironically, though they died in the cemetery, no stones mark their graves. Not only were the Jews of Lublin wiped out, the presence of past generations was largely obliterated.

I wander alone through the first cluster of tombstones. My delegation waits patiently, chatting in Polish. I approach the grave of Shalom Shakhna ben Joseph, who died in 1558.[3] I place some pebbles on the tombstone. I stand there in awe of the man whose remains lie somewhere under my feet—the first link in a now severed centuries-long chain of Talmudic scholars born in Poland.

On the tombstone his father's Hebrew name, Yoseif—Joseph—appears. But his father's gravesite is unknown. Like many Polish Jews of those times, his father was known chiefly by his Slavic name, Yosko. That Jews in Poland used Slavic as well as Hebrew names demonstrates that the boundaries between Jews and non-Jews in Poland were not as absolute as many think. At that time, and in later centuries, it was not unusual for Jews to be multilingual.[4]

Yosko was a financial agent of the Polish kings. He controlled other economic interests too, and when he died in 1507 his estate was entrusted to his wife, Golda. She enhanced the family fortune, and subsequently Shakhna's brother Pesah ran the family business, leaving Shakhna to engage in scholarly pursuits. In the 1520s Shakhna established a school in Lublin financed with his personal wealth. By so doing he helped to advance two traditions that became hallmarks of Polish Jewry: the existence of superlative academic institutions for the perpetuation and transmission of Jewish learning, and the investment of one's material resources for spiritual and intellectual continuity. In the generations that preceded Shakhna, Poland largely had been a wasteland of Jewish knowledge and learning. There were few of scholarly repute or ability. Schools for the training of rabbis and scholars were yet to be formed. Works demonstrating erudite scholarship were yet to be written. The establishment of Shakhna's academy in Lublin paved the way for demonstrating the accuracy of the statement of the seventeenth-century rabbi Nathan Hanover, who wrote, "throughout the dispersions of Israel there was nowhere so much learning as in the Kingdom of Poland. . . . There was scarcely a house in all the Kingdom of Poland where its members did not occupy themselves with the study of Torah."[5]

Shakhna studied with Rabbi Jacob Pollack, whom we shall encounter in a later chapter.[6] It was from Pollack that he learned the method of razor-sharp analysis known as *hilluk*. It was this mind-honing mechanism of clarification and debate that produced first-rate logical and legal minds. Shakhna wanted to prepare his students to adjudicate the manifold problems of Jewish law that would come before them once they took their place as teachers, judges, and communal rabbis. Shakhna carefully walked the line between theoretical exercises aimed at developing his students' intellectual capacities, and having them apply their acquired erudition and analytical skills to formulate independent opinions on concrete legal cases.

No ivory-tower scholar, Shakhna had the opportunity to apply what he taught. In 1541 he was appointed chief rabbi of "Lesser Poland" (Polish: Malopolska) by royal decree. In this capacity Shakhna had vast authority over the lives of Jews in the region of southeastern Poland. He was authorized to confirm appointments of communal rabbis in that area, without which they had no license to conduct marriages, approve divorces, or function as judges in legal disputes among their co-religionists. He even was authorized to apply corporal punishment to lawbreakers. In official Polish documents he is referred to in Latin as *Doctor Judeorum Lubinensium*, testifying to the widespread recognition of his erudition and authority.

Most of the luminaries of the next generation of the Polish rabbinate were trained by Shakhna. Among them was his future son-in-law, Moses Isserles, whose academy in Cracow would later eclipse that of his mentor and father-in-law. Students in Shakhna's academy who could not support themselves financially were sustained by his personal largesse.

Upon Shakhna's death his son Israel became head of the academy and the communal rabbi of Lublin. Since Shakhna was apparently more concerned with investing his energies in the development of his students, his school, and his community than with writing scholarly books, all we know of his teachings is what we may glean from the writings of his son and his students. Like his teacher Jacob Pollack, Shakhna left behind a legacy of learning but no literary corpus of his writings. He refused many requests to record his views, especially his legal decisions, because he feared that they might be accepted as precedents, thereby discouraging the expression of independent legal analysis and decision that he cherished so highly.

From Shakhna's grave I move a few yards and over 250 years to the most prominent tombstone in the cemetery. It dates from the early nineteenth century, which is unusual for the "old" cemetery, but when I read the inscription on the stone it becomes clear why this "more recent" grave is found here. It belongs to Rabbi Jacob Isaac, more commonly known as the Seer of Lublin.

Unlike other Hasidic figures who established family dynasties, the Seer (1745–1815) created a dynasty of disciples who eventually became masters. For thirty years (1785–1815) he was the acknowledged leader of Polish Hasidism. When he died, the rebbe of Ropshitz (Polish: Ropczyce), Rabbi Naftali, said, "The holy Seer is dead—how, then, can the world continue to exist? I don't understand it."[7] In times past, especially on the anniversary of his death (Hebrew: *yahrzeit*), thousands of Hasidim would visit his grave to pay their respects and to ask the soul of the Seer to intervene for them in heaven. But, in 1990, I stood there alone.

His teachings display erudition. His theology is sophisticated, complex. His sense of communal responsibility was intense. But he is best remembered for his alleged psychic, clairvoyant, and magical abilities. Not since the times of the biblical prophets had anyone been called *ha-Hozeh*, the Seer. Like his teacher Elimelekh of Lizensk

(Polish: Lejask), he believed that revelatory experiences were available not only in the past, but in the present as well.

It is told that he could read minds, predict future events, and gaze into a person's soul and reveal its various transmigrations as well as its *tikkun* (act of reparation and restitution) in each prior life—and in the present life, too. It is told that one of his teachers, Levi Yitzhak of Berditchev, once admonished him for making a public display of his powers. The Seer looked deeply into Levi Yitzhak's eyes and then said, "If you demand it, I shall never again use my powers."

Levi Yitzhak thought for a long time before saying, "No, I cannot ask you not to use so great a gift."

After Levi Yitzhak had left, one of the Seer's sons who had been there asked, "Father, if Levi Yitzhak had asked you not to use your powers, would you have complied?"

The Seer smiled and said to his son, "Thanks to my powers, I knew in advance that he would not ask me to stop using them."[8]

Among the Hasidim it was told that before the Seer's birth his soul asked God to be relieved of this gift because being able to see all of the evil in the world was too much to bear. His request was denied.[9] During his life the Seer worked unstintingly to combat that evil. According to some Hasidic legends he fought evil on a panoramic scale, trying to force messianic redemption.[10] In reality, his efforts were more modest; he simply tried to improve both the spiritual and the material lives of his followers. It is told that when a new Hasid came to the Seer, the Seer would clean the Hasid's soul of the rust that had accumulated upon it, thereby freeing it to pursue its spiritual development. Like earlier Hasidic masters, the Seer taught that there is more than one way toward spiritual fulfillment, and that an individual must find the path most compatible with his or her nature. For some it is prayer, for others study, for still others it is the spiritual elevation of mundane actions. Once a person finds the path, however, he or she must follow it relentlessly.[11]

The Seer once reflected on the meaning of the Talmudic statement I had recalled as we approached Lublin: "He who quotes the saying of a sage by name brings redemption to the world."[12] The Seer explained, "Do not our holy books, especially the Talmud, continuously quote statements in the name of their authors? Why then does messianic redemption not come? The Talmudic adage cannot therefore refer to the final messianic redemption. It must refer to another form of redemption—the redemption of the individual, individual spiritual self-fulfillment."[13]

Following earlier Hasidic teachings, the mission of the Seer was redemption—not of the world, but of his own self and his followers. For him, the two tasks were linked. Unless the master could achieve a high level of spiritual fulfillment, he would not be able to elevate either the spiritual or the material lives of his followers.

According to the Seer, the Hasidic master is one who has reached a higher level of consciousness than others because of his attainment of direct communion with God. Nevertheless, the Hasidic master must operate *simultaneously* on the metaphysical and the physical planes of existence. While remaining attached to God, he must accept responsibility for the material well-being of his community. In this paradoxical view, the Hasidic master is obligated to help provide for the economic sustenance of his community precisely *because* of his attachment to the upper worlds. The tzaddik's role has two foci: empathy with God's will and with God's need for human

righteousness, and empathy with the community and its need for economic sustenance. The tzaddik, according to the Seer of Lublin, is one who simultaneously is
influenced by and who influences the divine. The tzaddik, in the kabbalistic termi-
nology, is able to "draw down the divine influence to the world" precisely because of
his attachment to the upper worlds.

Paradoxically, through his attachment to a world devoid of materiality, that is,
to the completely spiritual realm, the tzaddik is able to draw down the divine influence that enables the members of his community to sustain themselves physically
and economically. The tzaddik is one who is able to combine physical asceticism
with intense involvement in human affairs. His life is characterized by having one
foot in heaven and one foot on earth.

According to the Seer of Lublin, poverty is an impediment to the goal of achieving spiritual fulfillment. It is the task of the tzaddik to lift the people from materiality
toward God, while simultaneously helping to ensure that the people are not so
crippled by poverty that they are unable to attend to religious duties that are aimed
at achieving communion with God.[14]

The Seer stressed the importance of performing deeds aimed at improving the
quality of life. He once offered the following schema of Jewish life in Poland: "Before
the Ba'al Shem Tov, the study of Torah was supremely stressed. With the Ba'al Shem
Tov, the emphasis shifted to prayer. But, with me, it has shifted to acts of loving-
kindness."[15] He also observed that his socially activistic approach was particularly
Polish. Making a pun on the words *po'alos* and *polishe*, he said, "We love teachings
about sacred deeds *(po'alos)* and this is a distinctly Polish *(Polishe)* teaching."[16]

Supplementing the teachings of his master, Elimelekh of Lizensk, with his own
embellishments, the Seer taught that the tzaddik cleaves to the upper realm for his
fulfillment and the Hasidim cleave to the tzaddik for theirs. There is a continuum
between the mystical experience of the tzaddik and the social welfare he bestows upon
his community. But social welfare is not an end in itself. It is merely a means, a prerequisite, for the spiritual elevation of the laity. Nor is "drawing down the divine influx"
a crude form of magic. In the words of the Seer, "I do not pray for anything unless I
see in advance that it is the divine will to pray for it."[17] The aim is a correlation between
the divine and the human will, a consistency between the spiritual and the physical.
Rather than drawing a wedge between the needs of the body and the needs of the
spirit, they are inextricably linked in the teachings of the Seer of Lublin.

When the Seer died, his followers wanted him buried next to Shalom Shakhna.
However, the rabbi of the town, who was not a follower of the Hasidic way, considered it an affront to Shakhna's memory. And so the Seer was buried some yards away,
next to "Abraham the Seller of Vegetables."[18]

Probably this Abraham, one of the first inhabitants of the cemetery, was little
more than a grocer who died in 1543. Legend, however, has it otherwise. It is told
that the Talmudic academy of Solomon Luria of Lublin was housed on the top floors
of the building where Abraham's grocery store occupied the bottom floor. Late one
night, while Luria studied in his academy, he heard noises coming from the store.
He went to investigate, and there he found Abraham the grocer studying the Talmud. He asked Abraham which passage he was studying. Abraham told him, and
Luria recognized it as an especially difficult text. Luria then questioned Abraham

regarding his understanding of the text, and to Luria's amazement Abraham understood it with incredible precision and depth, and he displayed a rare erudition of the Talmudic writings. When Luria later told others of Abraham's vast learning, they were astounded—not so much because a simple grocer was in fact a great sage, but because Luria had praised his Talmudic scholarship so highly, for it was Luria's wont to disparage the learning of his rabbinic colleagues if they did not prove equal to the high standards he set for himself.[19] In a community—the Jewish community of sixteenth-century Poland—that was replete with magnates of Talmudic learning, Luria was the greatest Talmudic scholar of them all.

I walk from the cluster of tombstones containing the graves of Abraham the grocer, Shalom Shakhna, and the Seer of Lublin to a second group of tombstones in the cemetery. The tombstone of Solomon Luria is there—broken into two pieces, one affixed to the earth and the other on the ground nearby: the work of vandals.

Luria lived in the sixteenth century, a time when one's genealogy was considered predictive of one's personal destiny. From this perspective, Luria had a most enviable pedigree. Many of the greatest rabbis of the time, such as Moses Isserles of Cracow and Judah Loew of Prague, were his relatives. The great kabbalist of Safed, Isaac Luria, was his cousin. His family roots could be traced back through the sages of Italy, Germany, and France to the greatest of all medieval Jewish commentators: Rashi, Rabbi Solomon Yitzhaki of eleventh-century France. From that pivotal point, the line extended back to the second-century Talmudic sage Rabbi Johanan ha-Sandlar, the student of Rabbi Akiva and a descendant of King David.[20]

Orphaned at a young age, Luria was raised and educated by his maternal grandfather, Isaac Klauber, in Posen (Polish: Poznan). After serving as a rabbi in Ostraha (Ostrog) and Brisk (Brzesc, Brest-Litovsk), he came to Lublin. At the time Shakhna's son Israel was the communal rabbi and director of the academy founded by his father. Almost immediately, controversy flared. Throughout Luria's life his brutally honest, firm, and uncompromising nature failed to win him affection. It did, however, win him respect. Yet Luria died a bitter man, feeling unfulfilled.[21]

Luria's disappointment with life was the result of his setting goals that exceeded the reach even of his own genius. His standards were high because, in his view, the stakes were even higher—the continuity of Jewish tradition, the forging of a Jewish community characterized by erudite scholarship, obedience to the Torah, and the greatest possible degree of moral rectitude.

Luria perceived his era as one of unique opportunity, as critical formative years in the spiritual development of Polish Jewry. Jewish learning had just begun to set down its roots in Poland. The country was strong politically and economically, and its defense seemed secure. Relatively stable and safe, the Jewish community had been granted unprecedented autonomy. Polish Jewry was, in effect, a nomocracy—able to rule itself by its own laws and traditions. For Luria, the challenge was how to apply Jewish tradition to Jewish communal life, how to apply the past to the present. To meet this challenge at least two prerequisites were necessary: knowledge of the tradition, and the intellectual and spiritual development of Jewish communal leaders, particularly of rabbis. In his academy Luria attended to the task of finding and training religious leaders. Most of the great Polish-Jewish scholars of the succeeding generation were his students. In his writings Luria addressed the first task—the definition of the nature of Jewish tradition, particularly of Jewish religious law. In doing this Luria had a clear vision that contrasted sharply with the reality he perceived around him. His mission, he believed, was to correlate that vision with reality. His point of departure was the Talmud.

For hundreds of years the Talmud had been the focal point of Jewish faith, authority, law, and tradition. The Bible could be accurately and authentically understood only through the refraction of Talmudic interpretation. What the Scriptures mean is what the Talmudic tradition takes them to mean. Judaism is not the Bible, but rather how Jewish tradition interprets the Bible. At the core of Jewish tradition is the Talmud—the formative, authoritative canon of early rabbinic teachings set down in the Land of Israel and in Babylonia, a vast literary corpus that took shape approximately from the time of the Maccabees to the time of Muhammad.

The Talmud is the foundation of Jewish faith and practice. It is what makes Judaism what it is and what distinguishes it from other religions. For Luria, the Talmud was the unimpeachable and crucial resource for Jewish teachings and living. The fate of the Talmud, therefore, determines the fate of Jewish faith, of Jewish spiritual existence. Luria felt compelled to expend all his energy, knowledge, and talent to clarify the teachings of the Talmud and to ensure that those teachings continually shaped and informed daily Jewish life. For Luria, ensuring the place of the Talmud as the touchstone of Jewish life, thought, and action required three things: a correct text, a correct understanding of the text, and a correct application of that understanding to the conditions of daily life.

A correct understanding of the text presumes an accurate text. Over the centuries, however, scribal errors had crept into the manuscripts of the Talmud and its commentaries. With the invention of printing from movable type, not long before Luria's time, these errors became standardized in printed editions of the Talmud. Incorrect texts led to incorrect interpretations, and to the development and practice of errant traditions. To rescue the Talmudic text from these corruptions Luria spent many years composing *Hokhmat Shelomoh* (*The Wisdom of Solomon*), a work in which he endeavored to establish correct readings of the text of the Talmud and of its two most prominent medieval commentaries—those of Rashi and of the Tosaphists—and to justify his textual emendations based upon his erudition, insights, and instincts. As the descendant of Rashi and of some of the Tosaphists Luria was, in effect, painstakingly restoring family heirlooms in order to ensure that the tradition could endure without the tarnishings and the textual abuses of the past.[22] In his writings Luria ridicules those scholars who regard old manuscripts as authentic and authoritative simply because they are old. For Luria, authenticity and rectitude are not synonymous with venerability. Boldly, Luria attacks certain precedents of the past as well as the positions of his own contemporaries that, in his view, distorted the tradition.

For Luria the authority of the Talmud is supreme. Therefore, every authentic Jewish religious law and tradition must be rooted in Talmudic text. Despite the weight of even centuries-old precedents, and in spite of the venerability of the earlier rabbis who established them, Luria held that the Talmudic text is the ultimate arbiter of the authenticity and correctness of any law, idea, or practice. In his major work, *Yam Shel Shelomoh* (*The Sea of Solomon*), Luria began the seemingly impossible task of tracing each Jewish law and practice to its Talmudic origin. Those that had no such roots were judged by him to be inauthentic; those that diverted from the Talmud or perverted its meaning were said to be in error. Relentless and unswerving in his task, Luria confronted and uprooted the views and precedents of even the most revered authorities of his own times and of times past. His remarkable erudition and penetrating powers of analysis resulted in a body of work almost invulnerable to attack. In *Yam Shel Shelomoh* Luria describes his method:

> I trace the law to its ultimate [Talmudic] source. I engage in an exhaustive research of all available authorities until I reach the very root of the matter. . . . I subject the validity of every decision to the closest scrutiny. All the pertinent precedents are collected before I formulate my own view. I supplement those studies with the opinions of my colleagues and students.[23]

In the development and application of his innovative and polemical method, Luria jumped headlong into the fray of contemporary controversy regarding four of the most volatile issues confronting the rabbinate in sixteenth-century Poland: the proper method for Talmudic study and decision-making in Jewish law, the authority of codes of Jewish law, the place of philosophy in Jewish tradition, and the role of the Jewish mystical tradition. Virtually all of the most prominent Jewish religious authorities of Luria's time and place articulated strong opinions on these issues.

Summarizing the achievements of Polish Jewry in the area of Talmudic scholarship, Heinrich Graetz, the greatest Jewish historian of the nineteenth century, wrote:

> It appeared as if the deep secrets of the Talmud were rightly understood and completely unraveled and appreciated only in Poland. Comprehensive erudition and marvelous insight were united in a surprising manner in the Polish students of this book, and everyone whom nature had not deprived of all talent devoted himself to study. The dead letter received new life from the eager inspiration of the Jewish sons of Poland; in this land it exerted an influence of great force, striking sparks of intellectual fire and creating a ceaseless flow of thought. The Talmudical schools in Poland henceforward became the most celebrated throughout the whole of European Judaism. All who sought sound learning betook themselves thither. To have been educated in a college of Polish Jews was of itself a sufficient recommendation; and all who did not possess this advantage were considered inferiors.
>
> The fame of the rabbinical schools of Poland was due to three men: Shalom Shachna, Solomon Lurya and Moses Isserles.[24]

Luria's confrontation with Shalom Shakhna's son Israel was not simply a battle for rabbinic authority in Lublin. It was a war with higher stakes—how the Talmud ought to be studied and how decisions in Jewish law should be made. Luria opposed the use of the casuistic method (Hebrew: *pilpul*), introduced by Jacob Pollack in Poland and spread by Shalom Shakhna, as an end in itself. For Luria, casuistry, once a means to clarity and understanding, had been reduced to an exhibitionistic game of trivial pursuit. As such, it perverted the very tradition it was supposed to analyze and illuminate. For Luria, hair-splitting exercises threatened to become a substitute for required erudition. As an alternative to pilpulistic gymnastics, Luria proposed his own method of textual and legal analysis and decision-making.

In Luria's time, codes of Jewish law proliferated. Luria perceived this as a danger, encouraging jurists to take the easy way out by consulting a code instead of engaging in the often difficult and laborious task of wading through precedents and reaching an independent decision. He saw the codes as potentially replacing the Talmud as the ultimate source of Jewish legal authority, and he perceived the publication of codes and manuals as potentially divisive, as creating many Torahs from one.

In attacking codification, Luria entered into conflict with the son-in-law of Shalom Shakhna, Moses Isserles of Cracow, who was one of Luria's relatives as well as one of his few friends. Later, tensions between the two mounted over the place of philosophy in Jewish tradition. Luria, in rebuffing Isserles's claim that Jewish philosophy is an integral aspect of Judaism, attacked Isserles for injecting Aristotle's philosophical views into Jewish thought. He further demeaned Isserles's enthusiasm for the philosophical teachings of Maimonides. For Luria, philosophy was a foreign graft on the tree of Jewish learning. At best, it was superfluous. At worst, it was a gateway to heresy. Mocking Isserles's notoriously poor Hebrew style of writing, Luria advised him to study Hebrew grammar rather than to dabble in philosophy.[25] With regard to Jewish mysticism (Hebrew: *kabbalah*), however, Luria took a much more supportive view. Luria saw kabbalah not as foreign but as integral to Jewish tradition. Like Isserles, Luria strongly opposed contemporary tendencies to popularize the esoteric teachings of the kabbalists. While he disagreed with Isserles's claim that "the wisdom of philosophy and the wisdom of kabbalah speak of the same thing with different words," he would have agreed with Isserles's observation that "laypersons who do not know their right from their left . . . who cannot interpret a simple verse of Scripture and who are ignorant of Rashi's commentary to the Bible, jump to study *kabbalah*."[26]

In *Yam Shel Shelomo*, in his responsa (case-law legal decisions), and in his other preserved writings, Luria treats virtually every aspect of Jewish life and law with his usual erudition and keen analysis. With equal facility, he treats issues of real estate transactions, contracts, torts, slander, wills, unfair competition, usury, financial transactions, marriage, divorce, bigamy, adultery, incest, spousal desertion, liturgical texts, Sabbath and holy-day observances, sorcery, and the history of rabbinic tradition. It is therefore easy to understand why the tombstone that I stand next to in the Jewish cemetery of Lublin says:

> Here lies the noblest of the noble,
> The king of the wisest of teachers.
> The great light who illuminated
>   Israel for all time by his work.

Later I learn of a story preserved by Polish families who have lived near this cemetery for generations. It is told that the sages buried in this cemetery continue their studies in undisturbed silent repose. Near the cemetery a Catholic monastery was built by monks committed to a life of silent meditative contemplation. Here, on this hill in Lublin, the spirits of the Jewish sages of past eras have become the neighbors of monks who join them in contemplative silence.

Though I wish to linger longer in the aura of the noble past of the Jews of Lublin, my companions urge me to leave. Our next stop is a powerful reminder of the ignoble deeds of a more recent past. We drive to the outskirts of Lublin to Majdanek, where hell came to earth. It is estimated that over 360,000 people met their deaths here, among them about 125,000 Jews. This place is known in German documents not as Majdanek but as the Lublin SS Concentration Camp (Konzentrationslager der Waffen SS Lublin). Inmates of 54 nationalities were murdered here — a united nations of starvation, disease, torture, beatings, slave labor, shootings, and gassings. Beginning in 1942, seven gas chambers and two crematoria functioned constantly.

I stand near pits not far from the crematoria. Here, on one day — "bloody Wednesday," November 3, 1943 — 18,000 Jews were shot to death. Their remains are gone, but horror still pervades the spot. The "new" crematoria that stood only fifty meters away, and that had been installed only months before, had been hungry to be fed. The mass execution of Jews spread on that single day to the auxiliary camps of Majdanek situated throughout the Lublin area. By midnight 42,000 Jews had been murdered. At Majdanek, as well as at other places in Lublin where the victims of this "factory of death" are memorialized, is the quotation: "I see my relatives in each handful of ashes."[27]

We walk through the camp. Everything is rotting away. A witness to history is disintegrating. Yet everything remains intact: the barracks, the barbed-wire fences, the crematoria. One can see how it was done. Ashes still remain in the crematoria.

We are running late. Our guide speaks only Polish and German. He tells us to hurry up. "*Raus*," he says. My back is toward him. The sound of this German word sends chills down my spine. I can hear the SS guards who were there years before yelling the same word in the same place. I can see the faces of the terrified inmates facing imminent incineration in the crematoria I had just visited.

We are late for my lecture. Rather than making a formal presentation, I tell the few hundred faculty and students about the Jews of Lublin who are there no more. I tell them Hasidic tales about the Seer of Lublin. After the talk the rector thanks me, commenting on how much we Jews and Poles have in common. The odor emanating from vats of kasha from the nearby kitchen where lunch is being prepared seems to confirm his remarks. I am reminded of Grandma's kasha.

A faculty member rises and says that hearing the tales of the Hasidic masters was like listening to the stories of Jesus in the Gospels for the first time. Other faculty ask more technical theological questions. The rector encourages the students to ask questions. A young man of about twenty politely asks me, "You are obviously a man of faith. From what you have told us, the Jewish nation has a great faith tradition. Why, then, here in Poland have the Jews become atheistic communists, people devoid of religious belief?" The question was sincere, an honest probing and not a confrontational affront. The rector intervened. It was time for lunch. But this question, which I encountered numerous times in Poland, remained with me. Perhaps the Jewish stereotype that Poles are anti-Semites was as problematic as the Polish stereotype that Jews are atheists and communists.

Before our departure from Lublin, we are given a tour of KUL, the Catholic University of Lublin. Pope John Paul II once taught philosophy there. We come to a magnificent, dignified building — the medical school of KUL. A plaque on the wall testifies to its original purpose, "This was the Yeshivah of the Scholars of Lublin."

In the 1920s Rabbi Meir Shapiro had a dream of restoring Lublin to its glory of yesteryear, when it had been the capital of Talmudic scholarship in Europe. Like Shalom Shakhna, he was a man of means with political connections, both within the Jewish community and the Polish government. He wanted to build a yeshivah where students would not be begging paupers as they were in most yeshivot, where those who labored to perpetuate the tradition would be given honor and respect, where the physical conditions would be as nurturing as the high intellectual ambience. This yeshivah would aim to train a rabbinic elite—a cadre of intellectually astute scholars whose primary mission would be to rekindle and to perpetuate the highest quality of Talmudic study. In addition, the yeshivah would be the focal point for a worldwide project in adult education called *Daf Yomi* ("A Page a Day"). According to this plan, individual Jews all over the world would study the same page of the Talmud each day. Over a period of about seven years, they would complete the entire Talmud.

In 1930, after six years of intensive effort by Rabbi Shapiro, the Yeshivah of the Scholars of Lublin opened its doors. The fame of the academy rapidly grew. All around the world, thousands of Jews began the project of "A Page a Day." Jewish newspapers around the world would announce which page was to be studied on a given day. Even today, thousands still are preoccupied with studying "A Page a Day." Within a few years after the founding of the yeshivah, however, unexpected forces led to the demise of Shapiro's great dream just as it was on the verge of being realized.[28] The first blow fell in 1934, when Shapiro died suddenly at the age of forty-six. Five years later the Germans invaded Poland, and in February 1940 a German newspaper proclaimed:

> It was a matter of special pride to us to destroy this Talmudic Academy, the largest in Poland. We threw out of the building the large talmudic library and brought it to the marketplace. There, we kindled a fire under the books. The conflagration lasted 20 hours. The Jews of Lublin stood and wept bitterly. We summoned a military band, and the triumphant cries of the soldiers drowned out the noise of the wailing Jews.[29]

The Jewish community of about forty-five thousand was decimated. Today, all that remains are graves, monuments, ashes, and memories.

We return to Warsaw, where I deliver some lectures and attend some meetings. The following day we journey northwest to Wloclawek for more lectures and meetings. Then, back to Warsaw. Early the following morning we leave by car for Cracow. On the way we make two short stops: Czestochowa, the home of the shrine of the Black Madonna, and Kielce, where on July 4, 1946, a pogrom broke out against the Jews— only months after the Holocaust had ended.

Late in the evening we arrive in Cracow, the first capital of Poland. The air pollution is overwhelming. This medieval city escaped destruction by the Germans and remains mostly intact. Our host is one of the priests who had attended the Chicago seminar. He is a Jesuit. We are housed at the Jesuit Academy of Cracow. In the seventeenth century, if a Jew walked by this academy he was fined. If he was on horseback the fine was larger. If she was in a horsedrawn carriage the fine was greater still.[30] Now I am lodging here as a guest. Perhaps things, at least some things, have changed. In the seventeenth century the Jesuits of Cracow were virulent opponents of the Jewish community—constantly agitating to stifle Jewish influence, always encouraging the persecution of Jews. Now the Jesuits of Cracow are at the forefront of encouraging religious dialogue with Jews, of combating anti-Semitism. One of them, a prominent journalist, had published a powerful manifesto calling for the "cleansing" of the Polish language of all anti-Jewish nuances. Until anti-Jewish stereotypes are rooted out of the Polish language, he contends, they cannot be exorcised from the hearts and minds of Polish people. It is Friday night. *Shabbat* begins. I usher in the Sabbath with my prayers at the Jesuit monastery. The next morning we shall attend Sabbath services at the Remuh Synagogue, the synagogue of the most famous intellectual magnate in the history of Polish Jewry—the Rema, Rabbi Moses Isserles, the protégé and son-in-law of Shalom Shakhna of Lublin.

The Spiritual Magnates of Cracow

We walk to Kazimierz, the district of Cracow that once was the matrix of Jewish life in that city.[1] We cross the peaceful municipal park, lined with chestnut trees and flanked by a large brick wall originally used to shield the city from attack. On Jewish Sabbaths before the Holocaust, when 25 percent of the city's population was Jewish, this park would be overrun with Jewish children at play, new mothers pushing baby carriages, young people dreaming of a better world, old people enjoying their only encounter with nature, married men thinking about how to provide for their families, and Talmudic scholars in an ongoing contest of debate and display of erudition. But now they are there no more. They are gone, vanished.

We pass apartment houses once crowded with Jews, streets once jammed with Jewish peddlers and their customers. There are faded Hebrew inscriptions and corroding Jewish symbols on many buildings that once were Jewish schools, hospitals, orphanages, publishing houses, meeting halls, study halls, synagogues, theaters and organizational headquarters.

As we emerge from the dim and narrow streets, a square opens up before us, a large rectangle, bordered by low-lying buildings. The remnants of an old well are set in the middle. On one end is the "Old Synagogue," once a center of religious life and local rabbinic authority, now a Jewish museum. Originally built in the late fifteenth century in gothic style, it is the oldest synagogue in Poland and looks like a medieval fortress. A plaque on the wall proudly proclaims that in 1794 Tadeusz Kosciuszko addressed the congregation from the pulpit, urging support in an uprising against the foreign invaders. Kosciuszko, as it happens, is buried not far away, in Wawel Castle.[2] We walk down the narrow streets and view the remains of other synagogues that in times past were packed with worshippers. The huge Reform synagogue on Miodowa (Honey) Street dwarfs the rest. But like the others it is vacant. From the square we can see the high spires of the churches of Cracow dominating the abandoned synagogues of Kazimierz.

A white structure stands before us. Hebrew letters over the door inform us that we have arrived at the synagogue of Rabbi Moses Isserles. It is smaller than I imagined it would be. In Isserles's time there were hardly more than 2,000 Jews in all of Cracow. Directly outside the synagogue is the old Jewish cemetery, littered with tombstones. There, Isserles is buried. Next to the Holy Ark of the sanctuary is a Hebrew sign that reads, "According to a tradition, this is where Rabbi Moses Isserles would stand to pray and to pour out his supplications before God." Even the most modest American synagogue dwarfs this one in grandeur and size, but no American synagogue can compete with the legacies that hover in this mostly abandoned place of Jewish prayer and memory. On this particular Sabbath, a group of young people from Israel have taken over the prayer service in the synagogue. Most are Ethiopian Jews, new residents of Israel. It is doubtful that Isserles either knew or conceived of the existence of black Jews.

The previous day had been the Jewish holiday of Lag Ba-Omer, also the anniversary of Isserles's death. In times past, thousands upon thousands of Jews from all over Poland would make a pilgrimage to study and to pray at Isserles's grave. Few other Jewish sages have been so honored. A handful of Hasidic Jews from Brooklyn had been there the previous day to represent the throngs that no longer come.

After lunch with the Jesuits we are given a walking tour of Cracow—Wawel castle where the kings once ruled and from where the Nazis governed Poland, the market square, the great churches, the museums, Jagiellonian University. Cracow is a city of rare charm and beauty. On Sunday morning, while my hosts are at prayer, I visit the old cemetery adjacent to the synagogue. Buried there is a constellation of many of the brightest stars of sixteenth- and seventeenth-century Polish Jewry. Greatest among them is Isserles himself. I wander alone among the stones, portals to a largely obliterated past, a congregation of abandoned spiritual magnates.

Even Solomon Luria, known as a miser when it came to the praise of his colleagues, recognized the towering achievements and abilities of his relative and friend, Rabbi Moses Isserles, known by the acronym of his name: "Rema." Despite points of violent disagreement between them, Luria wrote of Moses Isserles that "from Moses to Moses, there was none like Moses."[3] These words are inscribed on Isserles's tombstone. The tribute, originally applied to the twelfth-century Jewish philosopher and legalist Moses Maimonides, meant that from the biblical Moses to Maimonides there was none who could compare in learning. Some interpret the application of this phrase to Isserles to mean that he surpassed all of his predecessors in holiness, piety, and learning from the time of the biblical Moses until his own time.[4] Most, however, interpret it to mean that from the time of Moses Maimonides to the time of Moses Isserles, there was none of Isserles's scholarly stature. While poetic inscriptions on tombstones often lack historical accuracy, they do convey a shared attitude about the importance of the deceased.

Isserles came from a wealthy Cracow family. As a youth he was sent to study at the academy of Shalom Shakhna in Lublin. Shakhna was the first native-born Jewish scholar of note in Poland. His teacher was Rabbi Jacob Pollack. It was Pollack who launched the transplantation of Jewish learning to Poland, but it was Isserles who transformed Cracow into the capital of Jewish learning in eastern Europe. When Isserles died in 1572, still in his early forties, he left a legacy of scholarship that would make Cracow a focal point for the spiritual magnates of Polish Jewry for at least a century.

Like Shakhna, Isserles used his wealth to support his academy. His beneficence to the poor, his friendly demeanor and gentleness of spirit, became legendary. However, despite the enormous impact of his teachings, we know little of his life. The synagogue that bears his name was originally built by his father, Israel Isserl, in 1553 in memory of Moses' mother, Gitel, who died in 1552. After Moses Isserles's marriage to Shakhna's daughter Golda, he returned from Lublin to Cracow. The combined influence at the royal court of his father and his father-in-law won Isserles an appointment by royal decree as chief rabbi of Cracow, probably when he was still in his twenties. The same plague that claimed Isserles's mother also seems to have caused the death of his wife.

Shortly after Golda's death Isserles remarried. His second wife was the daughter of the wealthy Mordecai Katz of Cracow. Her brother was the scholar Joseph Katz, who is buried next to Isserles.[5] Joseph Katz had established a Talmudic academy in Cracow in about 1540. However, the academy founded by Isserles soon eclipsed both Katz's academy in Cracow as well as Shakhna's academy in Lublin. Among his contemporaries in Poland, only Solomon Luria could compete with Isserles in learning or rabbinic influence.[6]

Though neither Pollack nor Shakhna left behind a literary legacy—indeed, until the sixteenth century, Polish Jewry had not produced a single literary work of significance—Isserles, like Solomon Luria, was part of a generation in which the long dormant force of Polish Jewry's literary prolificacy suddenly burst forth. But unlike Solomon Luria, who focused his attention upon the Talmud and who opposed philosophy and the codification of Jewish law, Isserles concentrated much of his efforts on Jewish philosophy and the codes of law. Isserles's preoccupation with Jewish philosophy is most keenly reflected in his book *Torat ha-Olah*.[7] A large book, chaotically constructed, often vague and diffuse and written in Isserles's notoriously poor Hebrew style, *Torat ha-Olah* has neither the systematic structure, the conceptual crispness, nor the literary felicity characteristic of the works of the Jewish philosophers of medieval Spain. It is more a symbiosis of past views than an innovative work. Yet in this tome Isserles used his broad knowledge of philosophy, the sciences, and mysticism in an attempt to coalesce all aspects of past Jewish tradition into a single literary corpus. For Isserles, as for his rabbinic contemporaries in Poland, all truth is contained within the tradition, in the Torah. Isserles forged an inclusive view of that tradition, allowing it to encompass several forms of philosophical, mystical, and scientific speculation.

For Isserles, there is no conflict between Jewish philosophy and mysticism; they embrace the same ideas while using diverse vocabularies to articulate them. In contrast to many of his contemporaries, Isserles claims that philosophy is not a foreign graft on the tree of Jewish tradition, not an import from abroad. Isserles maintains that philosophy was initially developed by the Jews, who then taught it to the Greeks. It was then neglected by the Jews because of the travails of the exile. Reclaiming philosophy from the Greeks—who had corrupted it over the centuries—and restoring it to its original form constitutes in essence the recovery of a lost part of the Jewish heritage, of the Torah.[8] Isserles applies his reconciliatory nature to philosophy and to other branches of knowledge in a manner reminiscent of his gentle way of dealing with his students and colleagues.

Torat ha-Olah offers insight into Isserles as a persistent explorer of ideas and phenomena. Not content with passively accepting the views of the past, he describes human existence as a quest for understanding the world we inhabit. Accordingly, Isserles concurs with an earlier scholar who wrote that "one who has not enjoyed the pleasure of managing to find an answer to the doubts to which one's mind have given birth, has never known true joy in one's life."[9]

Isserles had a strong attraction, almost an obsession, with Maimonides's philosophical works. The structure of *Torat ha-Olah* is modeled after Maimonides's *Guide of the Perplexed*. Isserles claims that "one cannot detect a false idea" in the *Guide*, that Maimonides's words are like "a law revealed to Moses at Sinai" (Hebrew: *halakhah le-Moshe mi-Sinai*), and that the views of Aristotle incorporated by Maimonides are "all true."[10]

Isserles's views angered many of his contemporaries, especially Solomon Luria. To Isserles, Luria wrote:

> You constantly turn to the teachings of Aristotle . . . woe unto me whose eyes have seen, whose ears have heard that the words of this unclean one [i.e., Aristotle] have become the quintessence of delight . . . and a sort of spice for the Holy Torah in the mouths of the sages of Israel. May the God of mercy protect us from this great sin. . . . You mix [philosophy] with the words of the Living God. If their spirits [i.e., of young men] desire [philosophy] at all, then let them study it during the time they spend in the latrine.[11]

The debate between Isserles and Luria was not simply an abstract intellectual joust, nor was it a controversy limited to these two giants of Jewish scholarship; rather, it was a clash of the titans of Jewish learning who populated sixteenth- and seventeenth-century Poland. The ultimate issue was: What is the nature of Judaism? The leitmotif of the debate was the place of philosophy in Jewish tradition. The sages of the day were provoked to take a stand, and most did. The dispute raged for generations, and perhaps it continues even now among the spirits of the scholars buried in the old Jewish cemetery of Cracow.

Among the views that emerged, Isserles's position is a moderate one. His perspective is inclusive. For Isserles's classmate Rabbi Hayyim ben Bezalel, "the language of the Torah is one thing and the language of philosophy is something else."[12] For Luria philosophy is not inimical per se, but it poses two dangers. First, philosophy can serve as a conduit for the introduction of foreign and even heretical ideas into Judaism. It has the potential to pollute the essential core of Judaism. Second, it threatens to displace the centrality of the teachings and the authority of the Talmud. As such, philosophy needs to be severely marginalized. Luria was apprehensive lest Jewish philosophy define Judaism and try to fit the teachings of the Talmudic sages into its philosophically fabricated rubrics. For this reason, Luria opposed attempts by the medieval Jewish philosophers and by Isserles to formulate Jewish creeds, to identify "principles" (Hebrew: *ikkarim*) of Jewish faith. Just as Luria opposed Isserles's attempts to codify Jewish law, he took issue with Isserles's efforts to codify creed.[13] In Luria's view the Talmud must remain the ultimate focal point of Jewish life, learning, and authority. It cannot be usurped, displaced, or threatened by philosophical speculation or by credal formulations. Luria was apprehensive lest individual philosophical speculation supplant the higher truths inherent in the sacred tradition.

To be sure, sixteenth-century Polish Jewry was a traditional society in which the truths of revelation as transmitted by the cumulative tradition were considered superior to any verities that could be established by individual speculation; the tradition's presumed supernatural origin and nature was considered to be transcendent over knowledge available only through "natural" means such as empirical observation or rational analysis. According to Luria, Isserles had opened a Pandora's box. A far more radical perspective than Isserles's, however, was espoused by Rabbi Eliezer Ashkenazi, who lived in Cracow shortly after Isserles's death and who was perceived by many of his contemporaries as personifying the dangers that philosophical speculation posed to Jewish faith.

His grave is only yards away from that of Isserles in the crowded old Jewish cemetery of Cracow. On his tombstone there is a bas relief of a snake, indicating that he was a physician. However, for some of his contemporaries, like Judah Loew of Prague, the sign of the snake, symbolizing deception and an invitation to heresy, might have been interpreted to embody the nature of Ashkenazi's teachings.

Ashkenazi considered rational independent analysis to be a necessary feature of religious faith. He viewed unreflective faith as being sheer foolishness; it was his contention that religious belief that has not been subjected to rigorous analysis is an incomplete, truncated form of faith. Loew, on the other hand, thought that the kind of rational speculation advocated by Ashkenazi was dangerous at worst, superfluous at best. From Judah Loew's perspective, why should one who already has the truth need to demonstrate by logical analysis that it is true? Why should the verities of a revealed tradition be subjected to the limited intellectual capacities of the human mind?

Born somewhere in the Near East in 1513, Ashkenazi lived in many places—including Egypt, Italy, Cyprus, and Bohemia—before coming to Poland in 1578. Though his name indicates that he was of Ashkenazic origin, he spent much of his life in Sefardic communities and was influenced by his Sefardic teachers, including Joseph Karo and Joseph Taitatzak, in Jewish law and mysticism. He was widely acclaimed for his vast erudition both in rabbinic and secular knowledge, and is reputed to have known a dozen languages. In Poland, Ashkenazi lived in at least three cities: Poznan, Gniezno, and Cracow. In Poznan he served as rabbi of the city. In Gniezno, in 1580, Ashkenazi completed his magnum opus, *Ma'aseh ha-Shem* (*Deeds of the Lord*). In Cracow he lived as a private citizen. He died in 1586. According to a popular legend, when Ashkenazi served as a rabbi and a physician in Egypt he was accused of many plots and intrigues. He was in the middle of the Passover Seder when word reached him that a warrant had been issued for his arrest. At that point, the legend tells, a magical wind came, transporting Ashkenazi and his family to Cracow where they completed the Seder in peace.[14]

Ashkenazi was a trailblazer in the history of Jewish thought. It was perhaps for this reason that he was so vilified by some of his contemporaries, like Judah Loew of Prague. With direct reference to Ashkenazi, Loew writes:

> Behold I have heard that there was a certain individual in Poland . . . who filled his
> mouth with disputation and who disseminated lies and vanities without limit. All of

his efforts were aimed at honoring himself before others who themselves are ignorant, as is characteristic of the present generation. For they read works not imbued
with the spirit of the sages, works which are a tertiary variety of knowledge.[15]

In a text reminiscent of Luria's attack on Isserles, Loew lambastes Ashkenazi for
incorporating Aristotelian ideas into Jewish teachings. By so doing, claims Loew,
Ashkenazi casts doubts on traditional interpretations of vital religious beliefs such as
the nature of God and miracles. Yet, for Loew and others, Ashkenazi's approach poses
even deeper problems, which one can discern by focusing upon Ashkenazi's interpretation of two episodes in the biblical Book of Genesis.[16]

In his commentary on God's call to Abraham, Ashkenazi raises the age-old problem of how Abraham came to a belief in God. Ashkenazi describes the process of
philosophical speculation as one that begins with total doubt and that, by deductive
reasoning, leads to the establishment of certain assumptions that become the basis
for a system of thought. For Ashkenazi, it was precisely through the utilization of
such a method that Abraham arrived at the belief in God, and from that belief
Abraham then formulated the system of thought later known as Judaism. While it is
true that Ashkenazi admonishes his contemporaries against using Abraham's method,
and while he affirms the traditional belief that faith ultimately rests on revelation,
the cat was already out of the bag, for Ashkenazi himself appears to utilize the very
method that he ascribes to Abraham.[17] Historians of philosophy often proclaim
Descartes the founder of modern philosophy for his utilization (in his *Meditations*)
of the method that begins with total doubt and deductively establishes basic principles for a philosophical system. This honor, however, may more rightly be ascribed
to Ashkenazi, whose death predates Descartes's birth by a decade.

In his commentary on the story of the Tower of Babel, Ashkenazi introduces
the notion of religious pluralism. During an era characterized by religious absolutism, with each faith claiming a monopoly on the truth, Ashkenazi adapted a theory
of religious pluralism that sounds much more like one of our times than of his own.
Ironically, in 1580, the same year Ashkenazi completed the work in which he advocated religious tolerance, the Catholic church authorities in his town of Gniezno
enacted a number of ordinances severely restricting social intercourse between Catholics and Jews.[18]

Biblical commentators have always been perplexed as to why God punished the
people who built the Tower of Babel. These people are described by the text as being
united by a common language and common goals. What, then, was their sin? And
why did God punish them with the division of one language into many? According
to Ashkenazi, the people who built the Tower had not only one language, but one
religious language, one theology. They were all of the same faith as well as of the
same language. This, he suggests, leads to absolutism, which inevitably stifles free
thought, creative speculation, and authentic religious expression. A monolithic
society, according to Ashkenazi, often suppresses the individual search for religious
truth instead of encouraging it. Therefore, God divided the people into different languages, that is, into different faiths, so as to encourage the individual search for religious truth. In this view, religious absolutism is a sin, while religious pluralism is the
will of God.[19]

Ashkenazi further indicates that the biblical text describes Abraham, the parent of the monotheistic faiths, as discovering religious truth in the chapter directly following the story of the Tower of Babel. He takes this to mean that in the absolutistic and monolithic society of the Tower of Babel, Abraham's quest for religious truth was suppressed. Only with the emergence of religious pluralism could Abraham have the freedom to discover religious truth. As Ashkenazi writes, God "was obliged to separate them . . . since the proliferation of doctrines aids and stimulates the searcher for truth to attain the desired results." Such a "searcher" was Abraham, who "carefully investigated faith after faith . . . for the very existence of separate and different creeds side by side would cause spiritual awakening and thus truth would be found." For Ashkenazi, truth is not that which is imposed by religious absolutism, which stifles authentic religious faith. Rather, true religious faith is what comes through free intellectual investigation in an atmosphere of religious pluralism.

It is a Jewish custom to place "prayer notes" (Yiddish: *kvitlach*) on the graves of great saints and sages of the past. Many graves in the old Jewish cemetery of Cracow are littered with these prayer notes. Isserles receives so many that next to his grave there is a mailbox. But the grave of Eliezer Ashkenazi is usually bare. Religious Jews apparently do not perceive Ashkenazi as one who has the clout to intercede for them in heaven. Perhaps his views were too extreme for many, both in his own time as well as our own.

Running along the back cemetery wall lie the remains of a number of past chief rabbis of Cracow. One is Rabbi Joel Sirkes, known by the acronym "Bach," after the name of his most important work, the *Bayit Hadash* (*The New House*). He served as chief rabbi of Cracow from 1618 until his death in 1640. In close proximity is the grave of Rabbi Yom Tov Lipman Heller, whose tenure as Cracow's chief rabbi followed rabbinical appointments in Vienna and Prague. Heller died in 1654. With Sirkes and Heller, the debate concerning the place of philosophical speculation in Judaism continues, perhaps for all eternity.

In a famous legal decision, Sirkes deals with the case of a Jewish physician from Amsterdam who studied philosophy and who disparaged the Jewish mystical tradition. Sirkes unequivocally calls for the physician to be excommunicated. In formulating his position on this case, Sirkes reveals his attitudes toward philosophy and mysticism. For Sirkes, "the study of philosophy is the very essence of heresy . . . [and] since he [the physician] has rejected the wisdom of the Jewish mystical tradition and the teachings of the sages, it is fitting to be most stringent with him with even greater force."[20] By Sirkes's times, heresy in Judaism meant not only the rejection of certain core beliefs, but denial of the truth of the Jewish mystical tradition.

Though Sirkes lived about eighty years—almost twice as long as Isserles—little is known about his life. Probably born in Lublin, he occupied at least eight rabbinic posts during his career. Beginning with small communities, he worked his way up to serve the two greatest centers of Jewish life in contemporary Poland: Brisk (Brest Litovsk) and Cracow. During most of his early life he seems to have lived in poverty. Taking material advantage of his lucrative positions in the bigger cities in his later life, however, Sirkes apparently amassed a small fortune. Experience had convinced him that only financial stability could provide the tranquillity necessary for serious scholarship, and that the laity respects a rabbi more for his wealth than for his learning. Hence, to be an effective rabbi, both substantial learning and wealth are required. As Sirkes wrote, "The Torah is most concerned over the financial needs of Israel."[21] Very active in Jewish communal affairs both locally and nationally, Sirkes was especially concerned with reforming Jewish education, especially that of children. Though the rabbis of that time served as spiritual, legal, and juridical guides to their communities, they also oversaw the local Jewish educational system, from children first learning the Hebrew alphabet through the granting of rabbinic ordination.

Born in Wallerstein, Bavaria, Yom Tov Lipman Heller studied in Friedberg. At the age of nineteen he married into one of the most prominent Jewish families of Prague and published his first book. After serving as a rabbinic judge in Prague, then as chief rabbi of Moravia, and subsequently in Vienna, he returned in 1627 to Prague as chief rabbi of Bohemia. In 1629 Heller was imprisoned on the basis of vague charges and taken in chains on an imperial decree to Vienna, where he was incarcerated with hardened criminals. He was accused as a blasphemer against Christian faith. As partial evidence his praise of the Talmud was introduced. The death penalty was ordered. The Jewish community interceded and paid a large fine (that is, a bribe) for his release, which carried with it the condition that he never hold a rabbinic post in the territory ruled by the Austrian crown. He thus went to Poland—first Lublin, Brest, Nemirov, then Vladimir (Polish: Wlodzimierz) in Vollynia, and finally in 1643 Cracow. Though he wrote an account of his imprisonment, the full story remains to be told. Within the German, Bohemian, Moravian, and Austrian Jewish communities in which he lived during his early life, Heller was virtually without par or peer in Jewish learning. Still, within the orbit of seventeenth-century Polish Jewry he was but a single bright star among a constellation of supernovas.[22]

Unlike Sirkes, Heller was an advocate of the Jewish philosophical tradition. His grasp of Jewish philosophical ideas was unusually sophisticated for his time and place. He was also an expert in astronomy and mathematics. His writings display a broad erudition as well as a precise and articulate Hebrew style. No isolated bookworm, he was an active and provocative communal leader who would never compromise his integrity no matter what pressures were brought to bear. Unlike Sirkes, he was not an opportunist. Heller took a strong stance at the Council of Lands against those who bought their way into positions of rabbinical authority. The purchase of rabbinic positions, and the power and revenues that came along with it, was a widespread impropriety of Jewish life in sixteenth- and seventeenth-century Poland. Like Luria, Loew, and others, Heller attacked this communal corruption that threatened the integrity of Jewish religious, jurisprudential, and community leadership. Unlike Isserles and like Loew, he opposed the tactic of influencing the civil authorities to play a major role in the appointment of communal rabbis. Isserles had become chief rabbi of Cracow by royal decree, and in his work he defends the propriety of such a modus operandi. Heller's later appointment to the same post came without civil intervention and was based solely on his abilities.

It is curious that while battles raged among the knights of Jewish scholarship over the role of philosophy in Jewish thought, no one questioned the pedigree of Jewish mysticism. While these sages had reservations about making complex and recondite kabbalistic ideas available to the untutored masses, and the legal views of some of the kabbalists were overruled when they challenged established legal precedents, neither the sanctity nor the authenticity of the Jewish mystical tradition was ever challenged.[23] The sages insisted that one should first study the Talmud in depth before dealing with the difficult and complex teachings of the Jewish mystical masters. In the seventeenth century, when the teachings of Rabbi Isaac Luria, Solomon Luria's cousin, first reached Poland, they were opposed by some, not because they were kabbalistic but because they were perceived as being a diversion from earlier established kabbalistic views. Indeed, in the same row of the old Jewish cemetery of Cracow where Isserles is buried is the grave of the seventeenth-century rabbi and kabbalist Nathan Nata Shapiro, who was instrumental in disseminating Isaac Luria's teachings throughout the Polish lands.[24] The supreme reverence held by the rabbinic sages of Poland for the Jewish mystical tradition may have been summarized best by Sirkes when he wrote that whoever does not accept the wisdom of the kabbalah is a "denier" of the Jewish faith and deserves excommunication.

Despite the efforts of many sixteenth- and seventeenth-century scholars to limit the study of kabbalah to the spiritual and academic elite, the popularization and dissemination of Jewish mystical teachings was common by the end of the seventeenth century. Some kabbalistic ideas and practices also filtered down to the masses, often in a diluted form. As printing developed, the production of Jewish mystical books made a literature that had previously been circulated hand to hand, from master to disciple, readily available for popular consumption. The efforts of Judah Loew of Prague to express complex kabbalistic ideas in an accessible form of expression greatly aided the spread of Jewish mystical ideas. The incorporation of kabbalistic teachings into the written and spoken sermons of the day, biblical commentaries, and the popularly studied manuals of Jewish ethics and pietica facilitated their widespread dissemination.

When compared to the debate over the process of decision-making in Jewish law, the controversy over Jewish philosophy was a sideshow. In the largely autonomous Jewish community of Poland, observance of Jewish law (Hebrew: *halakhah*) was not a matter of personal preference, but an ongoing concern. The spiritual, commercial, and moral quality of Jewish life depended upon the accuracy and the quality of Jewish legal decision-making. Jewish law affected every aspect of daily life, from cradle to grave. The curriculum of the rabbinical academies often was no abstract matter: a text studied by a future rabbi could one day become the basis for a legal decision that could determine the disposition of a marriage, the validity of a contract, the propriety of a commercial transaction, the transmission of property to heirs, the presence or absence of certain foods on the dinner table, or the prayers that could be recited in the synagogue. No area of human behavior lay outside the jurisdiction of Jewish legal decision.

As we have seen, Solomon Luria waged a war to ensure the centrality of the Talmud in Jewish legal decision-making. Following Judah Loew of Prague, Yom Tov Lipman Heller focused on the early stratum of the Talmud, namely, the Mishnah, as being the foundation for all Jewish legal decisions. Indeed, Heller was the first Ashkenazic scholar to compose a complete commentary to the Mishnah. As a result of those efforts by Loew and Heller, local societies for the study of Mishnah sprang up all over Poland. Until the Holocaust one could find in Poland organizations like the Warsaw Coachmen's Association for the Study of Mishnah. Heller's erudite, precise, and insightful commentary greatly facilitated the widespread study of Mishnah around the Jewish world. For Heller, while the Mishnah was the ultimate basis for Jewish legal decision, he insisted that one also incorporate the authoritative views of the fourteenth-century rabbi Asher ben Yehiel, known by the acronym *Rosh*, into the process of legal decision making.

Rabbi Jacob was the third son of the *Rosh*. His magnum opus was the code of Jewish law called *Arba'ah Turim* (*Four Columns*). Unlike Maimonides's earlier code, the *Mishneh Torah*, which covers all aspects of Jewish law including the laws of temple sacrifices, Jacob's code deals only with the laws of his day. He divided his code into four parts, each dealing with a distinct area of Jewish law. For example, the section called *Hoshen Mishpat* (*Breastplate of Judgment*) deals with commercial transactions and tort law. *Orah Hayyim* (*Path of Life*) treats daily, Sabbath, and holy-day practices.[25]

To the chagrin of Solomon Luria and others, codes such as Jacob ben Asher's *Arba'ah Turim* and Isaac of Dureen's *Sha'are Dura* (primarily on the Jewish dietary laws) had become major textbooks used in the training of rabbis in the academies.[26] Luria believed that the codes deflected the authority of the Talmud and stifled independent research and legal reasoning. Isserles, however, saw the codes as critical tools for Jewish jurisprudence that, unlike the Talmud, provide a precise and organized presentation of legal decisions. For this reason, Isserles composed a commentary to *Sha'are Dura* called *Torat Hatat*. He subsequently began to undertake the much more formidable task of writing a commentary to *Arba'ah Turim*, often known simply as the *Tur*. He entitled this work *Darkhei Moshe* (*The Ways of Moses*).

While Isserles was in the process of composing *Darkhei Moshe*, the great Sefardic legalist and kabbalist Joseph Karo published *Beit Yoseif* (*House of Joseph*), his magisterial commentary on the *Arba'ah Turim*. Isserles's initial dismay faded after close analysis of Karo's work, when he realized that there was still much for him to do. Instead of identifying precedents and correlative decisions in case law prior to and subsequent to the *Tur*, and pointing out where his views differed from those of the *Tur*, as he had originally planned to do, Isserles recast his commentary as a critique of and a supplement to Karo's *Beit Yoseif*. Isserles's revised work was not only an analysis of when and why he differed with Karo, but it took into account a major component of Jewish law and practice largely ignored by Karo, namely, that of the Ashkenazic tradition.

Karo had based his work almost exclusively on the legal opinions of Sefardic scholars. Isserles adds Ashkenazic precedents and practices in his commentary. Here, as in his other halakhic works, Isserles defends two principles of Jewish law. The first is to consider the most recent precedent—representing the quintessence of what preceded it—to be the most authoritative one.[27] Against this position, Luria launched his clarion call of "Back to the Talmud!" The second principle, typical of Ashkenazic jurisprudence but virtually foreign to Sefardic thought, is the high regard and legitimacy afforded local custom and practice. For the Ashkenazic sages, "The custom of our forebears is Torah." Isserles rejects many of Karo's legal decisions on the basis of the customary practices of Ashkenazic Jews, even though some customs supplanted established laws. While Isserles recognizes that some customs may be simply mistaken (Hebrew: *minhag ta'ut*) or even foolish (Hebrew: *minhag shtut*), he generally upholds the legal status of local custom. However, here too he was attacked by his classmate Hayyim ben Bezalel, who claimed that while local custom usually has the force of law, Isserles had neglected local customs other than those then practiced in Poland; for example, the customs of German Jewry. Additionally, Isserles said that it is permissible, even desirable, to give the force of law to practices that are customarily observed, despite their having no textual precedent.[28]

As the *Tur* was a basic part of the curriculum of the rabbinic academies of Poland, many scholars wrote their own glosses to the text, probably as lecture notes for the classes they offered. Some were published; most were not. Except for Karo's commentary, the two most prominent commentaries on the *Tur* were Isserles's *Darkhei Moshe* and Sirkes's *Bayit Hadash*.

After spending about twenty years writing the *Beit Yoseif* and an additional twelve years reviewing it and adding supplements to it, Karo set to work to compile a precise synopsis. Entitled *Shulhan Arukh (Set Table)*, this new work follows the structure of the *Tur*. It simply and directly offers legal decisions in a series of short paragraphs without citing sources or precedents.[29] The *Shulhan Arukh* quickly became a handy manual for halakhic decisions on most daily matters. However, like the *Beit Yoseif* it neglects the precedents and practices of Ashkenazic Jewry, once again prompting Isserles to write a supplement in which the Ashkenazic tradition was represented. Isserles called his work *Mapah (Tablecloth)*, an appropriate companion piece to Karo's *Set Table*. The work was now ready for its universal acceptance as the definitive manual of Jewish law. In his characteristically gracious and inclusionary way, Isserles provided the means for the adaptation of a central body of law for all Jews. Over the years a number of basic commentaries, most of them generated by rabbis of the rabbinical academies of Poland, were added to this work, where Karo and Isserles stand together on virtually every page.

The growing momentum of legal codification in the sixteenth and seventeenth centuries stimulated a violent backlash. In Isserles's time, the leaders of the anticodification movement were Solomon Luria, Hayyim ben Bezalel, and Hayyim's brother — the preeminent Judah Loew of Prague. Those who opposed codification were more concerned with the dangers it posed to the process of decision-making in Jewish law than they were appreciative of the conveniences it offered. For the opponents of the codes, codification threatened the natural development of the tradition, the autonomy of competent contemporary rabbinical authority, and the authority of earlier precedents, particularly those of Talmudic origin.

The battle between these two camps raged on without a decisive conceptual victory on either side, although in practical terms the codifiers won out. What the opponents of codification expected may have been beyond the reach of the laity and even of most of the rabbis. Time was too short, the tradition too complex, to decide each case by an exhaustive review of precedents stretching back hundreds of years. It was easier to consult the codes. In unusual cases and unprecedented situations there remained the option of requesting a case-law decision, a responsum (Hebrew: *teshuvah*) from a legal authority. But usually the codes proved sufficient.

Opponents were apprehensive about how the acceptance and utilization of the codes would affect decision-making in Jewish law. Time has shown that their concerns were valid. Though the codes were meant to be guides to legal decision-making, they came to be regarded as binding precedents. Rather than furthering the process of the development of Jewish law, the codes stifled it; they not only codified but calcified the law, rather than allow its natural inner dynamic to develop freely. The codes and their commentaries threatened to become the basis for subsequent legal decision-making, thus supplanting the Talmud and interpretations of Talmudic texts as the foundation of Jewish legal opinion. By leaving the law in a state of suspended animation in the text of the codes, by paralyzing precedent in a single time and place, the codes robbed the law of life, growth, and change.

Isserles, who perceived a real danger in making the Jewish mystical tradition popularly accessible, did not seem aware of the inherent dangers of making Jewish law popularly available through the codes. By this action he in effect compromised the very rabbinic authority he labored so hard to defend. As the opponents of the codes pointed out, once the codes became popularly available any layperson who could read the codes could readily become his or her own legal decision-maker, and in so doing might err in the observance of Jewish law. The authority of the Talmud and of contemporary halakhic authorities would be subverted. The quality of Jewish scholarship would decline since the study of the codes would overshadow study of the Talmud. Writing to Isserles, Luria says:

> You impugn my authority to disagree with the codifiers. It is knowledge of the law that invests me with the prerogative to take issue with other halakhists and to expose their errors. . . . I am prepared to acknowledge my own errors only in the event that you prove my decisions are not found in the Talmud, or that my line of reasoning is not supported by the early post-Talmudic authorities (Hebrew: *gaonim*).[30]

Moving away from the debates over the codification of law and the place of philosophy in Jewish thought, I walk to a grave marked by a prominent tombstone. It is the grave of one of the chief rabbis of seventeenth-century Cracow. He succeeded Heller in that capacity, serving from 1654 to 1663. The name on the tombstone is very familiar to me. The name is Heschel.[31]

Born in Brisk, raised in Lublin, later chief rabbi of Lublin and then of Cracow, Abraham Joshua Heschel was known as a superlative scholar and as a person of extraordinary kindness and generosity. After the Cossack pogroms and the subsequent Swedish invasion of Poland, he spent almost two years in Vienna raising money to help the victims of those massacres. He had scores of disciples and was a gifted preacher and teacher. He was quick-witted, intellectually sharp and alert, yet modest and self-effacing. He had many famous descendants, including the nineteenth-century Apter Rav, named Abraham Joshua Heschel but popularly known by the name of his major work, *Ohev Yisrael*—lover of the people of Israel. But another one of his descendants was closer to me in time, place, and relationship. That person was my mentor, Abraham Joshua Heschel. Born in 1907 in Warsaw, he died in 1972 in New York. For six years in the late 1960s I was his student, disciple, protégé. He played a visceral role in molding my spiritual life, and the spiritual lives of many, many others as well.

Heschel is best known for his intense involvement in the social issues that preoccupied America in the 1960s. He was a close friend of Martin Luther King, Jr., and participated with King in the civil rights struggle. A few days before his assassination, King called Heschel one of the great prophets of contemporary America. Heschel was also at the vanguard of opposition to the war in Vietnam, which he considered a "moral monstrosity." He was one of the first leaders in the American Jewish community to call attention to the plight of Jews in the Soviet republics. He pioneered interfaith dialogue between Christians and Jews, and was instrumental in the drafting of Vatican II's 1965 schema on relations to Judaism in which the Catholic church radically redefined its relationship to Judaism and the Jewish people. Despite the enormous impact of his efforts in the social sphere, even more important were his extraordinary and enduring contributions to Jewish theology, spirituality, and scholarship. His erudition was startling. His personality was engaging, charismatic, charming. He developed a theology of Judaism that was both evocative and provocative. He wrote in an unusually beautiful poetic prose in four languages: English, Hebrew, German, and Yiddish. His writings had a freshness about them, yet they were firmly grounded in the vast Jewish tradition that he had already mastered as a child in Poland. At the core of his theology of Judaism is the idea of a divine-human partnership, that God is both in search and in need of human beings to realize the divine plan for the world, that the spiritual development of the individual self is the mission of each person, and that in our times the mission has been largely forgotten by us, the messengers. Many of his works have become classics.

Heschel taught that we must strive for meaning beyond absurdity; that one must be an optimist, even against one's better judgment; that a person should search for truth and integrity despite being surrounded by mendacity; and that one must believe fiercely in God despite the often ferocious and cruel quality of historical experience.

The subject of Heschel's last book was the Hasidic master Rabbi Mendel of Kotzk. The rabbi of Kotzk had taught that there are three ways to respond to sorrow. One can scream. One can be silent. Or one can transform sorrow into a song.[32] Following this teaching, Heschel marshaled his immense literary abilities, his keen intellect, and his profound spiritual capacity to help ensure the continuity of the *niggun*, the melody of the Jewish spirit, snuffed out during the Holocaust in his native land. While no one could restore the lives that were lost, one could try to maintain and transmit the surviving keys to the spiritual treasures of the Jewish soul. The alternative was to surrender a bounty of inherited insights, wisdom, and experience to oblivion. To permit the bequest from the past to be irretrievably lost was, for Heschel, tantamount to a second Holocaust. Despite what had happened, precisely because of what had happened, Judaism could not be forgotten; the surviving remnant of the Jewish people, especially the diaspora of Polish Jewry, could not afford to forget the message they had been charged to convey.

Abraham Heschel was my mentor, my master, my teacher. For Judaism, the master-disciple relationship is the holy of holies. What transpires within the sanctity and the intimacy of its precincts determines whether the wisdom of the past will be perpetuated or whether it will atrophy. What is at stake is the perpetuation of tradition, the continuity of Judaism. The master who has acquired an embarrassment of riches from the past is obliged to convey that legacy to the future. The disciple represents continuity, life after death. Among other things, Heschel was a physical and spiritual conduit between the lost Atlantis of Polish Jewry and the present situation of contemporary Jewry. He was a link between the world of my physical and spiritual forebears and myself.[33] On a subsequent trip to Poland I would visit the huge Jewish cemetery in Warsaw. There, quite by chance, I came upon the grave of Moshe Mordecai Heschel, the descendant of Abraham Joshua Heschel of Cracow and the father of my mentor.

The plan is to drive that evening to Oswiecim, to Auschwitz, and to spend the night there in preparation for a reunion of the group of Polish priests that came to Chicago in 1989. I refuse. The thought of spending a night there terrifies me. I deliver a lecture at the Jesuit Academy in Cracow on "Faith in Jewish Theology," wondering how I shall respond the next day to being in the single place on earth that offers the most poignant challenge to religious faith. The following morning we take the drive to Oswiecim, less than an hour from Cracow. For most of my life I had studied the horrors of the Holocaust and had become obsessed by them. I had read, written, and taught about the Holocaust, but visiting the capital of the Holocaust Kingdom would be something altogether different from what I had learned from books and from talking to those who had been there during World War II. This visit to Auschwitz will be discussed in a later chapter. Happy to leave that place, we take the long drive back to Warsaw. After a few more days of lectures and meetings in Warsaw, I am glad I have come to Poland but I am anxious to leave. We return to Chicago, but Poland stays with me. Surprisingly, I find myself wanting to return. But before traveling there through space, I travel there through time. My time portal is a tombstone in a cemetery in Queens, New York.

Transmigrations of a Name

My omnipresent dybbuk obsessed me. There was much more to see than I had seen in Poland. There was more to know about what I had seen. Somehow, I felt rooted there, strangely at home in that strange land. I decided to find out why. I decided to search for the Makower Ruf. Perhaps recovery of my family's past there, my genealogy, was a way of appeasing this demanding dybbuk.

If genetics can determine the complexion of one's face, why can we not assume that genealogy plays a crucial role in determining the complexion of one's life? If genealogy is a basis for continuity, perhaps the starting place to climb both back to the past and ahead toward the future is on one's own family tree. If life is a text in search of a commentary to give it coherence and meaning, it may be that the commentary was composed even before the text had been conceived. In filling out the jigsaw puzzle of one's life, one's family history may provide an otherwise absent piece of the complete picture. Without this piece, the key to decoding the meaning of otherwise inexplicable actions, otherwise unfathomable commitments, remains out of reach.

Consider a son who never knew his father. The son grows to adulthood, marries, and becomes a father. One day the son finds his father—and other members of his family as well. The son discovers that he has much in common with them; he also notices resemblances between his own children and members of his newly found family. Suddenly, the son's life acquires a new level of understanding. The son's children now have a past somehow connected both to their present and their future. Genealogical research is like meeting one's parents for the first time. Many inexplicable events in one's life suddenly become clear.

A tombstone standing in a cemetery in Queens, New York, served as the gateway to my past. Toward the west, the silhouette of the Manhattan skyline was barely visible. Toward the east, in a land far away, my ancestral past began to come into focus. When last I was in this cemetery, a crowd of people surrounded the line of granite stones. There were tears and prayers. It was 1968 and Grandma was being laid to rest. Nearby, Grandpa's tombstone, placed in 1963, waited. Now he was no longer alone. Yet this time there was no crowd, only my tears, my memories, and my resolve to pry open the door to the past.

When Grandma's mother died in 1937, Grandma had a partial genealogy inscribed on her tombstone. She did not want the past of which she was so immensely proud to be forgotten. Hastily I copied the inscription on my great-grandmother's tombstone:

> Here lies Esther Yashanofsky, daughter of Yehudah Dov. From noble forebears: the granddaughter of Rabbi Hayyim Dov ha-Kohein Feigenbaum, Chief Rabbi of Wyszogrod—Vengravi, descendant of Haham Zevi, and in-law of the righteous Itzele Platzker. And also, the granddaughter of the pious rabbi, Ephraim Fishel Solomon, Chief Rabbi of Makow.

Here, finally, was the name of the Makower Ruf—Ephraim Fishel Solomon. The portal had been opened, but only a crack. This was a lead but far from a destination.

Within a few weeks, the *yizkor bukh*, or memorial book, for Makow-Mazowiecki that I had ordered arrived from my book dealer in Tel Aviv. During the 1950s and 1960s, survivors of Jewish communities destroyed by the Nazis compiled *yizkor bukhs* for many of these towns and cities.[1] In 1969 the volume for Makow was published in Israel.

I opened the volume, fearful that Ephraim Fishel Solomon might not be mentioned. Clippings from an Israeli newspaper fell out of the book, diverting my attention. There is a photograph of a short, gray-haired man in a business suit, carrying a suitcase, coming off a plane. The caption reads: "August 10, 1982. Admiral Hyman Rickover, eighty-two years old, father of the nuclear submarine, arrived in Israel yesterday morning. Upon arrival, the admiral observed: I was born in Poland in the town of Makow, near the Catholic church erected in 1615. Like many Jews, we left Poland in a concealed wagon past the German border, and from there we came to the United States." Rickover grew up in Chicago, where I now live. Later I would learn that Léon Blum, the socialist anti-Fascist premier of France in the 1930s, also was a Jew from Makow.

That Admiral Rickover, the mentor of former president Jimmy Carter, came from Makow was evidence enough that Makow was not simply a place that existed in the tales of my grandmother. As I turned the pages of the book, I sought documentary proof that the Makower Ruf was real as well. The opening chapter offers a schematic history of the Jews of Makow, from the first Jewish settlement in the sixteenth century through the destruction of the community by the Nazis. There, between the promising beginning and the tragic end in Treblinka (only a few kilometers from Makow), was a page-long section entitled "Rabbi Ephraim Fishel Solomon." It began:

> Rabbi Ephraim Fishel Solomon was installed as rabbi of Makow in 1855. Because of his wisdom, kindliness and altruism, he was beloved by all the inhabitants of Makow, including the non-Jews. He was renowned as a scholar. . . . At his initiative—mostly from his own funds, the new Study House was built adjoining the synagogue in 1858. He and his family lived above the Study House where the rabbi taught his students. Active in communal affairs, Rabbi Ephraim Fishel organized and led the Jewish community for twenty-five years. . . . He died on Shevat 20, 5641 (1881). Over his grave an *ohel* was built. Until recent times, on the anniversary of

his death, candles were lit in the Study House and Talmud was studied in his memory, and many went to his grave to recite Psalms. In 1885, his wife Rivkah died. The pious women of the town always referred to her as "Rivkele, the Righteous."[2]

The text goes on to say that some years later Ephraim Fishel's son-in-law, Rabbi Mordecai Neuman, became rabbi of Makow. His grandson, Rabbi Ephraim Fishel Neuman, emigrated to New York and served as rabbi of the Makower synagogue in Manhattan. Toward the end of the book there is a photograph and a review of the life and work of Rabbi Ephraim Fishel Neuman, who died in New York in 1952. Unlike his namesake, he had written a number of books. I managed to obtain most of them through interlibrary loans. An appendix to one of his books jolted open a door to the past. The book, *Darkhei Hayyim*, is dedicated to his relatives, listed by name, who were killed by the Nazis. To preserve their memory, Neuman also felt obliged to sketch his family genealogy.[3] In his view, the Nazi genocide was an assault on all the generations of Polish Jewry that had preceded the victims themselves. At Treblinka, an attempt had been made not only to annihilate the current generation and the future generations of Polish Jewry, but to erase from memory the past as well. Genocide meant the end of genealogy, the obliteration of the legacy of the past, the annihilation of memory of the giants of the spirit who, for so long, had populated the landscape of Polish Jewry.

Neuman could not restore what had been lost. But he could record what otherwise might be lost—the story of a family. The task he began became mine to complete. Between my annual visits to Poland over the next few years, I initiated, through my research, a conversation with my ancestors. There was much more to discover than I had imagined. Like Alice in Wonderland, I walked through the pages of books to find a lost land, the native land of my forebears.

On a subsequent visit to Poland, I come to Lodz. I find there a magnificent Jewish cemetery, but few other reminders of the Jewish community that once made up a third of the population of that metropolis. The now neglected gigantic marble monuments that populate the Jewish cemetery point to an affluence shared by only a few throughout history. Among the many graves there is the grave of one of the greatest Polish poets, Julian Tuwim. During World War II, Tuwim was in America. I recall the words of his poem "Mother":

> In the cemetery of Lodz
> In the Jewish cemetery
> There is the Polish grave of my mother,
> My Jewish mother . . .
> A Nazi shot and killed her,
> When she was thinking about me.[4]

The buildings that housed textile factories that helped bring Poland into the industrial age in the nineteenth century, as well as the mansions of the owners of the factories and the minute rowhouses of the workers, point to a bygone age primarily of interest to historians and to filmmakers in search of a ready-made historical setting. Lodz is the second largest city in Poland, after Warsaw. Like Chicago, it suffers from "second-city syndrome." Writing in the 1930s, the great Yiddish novelist Sholem Asch described the Jews of Lodz as a forest of thin, black Jews. Some pass hastily with rolls of cotton under their arms; others stand comfortably in groups before shops and flourish their thin walking sticks. Amidst all this appears now and then a patch of color from a peasant-woman's headcloth, a bright gleam of a peasant's coat; they relieve the colorless monotony of black caftans and the dark buildings like a cluster of flowers in a sandy waste. . . . Charged with power like a great dynamo, overladen with human energy, covered with sweat, blackened with coal-smoke, the city quivers with perpetual movement, with constant haste.[5]

I feel queasy. A sense of dread suddenly comes over me. My hosts, concerned, ask if I am ill. They continue the tour and inform me that we are now in the section of the city where the Lodz ghetto once was. The cause of my discomfort is now explained. Before the Holocaust about 250,000 Jews lived in Lodz. During the Holocaust, the Jewish population of Lodz increased because of the forced deportation of thousands of Jews to Lodz from other European cities. On January 19, 1945, when Lodz was liberated, less than 900 Jews remained.[6]

Chaim Rumkowski, the leader of the Lodz ghetto, believed that working for the Germans would save the Jews of Lodz from extermination. He was wrong. Although he went to the death camp in a furnished caboose, the result was the same for him as it was for those who went huddled in cattle cars. Rumkowski had believed he could save the many by surrendering the few. At one crucial point he ordered all parents to hand over their children to the Germans, thus condemning them to death. The children could not work. Their sacrifice, he said, was necessary.[7] I think of my son and a wave of depression hits me. I am then introduced to the young daughter of my hosts. She is four years old. Had she been alive and Jewish then and there, she would have been taken from her parents and sent to her death. I promptly fall in love with her. She is exquisite and alert. Somewhat self-consciously, she introduces herself.

"My name is Kasia," she says proudly, "and this is my friend Bugs Bunny." She points to a blown-up plastic replica of the famous rabbit clutched tightly in her small arms. "He lives in America. Do you know him?" she asks.

"No, he lives in California and I live in Chicago. California is very far away from Chicago."

"Well, if you ever meet him," she says, "tell him that Kasia says hello." Then, after a moment, she asks me, "What's your name?"

I tell her my name. She looks puzzled and asks her mother, "Is that an American name, like Bugs Bunny? Does he have a Polish name?"

Her mother says, "I don't know."

Kasia turns to me and asks, "Do you have a Polish name?"

"I don't know," I reply.

Though I may not have a Polish name, I do have a Jewish name that I inherited from my great-grandfather who came to America from Poland.

It is the custom among east European Jews to name children after a deceased relative. In that way, names never die; the past lives on in the present. I was named for my great-grandfather Beryl Yashanofsky (Polish: Jesionowski), who was born in 1869 in the town of Kossov (Polish: Kosow) near Lomza in eastern Poland. He arrived in New York in 1906 and died there in 1942. I inherited my name from him, a man I never met, a man whose history was somehow my own. Like him, my Yiddish name is Beryl, Dov in Hebrew. Both names mean "bear."

Beryl Yashanofsky was my mother's mother's father. His surname came from *jesion*, which in Polish means "ash tree." His family raised timber crops for lumber in Poland. They were people of means. His marriage to my great-grandmother, Esther Rosenstreich of Warsaw, was an arranged union. He brought wealth to the match. She brought *yihus* — genealogical status, a string of prominent rabbinic forebears. Her grandfather was the Makower Ruf. The match was an unhappy one, especially once they came to America, for in America *yihus* meant little. In Poland, his inherited wealth somehow disappeared. He barely eked out a living as a pants presser on New York's Lower East Side.

My genealogical research hit a dead-end with Beryl. I could not trace the name we shared further back than him. However, through Esther it was easier. The Ashkenazic Jews, who cherished *yihus*, carefully preserved the genealogical records of their rabbis. Since Esther came from a rabbinic family, I was able to follow the trail of names that constitute the leaves on her — on my — family tree. The name that consistently transmigrated throughout her lineage was Ephraim Fishel. As I climbed backward toward the roots of that tree, back to its initial planting in Poland in the fifteenth century, I met many ancestors who shared the name Ephraim Fishel (see Fig. 1).

As was already mentioned, the name of the Makower Ruf was Ephraim Fishel Solomon. He died in Makow in 1881. He was my great-great-great-grandfather. His grandfather was Ephraim Fishel of Ludmir, whose great-great-grandfather was also Ephraim Fishel of Ludmir. The grandfather of this Ephraim Fishel of Ludmir was Ephraim Fishel of Lukow, whose grandfather was Ephraim Fishel of Brisk. The great-grandfather of Ephraim Fishel of Brisk was Ephraim Fishel of Cracow, who died in 1530. The grandfather of Ephraim Fishel of Cracow was also Ephraim Fishel, who died in Cracow in the 1470s. It is with this Ephraim Fishel — fifteen generations before Ephraim Fishel of Makow and twenty generations before me — that the history of our family in Poland begins.

Ephraim Fishel definitely went to Cracow, then the royal city, the capital of Poland, but where he came from is not clear. Some say Prague. A few say Frankfurt. I agree with those who say Nuremberg, a city in south-central Germany, in Bavaria. In the third or fourth decade of the fifteenth century he seems simply to have had enough of the massacres, expulsions, persecution, extortion, restraint of trade, and restraint of living that characterized Jewish life in Germany at the time. Compelled to listen to Christian preachers trying to apostasize him, weary of paying extortion and carrying debt disguised as "taxes," sick of watching fellow Jews burned at the stake for crimes they did not commit, he left — and not too soon. By profession a banker, Ephraim Fishel may have anticipated the Nuremberg municipal code of 1479 that forbade Jews to charge interest on loans to non-Jews. He may have previsioned the royal decree of Maximilian I in 1499, expelling the Jews from Nuremberg. Or perhaps in some way he foresaw the Nuremberg Laws of a later era that were to lead to the Final Solution — to the Holocaust. In leaving, he not only ran from, he also ran toward — to Poland, the new land of Jewish refuge, the land of opportunity for Jews.

In the mid-fifteenth century the economic, political, and social conditions in the German lands and in Bohemia were in a state of rapid decline, especially for Jews. Money-lending had declined as a Jewish profession in Germany. The economy there was in ruins. Jews were constantly being expelled or threatened with expulsion

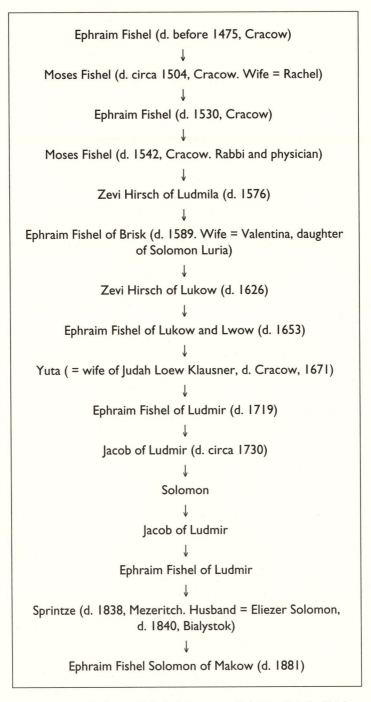

Ephraim Fishel (d. before 1475, Cracow)

↓

Moses Fishel (d. circa 1504, Cracow. Wife = Rachel)

↓

Ephraim Fishel (d. 1530, Cracow)

↓

Moses Fishel (d. 1542, Cracow. Rabbi and physician)

↓

Zevi Hirsch of Ludmila (d. 1576)

↓

Ephraim Fishel of Brisk (d. 1589. Wife = Valentina, daughter
of Solomon Luria)

↓

Zevi Hirsch of Lukow (d. 1626)

↓

Ephraim Fishel of Lukow and Lwow (d. 1653)

↓

Yuta (= wife of Judah Loew Klausner, d. Cracow, 1671)

↓

Ephraim Fishel of Ludmir (d. 1719)

↓

Jacob of Ludmir (d. circa 1730)

↓

Solomon

↓

Jacob of Ludmir

↓

Ephraim Fishel of Ludmir

↓

Sprintze (d. 1838, Mezeritch. Husband = Eliezer Solomon,
d. 1840, Bialystok)

↓

Ephraim Fishel Solomon of Makow (d. 1881)

FIGURE 1. From Ephraim Fishel of Cracow to Ephraim Fishel of Makow

from German cities and towns. Perpetually subject to punishments for spurious crimes—poisoning wells, desecrating the Host, killing Christian children to use their blood in religious rituals—the Jews of Germany looked to Poland for refuge. Poland was the land of economic opportunity and expansion, and of relative freedom and safety. From the west not only Jews, but non-Jews as well—Scots, Germans, British, and others—streamed into the Polish lands. Though Poland was not yet the land of Jewish learning it was later to become, German Jews like Ephraim Fishel took what they could, and journeyed eastward. Like so many immigrants he migrated not for spiritual or intellectual reasons, but for pragmatic ones. As a husband and father, he wanted a safe place to raise his family. As a Jew, he wanted to live without persecution. As a businessman, he wanted an environment where money could be made and retained.

Poland welcomed the Jews because their talents and experience could help develop the then incipient Polish economy. Seen from this vantage point, it was a marriage of convenience. But a marriage of convenience is still a marriage. Indeed, the contemporary view of Poland as a land endemically inhospitable to Jews runs sharply counter to much of historical experience. For most times and in most places during the thousand-year residence of the Jews in Poland, Polish Jews generally acknowledged the following: 1) the Jews had resided in Poland for a long time; 2) the residence of the Jews in Poland was a permanent arrangement—Jews were a fixed and continuing part of the social and geographical landscape of Polish territory; 3) the residence of Jews in Poland was an expression of divine grace; and 4) Polish Jews were Jews *of* Poland, not simply Jews *in* Poland, and as such they had certain extensive and well-defined rights and privileges that were protected by the Polish civil authorities.[8]

In the words of historian Gershon Hundert:

> Among Jews in the Polish Commonwealth, there developed an undeniable Polish self-identification. . . . There was also a sense of permanence and rootedness about the Polish Jewish community itself; its members did not see themselves as mere sojourners. They lived in Poyln, a land suffused with the fear of heaven and study of Torah. . . . Indeed, only the miraculous appearance of the messiah would bring an end to their residence in Poland. This perception of the Polish Jewish community as a permanent part of Polish society was shared by non-Jews in the commonwealth. . . . Jews were different; they were an integral part of the Polish social landscape. In their own eyes, in the eyes of Jews from elsewhere, and in the eyes of non-Jews, Polish Jews were an identifiable group, and that identity was incontestably Polish. . . . It would defy all logic to speak of them [Polish Jews] as living in a world apart. . . . Jews and Christians met and interacted. Their histories are not separate ones. They interlock, and they need to be understood in the light of that relationship.[9]

The Jews who came to Poland in the generation of Ephraim Fishel of Cracow were not the first Jews to populate the Polish lands. When the first Jews came to Poland is unclear, but some historians place it as early as the ninth century, near the dawning of Polish national history.[10] What is clear is that by the fourteenth century Jewish emigration to Poland accelerated as Jews sought refuge from persecutions and plagues, and as economic opportunities became increasingly available in the Polish lands.

By the sixteenth century Poland was not only a major Jewish population center, but a heartland for Jewish learning and spirituality.

According to the greatest Jewish historian of the twentieth century, Salo Baron, the description of a Jewish community properly opens with numbers. A community's feeling of rootedness, of being at home, is reflected in the size and growth of its population. From the trickle of Jews that came to Poland in the fourteenth century, a flood of Jews from the west followed. The growth rate, both through immigration and internal Jewish population expansion from the sixteenth to the eighteenth century, was explosive. By the late eighteenth century, despite the havoc wrought by invading armies, almost a million Jews dwelt in the Polish lands. In the eighteenth century the Jewish birthrate eclipsed that of other native groups; Poland was home to more Jews than any other country in the world.[11] For centuries Polish Jews exhibited a low level of what may be called "exilic consciousness." Poland was their home, their only home. As a number of historians have observed, if things were so bad for Polish Jewry, how come the Jews of Poland were so content for so long? How did they manage to create so vital a communal existence? Certainly everything was not always good, but neither was the experience one of unrelieved gloom.[12]

Though expelled from many "enlightened" and unenlightened lands, the Jews were never expelled en masse from Poland. The Statute of Kalisz, granted in 1264 by Boleslaw the Pious and renewed in 1334 by Casimir the Great, established the legal basis for the privileges and rights to be enjoyed by Jews in Poland. Though these statutes have been applauded by some Polish and Jewish historians and depicted by Polish-Jewish artist Artur Szyk as the epitome of Polish receptivity to the Jews, the fact is that they were not endemic to Poland, but were closely modeled after statutes previously granted Jews in other lands, most notably in Austria in 1240.[13] Nonetheless, the implementation of these statutes played out in a unique fashion in Poland as it quickly became the demographic epicenter of Jewish life.

Life in sixteenth- and early-seventeenth-century Poland often has been described as "a heaven for Jews, a paradise for noblemen, and a hell for serfs." It is indisputably true that during that time Jews in Poland enjoyed unprecedented economic and social freedom. Jewish autonomy was broadened to the point that the Jews were largely self-governing. The Council of Lands that functioned during that time had powers of self-governance that went considerably beyond that which other European Jewish communities enjoyed. It was also during this period that Jewish intellectual and religious life flourished in a manner virtually without precedent and certainly without later duplication. The Polish masters of Jewish law and Talmudic commentary became dominant in the Jewish world. What had once been the provenance of an intellectual elite now percolated down to the masses. Poland became both the largest consumer and the largest producer of Jewish learning in the world. Even some of the most recondite kabbalistic teachings reached the literate masses. The study of astronomy, mathematics, medicine, and philosophy found its way to Poland and was reflected in the writings of leading Jewish scholars. Yiddish was transformed from a dialect into a language not only of daily converse but of sophisticated literary expression. Far more than in any other European country, Polish Jews were encouraged to participate in a wide range of trades, crafts, and other skilled professions. They managed many of the estates of the nobility and served as indispensable craftsmen in the rural communities. As itinerant peddlers, they helped to disseminate not only new goods, but also the books that spread the emerging Polish literature throughout the land.

The current proclivity to impose contemporary rubrics upon the past, to evaluate the events in previous centuries by the sociopolitical criteria of our own times, to force historical perceptions into modern ideologies and stereotypes distorts the past to satisfy the perceived needs of the present. Rather than force our contemporary expectations upon past generations of Polish Jewry, we should try instead to understand the experience of Polish Jewry from the perspective of those who lived it, to see how Polish Jews of the past understood their own situation.

From the impression offered by some historians and by views that seem to have captured the popular imagination of Jews today, the Jews of Poland throughout their history manifested a sense of helplessness and despondency in response to continuous persecution and violence. In this view, Polish Jews despaired of their cruel fate, praying for relief from the harsh travails of everyday life in a land inhospitable to Jewish existence, in an atmosphere that stifled Jewish creativity, and in an environment that severely restricted not only their ability to make a living but even to live. Yet even the most casual perusal of the history of the Jews in Poland indicates that, more often than not, the opposite was the case.

Contrary to contemporary perceptions, Polish Jews for much of their history seem to have been presented with more economic, social, and cultural opportunities than were much of the general population of the Polish lands. The restrictions under which Jews lived were neither onerous nor unusual for the time and place. The discriminations they endured were shared by other minorities. Although nowhere near as privileged as the nobility or the Catholic elite, Jews found themselves in a comparatively advantageous situation—and they knew and appreciated it.

Security was always illusory in Poland. As a minority Jews were more vulnerable than others; for example, during the Cossack uprisings of the mid-seventeenth century, somewhere between 25 and 50 percent of the Jewish population of Poland was annihilated. This was not done by Poles, however, but by invading enemies. Indeed, most of the Poles in the region overrun by the Cossacks were also killed.[14]

Polish Jews did not view themselves as guests living in someone else's home. They felt little need to dissipate their energies in religious polemics with the more numerous Catholics. They did not feel compelled to apologize to princes or priests for who they were or for what they believed. They suffered from no inferiority complex regarding their heritage as compared to others.[15] While peasants and even noblemen throughout Poland tended to view themselves as inhabitants of the local areas in which they lived, the more mobile Polish Jews tended to view themselves as permanent inhabitants of the Polish lands. It very well may be that the Jews in Poland were the first group there to consider themselves "Polish nationals."[16]

It has been a tendency of Jewish historians to describe the history of the Jews in Poland as if it were detached from the events that form the history of Poland. However, the nature of the Jewish experience in Poland has to be seen in the context of the environment in which they lived. Social, political, and economic realities were in constant motion. The boundaries of Poland regularly changed. If the Jews in interwar Poland were generally poor, it was because Poland was then a poor country.

If the Jews suffered greatly during invasions by Tatars, Russians, Swedes, and others, it was because all of Poland was devastated by those invasions. If the Jews prospered during the sixteenth century, it was because the Polish economy experienced extraordinary growth in that period. If the Jews lost their autonomy during the modern period, it may be related to the fact that Polish national autonomy was greatly compromised for most of its modern history by a series of partitionings among various foreign powers.

In our quest to understand Jewish life in Poland, it is instructive to look at how Polish Jews understood themselves.[17] For example, in the sixteenth century German rabbis compared their own undesirable situation to the "haven" Jews had found in Poland. Writing from Germany to Moses Isserles in Cracow, Rabbi Hayyim ben Bezalel of Friedberg states that in Poland, "Jews are not despised and despoiled. Therefore a non-Jew coming into the Jewish quarter has respect for the public and is afraid to behave like a villain against Jews, while in Germany every Jew is wronged and oppressed the day long." This perspective is affirmed by Isserles, who writes, "In [Poland] there is no fierce hatred of us as in Germany . . . you will be better off here . . . you will have peace of mind." Writing in 1550, Isserles further says, "Had the Lord not left us this land as a refuge, the fate of Israel would have been indeed unbearable. But, by the grace of God, the king and his nobles are well disposed toward us."

In his massive commentary to the Talmud, Luria describes Polish Jews as having the privileges of free men, "like noblemen." He praises the kings "who many times are kind to the Jews." The chronicler Nathan Hanover describes King Sigismund III as one "who loved justice and loved Israel." In the eighteenth century, Pinhas of Koretz (Polish: Korzec) argued that "it was the Jews of Germany who suffered the bitterest exile of all," despite the fact that German Jewry was then westernized, modernized, somewhat emancipated, and "indistinguishable from the Gentiles in their language and dress." "In Poland," writes Rabbi Pinhas, "where both our language and dress are different from the Gentiles, the exile is less bitter than anywhere else." Describing the Russian incursions into Poland, Pinhas championed the Polish cause, describing Russia as a land "where one became steeped in filth." Pinhas tried by his prayers to forestall the Russian annihilation of Poland. After he died his disciple, Rabbi Raphael, said, "Had Rabbi Pinhas only lived two more years, he would have destroyed the Russians, as well as the Kaiser and the French."[18]

Further indication of the confidence of Polish Jews in their relative social security comes from economic records. A lack of confidence would express itself in financial liquidity and short-term deals. Yet long-term economic investments were common in sixteenth- and seventeenth-century Poland. Jews were engaged in tax farming, estate leasing, and commercial enterprises, building substantial homes and other capital investments with the aim of passing them down to their children and grandchildren. Both the rabbinic writings that express approval of the economic attainments of Polish Jews and those that condemn the headlong pursuit of wealth reveal a positive attitude toward the security, comparative prosperity, and long-term opportunity that dwelling in Poland provided.[19] Furthermore, the privilege to pursue their own way of life, to be governed by Jewish tradition, and to enjoy autonomy was widely perceived by Polish Jews as an indication of divine grace bestowed upon the Jewish community in Poland. For the rabbinic elite in Poland, the favorable conditions of Jewish life in that land offered a unique opportunity to ensure Jewish continuity with the past, to maintain the integrity of Jewish religious tradition, and to convey that tradition — enriched by contemporary scholarship and creativity — to future generations of Polish Jews. Writing after the Cossack invasions, Nathan Hanover compares the destruction suffered by Polish Jewry to that of Jerusalem in ancient times, and he likens the rabbinic courts of Poland to the Sanhedrin of the early rabbinic period. Hanover also describes many valiant efforts on the part of Polish noblemen and military leaders to protect and support the Jews in that time of need.

The myth of Jewish passivity in the face of attacks cannot stand up to rigorous historical analysis. Self-defense, armed or by other means, was not rare among Polish Jews. During the Cossack invasion, Jews and Poles fought together against the common enemy. In Poznan in 1687 the Jews defended themselves against attacks by Polish students and artisans. According to a contemporary Jewish chronicler, "Every time they came back to our street with drawn swords, the Jews drove them back frightened into the marketplace." During Kosciuszko's 1794 insurrection against the Russian occupation forces, Polish Jews furnished financial support for the rebellion, joined militia groups, and formed a special Jewish regiment.[20] Jews also sought remedies in the courts for violent or discriminatory acts. When a Jew was murdered, the Jewish community pressed the authorities to apprehend and punish the criminal. For instance, a seventeenth-century rabbi wrote, "And so did we behave many times and we arranged with the community leaders that they should prosecute the murderers . . . in order that it be know that Jewish blood is not free for all."[21]

An old Jewish legend tells that when the Jews traveled eastward seeking to escape from plagues and persecutions, they arrived in a land where they received a letter from heaven. On the letter were two Hebrew words: *po lin* — dwell here. This is how, the legend tells, Poland (in Hebrew, *Po-lin*) was named. On the leaves of the trees of that land, the story further tells, were inscribed sacred names and in the branches were hidden errant souls seeking deliverance by the sacred deeds of Jews that would henceforth be performed in that land. According to another tradition, Poland in Hebrew is *Po-Lan-Yah*, meaning "here God dwells."[22]

The portrait of Poland as a land forever inimical to Jews and Judaism would not have been understood by the first Ephraim Fishel or by most of his descendants. When, in about 1470, Ephraim Fishel died, he died in peace. He had acquired wealth and status. He had something to pass down to his children — not piety or learning, but qualities he had not known during his years in Germany: stability, tranquillity, and life without fear. He seems to have instilled into his family the lesson that the acquisition of wealth and power ensured security, and it was this legacy that his children cultivated, refined, and expanded.

Comparative newcomers in Cracow, the Fishel family soon eclipsed the earlier settlers as the economic, social, and political powerhouse of Jewish Cracow. Within two generations, they would consolidate their leadership by absorbing rabbinic authority as well as expanding the vortex of their political and economic power and influence. Ephraim Fishel had begun the family's rise to power by forging economic links with the Polish nobility. His son Moses extended these links to the royal family. "Make kings your debtors," one can envision Ephraim Fishel telling his son, "and they will remain in your debt."

Despite initial opposition and hostility from the Jewish leadership of Cracow, by the late 1470s Moses Fishel, tightly controlled Jewish communal affairs. As he increasingly acquired leases on royal franchises and customs revenues, his fortune and influence grew. In 1483 Moses's wife, Rachel, known in Polish as Raska Moyzeszowa, was establishing herself as a banker—one of the first women bankers in Poland. Upon her husband's death, she became a power to be reckoned with in her own right.

Like a patient in remission, always afraid that the disease might return, the Fishels must have wondered if the oppressive measures taken against Jews in Germany would follow them to their new home. Such fears were realized when, with the opening of Poland toward the west, the "high culture" of Spain, France, and Germany seeped into Poland, and with it the depravities of anti-Semitism. Anti-Jewish literature and teachers to impart it came to Poland from France. An alliance of Catholic clergy, immigrant German burghers, and native Polish merchants formed a coalition to pressure the Polish kings to emulate other European monarchs by withdrawing the privileges they had granted the Jews. Alternatively, the kings were urged to expel the Jews, as the French king had done in 1372, and various Bohemian and German rulers had done throughout the fourteenth and fifteenth centuries.

But the Polish kings stood firm; the promises made to the Jews were mostly honored, despite opposition from certain quarters. For example, when King Casimir IV signed a writ in 1453 renewing and expanding Jewish privileges, the powerful Polish cardinal Zbigniew Olesnicki wrote to the king demanding, "Your royal highness, correct your behavior, show respect to the Catholic faith and deign to withdraw and nullify the privileges granted its enemies." The itinerant preacher John of Capistrano, who had enjoyed enormous success as a Jew-baiter in Germany, joined Olesnicki's crusade to have the royal privileges revoked. Writing to Pope Nicholas V on October 13, 1454, Capistrano stated, "The King of Poland did not listen to my advice about the Jewish privileges, a copy of which I am sending to Your Holiness together with other books against these descendants of the devil." Finally, under the threat of a revolt by the nobility, the king nullified some of the privileges he had granted the Jews.[23] But compared to what they had known in Germany, such events must initially have struck members of the Fishel family as expected inconveniences rather than portents of a coming catastrophe. Despite the suspension of certain royal privileges, their contracts to collect royal revenue were still in force. Despite pressures from the Cracow burghers that forced the Jews to move from "the Jewish street" (now St. Anne's Street) to other places in Cracow, there seemed no real threat of expulsion, no omnipresent fear of massacre. They felt secure while remaining vigilant.

A 1485 document in Hebrew and Latin translation—still preserved today in the Cracow municipal archives, with four signators of the leading Jews of Cracow, including Moses Fishel and his brother Jacob—states that the Jews of Cracow "willingly [?] agreed to severely restrain Jewish commerce and trade in Cracow." Here was a small but significant victory for the German burghers who had migrated to Cracow.[24] The Jews mostly ignored the 1485 agreement, but in 1492, when the writ restricting Jewish commerce in Cracow was translated into German, the German burghers stepped up their efforts to introduce anti-Jewish measures. Their success was limited, however: Poland was not Germany.

The expulsion of the Jews from Spain in 1492 sent shock waves through Jewish communities around the world. What was once the most socially and economically secure Jewish community on earth now consisted of exiled wanderers. Yet the Jews of Poland did not feel especially threatened. In other countries, expulsions were commonplace; in Poland, Jews might be compelled to move from place to place within the country, but this was their home and they intended to stay.

In June 1494 an envoy from the sultan of Turkey arrived in Cracow. Turkey had become a central place of refuge for Jews exiled from Spain. The Turkish sultan had mocked the Spanish king for exiling the Jews, for casting out a valuable economic asset. "How could Spain expect to remain prosperous without Jews?" the Turkish sultan had asked. In his view, Spain's loss was his gain. (History was to prove him right: with the expulsion of the Jews, Spain irreparably compromised its economy.) Jews who served the Turkish court interceded at the courts of kings and princes around the world to protect their fellow Jews. No doubt several Jews were attached to the Turkish delegation.

With the Turkish envoy came twelve camels, animals never before seen in Cracow. Crowds gathered to gape at the strange animals and at the exotic costumes of the people in the entourage. The Polish king waited to receive his guests.

Suddenly, there were shouts of "Fire." Panic broke out as flames rose. Smoke was seen coming from the nearby Church of St. Mark's. Both Jewish and non-Jewish homes and shops were burning, yet the cry "The Jews are burning our homes" came from the crowd. Jewish residences and places of business were pillaged. Jews were beaten and robbed. Casualties mounted as Jews tried to defend themselves, with more injuries occurring in the fighting than from the fire.

When both the fire and tempers had been brought under control, two separate delegations — the members of the city council and the leaders of the Jewish community of Cracow — lodged their complaints before the king, Jan Olbracht. The king acknowledged the claims of the city council and incarcerated the leaders of the Jewish community, who were held responsible for the damage done by the fire and the subsequent riots. Among those imprisoned were Moses Fishel and his son-in-law, Rabbi Jacob Pollack. Locked in the castle dungeons, they waited while investigations and inquiries dragged on.

Relief came from an unexpected ally — the Jewish leaders were freed from prison at the urging of the renowned humanist and the prince's tutor Filippo Buonacorsi, and the king began to manifest a supportive attitude toward the Jews.[25] No doubt Moses's wife Rachel, a lady-in-waiting of the Queen Mother Elizabeth, was instrumental in bringing the matter to its fortunate conclusion.

The town burghers appealed to the king's brother, Cardinal Fredrick of Gniezno, the primate of Poland (and later elevated to sainthood). As a result of his intercession, the burghers' lost battle in their ongoing war against the Jews now turned into a victory. In 1495 the king, having consulted with the city council as to how to solve Cracow's "Jewish problem," ordered the Jews from Cracow. Most moved to Kazimierz, a town a few miles from the center of Cracow (it is now a section of Cracow). Only one Jewish home seems to have been explicitly exempted from this decree — that of Rachel, the wife of Moses Fishel. Yet, a number of Jews remained in Cracow without direct royal protection.[26]

Moses Fishel, apparently weakened by his incarceration, died soon after his release from the dungeons of the king he had served and enriched. It was probably expected that Moses's brother would become the family leader. But instead this role was assumed by Moses's wife, for Moses's brother had divorced himself from his family and his people when he accepted baptism into the Catholic faith.

Moses's brother was named Ephraim Fishel, but to posterity he is known by his Christian name, Stefan Powidski. Adopted by Jan Laski, the vice-chancellor of Poland (later archbishop and chancellor), Stefan was eventually ennobled. Two of his sons followed him into his new life and were baptized as Jan and Stanislaw. However, his wife and his other children remained Jews. Stefan soon abandoned his Jewish wife and took a gentile wife. Ironically, while Stefan had deserted the faith of his fathers, he retained their profession, apparently continuing to collect fees from leases granted to his father and his brother. By the eighteenth century his descendants had acquired large landed estates throughout Poland and were established and powerful members of the nobility. His descendants live in Poland to this day. Often I wonder if they, like I, are seeking the roots in Poland of the family tree we share.

Stefan surely knew that he was not the first Jew in Poland to choose a different faith, nor would he be the last. Despite the popular portrait of Polish Jews as an isolated and insular community, Jews in Poland converted to Christianity throughout the centuries. Their numbers were not large, their percentage remained minuscule, but a small stream continued from medieval to modern times, usually for self-serving reasons, sometimes out of conviction, but rarely by force. Jewish converts to Christianity came from all strata, including those close to the core of Jewish religious and intellectual life. An example is the Helitz brothers, who in the early 1530s introduced the printing of Hebrew books to Poland. The new publishing house had the promise of becoming a vital cultural factor in the Jewish community of Poland. In 1537, however, for reasons that remain unknown, the brothers converted to Christianity.[27]

Two of Rachel's daughters had married rabbinic scholars of unusual intellectual potential and capacity. Her daughter Esther was married to Rabbi Jacob Pollack; Hendel Fishel was married to Rabbi Asher Lemel. Like the Fishel family, Jacob Pollack probably hailed from Bavaria. Even in his youth Pollack was known as a profound Talmudist. Before coming to Cracow he had served as a rabbi and member of the Jewish ecclesiastical court in Prague. It is possible that the Fishel family came to Cracow via Prague, and that the match between Pollack and the daughter of Rachel and Moses Fishel took place there. When the Fishels left for Cracow, Pollack and his wife went as well.

As we have seen, Pollack's arrival in Cracow was a watershed in the history of Polish Jewry. The long and unsurpassed tradition of Talmudic scholarship in Poland—the hallmark of the religious life of the Polish Jew—began when Pollack established the first yeshivah in Poland soon after his arrival in Cracow. At that time, Poland was devoid of the intensive and extensive rabbinic learning for which it would later gain fame. It was Pollack who forged the foundation of Jewish scholarship in Poland. His students fanned out throughout Poland to establish centers of Jewish learning that would sustain the religious and the intellectual life of Polish Jewry until the Holocaust.

While Pollack's passion was scholarship, Rachel Fishel's passion was power. Whatever feats of intellectual acumen Pollack was able to perform, however many students he was able to train in his unique method of Talmudic analysis, called *hillukim*, must have remained irrelevant to her. Pollack was part of the Fishel family and as such he was obliged in Rachel's view to help consolidate the family's power, influence, and control over the Jews of Poland. While Pollack was a master in the realm of ideas, in the world of realpolitik Rachel Fishel had few peers.

Pollack's Talmudic scholarship and expertise in Jewish legal decision won him the support of the Jews of Cracow-Kazimierz. But this was not enough for Rachel Fishel. Apparently it was at her urging that King Alexander, on June 21, 1503, appointed Jacob Pollack the first chief rabbi of Poland.[28]

It does not seem coincidental that shortly after Pollack's appointment, a substantial debt owed the Fishels by the king was abruptly canceled. But Rachel deftly found a way to make a profit from the king despite the cancellation of the debt. At her request, the king ordered the royal mint to produce coins of the realm from silver bars provided by Rachel Fishel. The bars she submitted were worth a thousand florins, but the coins she received were worth sixteen hundred florins.

Rachel's machinations must have given her great satisfaction, but they caused only difficulties for Pollack. Already in 1492 Rachel had pushed Pollack into a dispute that threatened to undermine his rabbinic status and authority.

Rachel had married off her daughter Sarah to David Zeners of what is now Budapest. Zeners was from a wealthy Hungarian Jewish family. At the time of the marriage Sarah was a minor, that is, she was under twelve years of age. This was not unusual in those days, when marriages were arranged by the parents usually for reasons of status, wealth, or both. According to Talmudic law, in such a case the child-wife has the right of *me'un*, of freeing herself from her husband, usually before the consummation of the marriage. In the mid-fifteenth century, however, a rabbinic decree was issued in Germany abolishing the right of *me'un*. Nonetheless, Pollack upheld the right of his sister-in-law both to leave her husband and to remarry. No doubt the influence of Rachel Fishel played a central role in his legal decision. As a result of this decision, Pollack was attacked by most of the great contemporary rabbinic scholars of the time. Bans of excommunication were written against him, and Pollack's status as a rabbinic judge was severely impugned. For, as it happened, the issue was not simply whether contemporary scholars had the right to overturn Talmudic precedent; nor was it whether a child had the right to refuse a repulsive marriage. At issue was the propriety of using political clout to secure a rabbinic appointment. As we have seen, the appointment of rabbis by civil authorities influenced by wealthy Jews was to become a matter of bitter Jewish communal dispute. Such actions were defended by no less a figure than Moses Isserles and attacked by leading scholars such as Solomon Luria, Judah Loew, and Yom Tov Lipman Heller. A second issue was whether Pollack was trying to manipulate the law to cover up the improprietous behavior of his sister-in-law, Sarah.

Though young, Sarah was not completely innocent. While married to Zener, she had fallen in love with a younger man—a student and poet who lived as a boarder in her house. This affair of the heart appears to have been conducted with little discretion. Indeed, it was so well known that ballads were written about it and sung in marketplaces and homes. Meanwhile, Rachel's son Ephraim Fishel had received from the king the authority to levy and collect the taxes due to the Crown from all the Jews of Poland. With the establishment of a flat tax, rather than having each Jewish community levy and collect their taxes separately, a single collector was named. This task—and the power and lucrative commissions that went with it—fell to Ephraim Fishel.

With Ephraim Fishel in control of Jewish communal finances and with Jacob Pollack in control of the religious and intellectual life of Polish Jewry, the subservience of the Jewish community of Poland to the Fishel family seemed complete. The achievements of Rachel Fishel far surpassed even the wildest dreams of her father-in-law, Ephraim Fishel, or of her husband, Moses Fishel. For almost a century the Fishel family was to play a dominant role in the economic, political, religious, and social affairs of Polish Jewry.

The Fishel family was caught in the nexus of a debate—still current in our own time—between those who favor centralized control of communal affairs and those who favor a decentralized communal structure. Ultimately, those who fought for local decentralized communal control prevailed. What they found suspect was the role of a Christian king in determining who would be the social and religious leaders of Polish Jewry. But Rachel Fishel saw things differently. She believed that without first fortifying the physical security of the Jewish community, other concerns were of little consequence. And the best source of such security was an alliance with the royal court.

While Ephraim Fishel managed to cope with the social and political pressures of his position as royal tax collector, his brother-in-law, the abrasive and controversial Jacob Pollack, retreated from the attacks of his colleagues. Pollack's tenure as chief rabbi was short-lived. Because his post had been granted by the king, his authority had never been recognized by the Jewish community. The proliferation of bans of excommunication issued against him by the leading rabbis of his time further undermined his status as an objective and honest arbiter of Jewish legal problems. The case of his sister-in-law, Sarah, continued to plague him. Eventually Pollack was forced to leave Cracow and to wander homeless from land to land, stripped of his status. The period of his imprisonment in the royal dungeons might have seemed a luxury compared to his subsequent situation. But Rachel Fishel would not tolerate this indignity. At her request, on August 2, 1509, King Sigismund I (Zygmunt I Stary) issued an "iron letter" making it possible for Pollack to return to Cracow under the protection of the king himself. Anyone trifling with Pollack would now have to answer to the king. Despite royal protection Pollack was unable to resume his position as a communal rabbi and an arbiter of Jewish legal disputes, but he was perhaps content to return to the post he cherished most—head of the first Talmudic academy of Poland. Liberated from the fray of political and social disputes, he was now free to teach students who would lay the foundations of rabbinic learning in Poland. Though no longer chief rabbi of Poland, he was able to become the progenitor of Jewish scholarship in the Polish lands. Though he produced no published writings, Pollack did produce great scholars. Foremost among them was Shalom Shakhna, who would establish the great yeshivah of Lublin. Shakhna also would marry Pollack's daughter, thereby perpetuating the influence of the Fishel family in the sphere of Jewish education in Poland.

It was not Pollack's nature to let well enough alone. In the 1520s he felt compelled to become involved in a scandal that rocked the Jewish community of Cracow-

Kazimierz. In the affair of his sister-in-law, he was accused of encouraging adultery. Now he was accused of trying to stop it. Yet here, too, he pitted himself against the wrong opponents.

The second wife of King Sigismund I was the despised Italian princess, Bona Sforza, who brought with her to Poland both the corruption and the culture characteristic of the Italian Renaissance court. Among those to accompany Bona Sforza to Cracow after her 1518 royal marriage was her Jewish physician, Samuel ben Meshulam, who wasted no time establishing both social and financial relations with the leading local Jewish families of Cracow, including the Fishels. Soon, Ephraim Fishel's wife, Hava (Polish: Chwalka), and his daughter-in-law Esther became ladies-in-waiting to Queen Bona.[29]

Samuel the physician's closest new friends in Cracow were a local merchant named Moses and Moses's wife, Klara. Samuel entered into a number of commercial ventures with Moses and was often seen socially with Moses and Klara. But more seemed to be going on. In the small inbred Jewish community, rumors began to proliferate about a passionate and not-so-secret love affair between Samuel and Klara. Rabbi Jacob Pollack charged Samuel and Klara with committing adultery, and on April 23, 1522, a hearing was convened in Cracow to consider countercharges by Samuel, Moses, and Klara against Jacob Pollack for defamation of character. Afraid of the power wielded by Samuel at the royal court, Pollack once more left Cracow. He returned, however, and suits and countersuits went on. It is unclear how the matter was finally resolved, but it seems that Samuel prevailed. According to one source, Pollack eventually left Poland for good, journeying to the Holy Land, where he died less than a decade later. Another source holds that Pollack followed his son-in-law and disciple Shalom Shakhna to Lublin where he taught until his death in the yeshivah established by Shakhna.

Despite the successful attempt of the Jewish community of Cracow to unseat Pollack as chief rabbi of Poland in 1505, Rachel Fishel still managed to retain family control of key rabbinical posts. By 1507 Rachel's other son-in-law, Asher Lemel, was serving as the chief rabbi of Cracow. Married to Rachel's daughter Hendel, Asher was known by his mother-in-law's name, Rabbi Asher Rachele. Asher Lemel and Hendel were to become the progenitors of one of the most prominent rabbinic families in Poland. Their most famous descendant would be their grandson, the preeminent Rabbi Meir, known as the Maharam of Lublin. Whereas Pollack was the first great Talmudist in Poland, Lemel is often depicted by historians as Poland's first important kabbalist.

The grave of the Maharam may still be found in the old Jewish cemetery of Lublin. At the age of twenty-four he served as the head of the Jewish academy of Lublin and died there in 1616 when in his late fifties. He also served in Cracow and Lemberg (Polish: Lwow). Wherever he settled, he founded rabbinical academies that attracted many students. He welcomed and received inquiries from rabbis from all over Europe on legal matters. Despite his occasional use of casuistry, his many writings were clear and precise. Like his grandfather, he was conversant with the Jewish mystical tradition and two of his students—Nathan Nata Shapiro and Isaiah Horowitz—emerged as leading kabbalists. Like many of his contemporaries, he was reluctant to publicize kabbalistic teachings. Also like many of his contemporaries, he strongly opposed the authority of the Jewish legal codes. In this regard, he wrote, "It is not my custom to occupy myself with [the study of] the *Shulhan Arukh*, and surely not to base any legal ruling on an inference from its language."[30] Among his closest disciples was Rabbi Abraham Joshua Heschel of Cracow.

Opposition to Lemel's appointment as chief rabbi of Cracow did not come primarily from the longtime Jewish residents of Cracow-Kazimierz, as might be expected, but from the recent Jewish immigrants who flowed into Cracow after their expulsion from Bohemia. Tensions soon erupted between the new arrivals and the established residents. The Bohemian Jews tried to take over control of the synagogue in Kazimierz and to replace Lemel with a rabbi of their own choosing. However, the Bohemians underestimated Lemel's leverage at the royal court. In 1519 King Sigismund reaffirmed both the rights of the established Jews to their synagogue and the previous appointment of Lemel as rabbi of Cracow. Though they were compelled to accept the king's decree, the Bohemian Jews nonetheless appointed a certain Rabbi Peretz for their own community. Again, the Fishel family saw fit to assert and to expand its influence, this time at the hands of a new Moses Fishel—the grandson of Rachel and Moses.

Born soon after the death of his grandfather, Moses Fishel inherited both his name and his position of communal leadership. But unlike his grandfather, this Moses Fishel manifested little interest in the commercial and financial dealings that had served for three generations as the basis of his family's influence. In his early youth Moses studied Talmud with his uncle, Jacob Pollack, and became a rabbinic scholar of some substance. Later, he went to Italy where he became a physician.[31] As historical scholarship has demonstrated, interaction between Poland and Italy—and between Polish and Italian Jewry—flourished during this period.[32] Jewish students from Poland went to study medicine in Italy, particularly in Padua. Jewish students from Italy populated the rabbinical academies of Poland. The flow of Italian culture into Poland brought with it ideas of the Renaissance that infiltrated into Jewish life and thought. At the same time, Hebrew books published in Italy and brought to Poland introduced new concepts of Jewish mysticism. The harsh polemical style characteristic of sixteenth-century Jewish literature, where not only an opponent's intellectual position, but his entire being was ridiculed, may have been an outgrowth of the intermingling of Jewish culture with Italian Renaissance thought. It may be that some of the battle over the place of philosophy in Judaism reflected a conflict over a broader issue, namely, whether Polish Jewry should be receptive at all to the ideas being exported from Italy. Did those ideas promise to fortify and expand, or to threaten and subvert, the integrity of Judaism as it had developed in Poland?

After serving as the personal physician of the archbishop of Poznan, Dr. Moses Fishel returned to Cracow and, probably through family influence, became in 1523 a court physician to King Sigismund I. After the death of his uncle Asher Lemel in 1532, he was also appointed to Lemel's post as chief rabbi of Cracow. In 1541 Rabbi Dr. Moses Fishel and his cousin Shalom Shakhna of Lublin were appointed by the king to be co–chief rabbis of Poland (Shalom Shakhna was married to Moses Fishel's cousin—the daughter of Jacob Pollack and Esther Fishel). The authority granted to Fishel and Shakhna far exceeded that granted to Jacob Pollack. With the appointment came not only considerable power but also substantial financial compensation. Immediately, local Jewish communities—beginning with the Jews of Cracow-

Kazimierz—tried to sabotage these appointments and to restrain the powers granted by royal decree. Although Moses Fishel's appointment was for life, that life soon came to an abrupt and unexpected end.

By the 1520s the effects of the Protestant Reformation were being felt in Poland. There, as in Moravia and Lithuania, it was not the Lutherans or the Calvinists who posed the greatest threat to the entrenched Catholic Church; rather, it was representatives of what has been called the "radical reformation" who had begun to make substantial headway in Poland. These reformers were attacked by Catholics and Lutherans alike. The charge against them, whether made by Catholic bishops or by Martin Luther, was the same: Judaizing, that is, stripping Christian teaching of its most fundamental ideas and returning to Jewish ideas and practices. Some followers of these new sects abandoned Sunday Sabbath observances for Saturday Sabbaths. Others practiced circumcision. The greatest threat, however, came not in practice but in ideas, including rejection of the Holy Trinity and the divinity of Jesus Christ. Some carried their commitments to what they considered the logical conclusion and sought instruction in Judaism. A few even sought conversion to Judaism.

Among those swayed by the winds of the radical reformation was Catherine Weigel Zaluszowska, the wealthy widow of Melchoir Weigel—a merchant and member of the Cracow city council. In 1530 she had been accused of Judaizing, but she recanted under threats of torture. Nine years later she was accused again, but refused to recant. Consequently, at about the age of eighty, she was burned at the stake in Cracow. According to eyewitnesses of her execution, she was asked, "Do you believe in God's only son, our Lord Jesus Christ?" She replied, "God has neither need for a wife or son, for only mortals need sons. . . ." Whether Catherine Weigel Zaluszowska was a secretly converted Jew or a radical anti-Trinitarian, her execution made a great impression on both the civil and religious authorities, who suspected Jews of trying to convert Christians. Soon after the "Weigel affair," the king ordered the arrest of a number of Jewish communal leaders in Cracow. Despite family influence at royal court, Dr. Moses Fishel was jailed and probably tortured. He died in 1542, shortly after his release, probably as a result of injuries suffered during his imprisonment.[33] He had served as the chief rabbi of Poland for only about a year. By 1552 the office of chief rabbi of Poland had been abolished. Tax collection had been decentralized. The power of the dynasty established by the refugee Fishel from Germany had declined, but it had not ended. The descendants of Rabbi Moses Fishel, the physician, would spread throughout the Polish lands, and they would be heard from soon again.

With the generations of Pollack, Shakhna, Lemel, and Isserles, the spiritual heritage of Polish Jewry began to take shape. Fortunes were accumulated and lost. The favor of kings was cultivated and surrendered. The tradition of learning and piety had become deeply rooted—only to be swept away centuries later by the flood of fire called the Holocaust.

King for a Night

Some aspects of the tumultuous career and the tragically ironic life of Rabbi Jacob Pollack have been discussed in the previous chapter. Though a failure in many of his endeavors, Pollack was an enormous success in the training of scholars. His two greatest disciples were Shalom Shakhna and Meir Katzenellenbogen. Shakhna married Pollack's daughter and established the great yeshivah in Lublin. Shakhna's daughter would marry the preeminent Rabbi Moses Isserles. Meir Katzenellenbogen is known to posterity as the Maharam of Padua. The rabbinic dynasty he founded in the early fifteenth century would spread throughout Europe. One of his descendants, Rabbi Saul [Katzenellenbogen] Wahl, would be known to future generations as King Saul, for according to a well-documented legend Saul reigned as the king of Poland, albeit for a single night. Other descendants of Meir Katzenellenbogen are also known to history. One is Karl Marx. Others are the great Jewish philosopher Moses Mendelssohn and his grandson, the composer Felix Mendelssohn-Bartholdy. Still others include the Jewish philosopher Martin Buber, and the "queen of cosmetics," Helena Rubenstein. But my interest in the Katzenellenbogen family is based mainly on my discovery that I, too, am a descendant of Rabbi Meir Katzenellenbogen. Five lines of my lineage flow into the Katzenellenbogen family: the Fishels, the Klausners, the Shors, the Shakhnas, and the Lurias.

The Katzenellenbogen family can be traced to the German town of that name. Rabbi Meir was born there in 1482. With his father-in-law, Rabbi Abraham Mintz, Meir migrated to Italy where, after a long and distinguished career, he died in 1565. Meir was succeeded by his son, Rabbi Samuel Judah Katzenellenbogen, who served as chief rabbi of the Republic of Venice until his death in 1597. Saul Wahl was the precocious son of Samuel Judah Katzenellenbogen.[1] Fortified with sacred wisdom imparted by his father and secular wisdom acquired at the University of Padua, Saul was sent to augment his Jewish learning at the great yeshivah in Brisk (Brest-Litovsk) in Poland. The branch of the Katzenellenbogen family established by Saul there (he was never to return to his native Italy) was to become one of the great rabbinic dynasties of eastern Europe.

Though then in Lithuania, Brisk is nonetheless well within the borders of the historical lands of Poland.[2] In 1386 the Grand Duchy of Lithuania became part of the Polish kingdom. The borders of the kingdom (later the republic) of Poland-Lithuania constantly shifted through the centuries, remaining expansive until the series of the partitions of Poland among various foreign powers beginning in the late eighteenth century. From the time of the first partition in 1772 until 1918, Poland was wiped off the map. From the late fourteenth century until the late eighteenth century, however, the geographical area of Poland was considerable, and the population of Polish Jewry constantly shifted within those borders.

The historical lands of Poland, and not the current borders of the Republic of Poland, represent the boundaries both of Polish history and culture, and of the social and spiritual heritage of Polish Jewry. While Cracow, Lublin, Poznan, Warsaw, and Bialystok are currently within the borders of the Republic of Poland, great Polish cities—leading centers of Polish Jewry—have been absorbed by other countries. For example, included as part of the legacy of Polish Jewry is the culture and learning produced in the prominent Galician (now Ukrainian) city of Lemberg (Polish: Lwow). Included as well are other cities and towns of Ukraine like Berditchev, Korets and Chernobyl, where Hasidism thrived. In Lithuania there are the cities and hamlets where the opponents of Hasidism flourished, including Vilna and Valoshin. There was Podlasie (Podlasia), between Byelorussia (now Byelarus) and Lithuania, where Jews populated towns like Lukow and Grodno. In Podole (Podolia), Hasidism was born and in Volhynia (Wolyn) it flourished. In Byelorussia (Polish: Bialorus) were the cities of Minsk with a 90 percent Jewish population and Vitebsk (Polish: Witebsk), the birthplace of Marc Chagall. Northward, the kingdom of Poland-Lithuania stretched far beyond Vilna (Wilno). Eastward, it bordered on the Muscovite kingdom. In the west, Poznan (German: Posen) was near Poland's western frontier with the Germanic lands.[3]

During these centuries, Poland was far from being ethnically or religiously monolithic. For example, while today about 96 percent of the population of Poland is Catholic, Catholics accounted for about 54 percent of the Polish population in 1793 and 65 percent in 1931.[4] Describing pre-partition Poland, historian Norman Davies writes:

> To the objective observer, the most outstanding feature of pre-partition society in Poland-Lithuania was its multicultural character. Within the confines of the old Republic, there flourished a profusion of peoples, a riot of religions, a luxuriance of languages. . . . The cultural variety of old Polish society encouraged a number of specific attitudes. It prepared the ground, if not for universal tolerance, then at least for practical toleration.[5]

When Saul Katzenellenbogen came to Brisk (currently in Byelarus) in the sixteenth century, he found there a well-established Jewish community. Jews had first settled in Brisk in the mid-fourteenth century. The great-grandfather of Rabbi Solomon Luria had served as the first rabbi there. His name was Yehiel ben Aaron Luria, and he died in 1470. Yehiel Luria was also the great-grandfather of Rabbi Moses Isserles. It seems that before going to Lublin, Solomon Luria served as a rabbi both in Brisk and in Ostraha (Polish: Ostrog). In the seventeenth century the yeshivah of

Ostraha, under the leadership of the masterful Talmudic commentator Rabbi Samuel Edels, became the most important Talmudic academy of eastern Poland.

Both Jewish and Polish sources offer many versions of the legend of Saul Katzenellenbogen. The most reliable account is found in a manuscript by his great-grandson, Pinhas Katzenellenbogen. This manuscript can be found today in the Bodleian Library at Oxford University.[6] One indication that the legend of Saul Katzenellenbogen's election as the king of Poland has been taken seriously by subsequent generations is the fact that he is known to posterity as Saul Wahl. *Wahl* is Yiddish for "elected."[7]

Most versions of the legend begin by telling how Prince Nicholas Radziwill of Poland-Lithuania met Saul's father, Rabbi Samuel Katzenellenbogen, in Italy. According to one version, Nicholas's father had scandalized the family by converting to the Protestant faith. To restore the family's religious standing, Nicholas not only reaffirmed Catholicism but took upon himself a penance to atone for his father's sin. The form the penance took was a pilgrimage to the Holy Land. On his return home, the prince passed through Italy, where he was attacked by brigands and robbed. Starving, ill, and on the verge of death, the prince somehow staggered to the home of Saul's father, Rabbi Samuel. When the rabbi opened the door, the prince collapsed in his arms. Samuel nursed the prince back to health.

At this point in all versions of the legend, a conversation takes place between the prince and the rabbi. The prince is ready to leave for home, but before he departs, he asks the rabbi, "Now that you have done so much for me, what can I do for you?"

"My son, Saul, lives in your native land," the rabbi answers. "I will give you a letter from me for him. He is a man of great abilities, and may be able to be of service to you."

Upon his return home Nicholas located Saul, whom he immediately recognized as a man of high culture. He noticed that Saul was literate in many languages, that he was knowledgeable in the humanities and the sciences, and that his acumen for commerce was considerable.

Nicholas found Saul to be a man of honesty and integrity, and Saul became the prince's chief advisor in commercial and political affairs. Soon, other nobles sought Saul's advice and counsel, and Saul became known and respected among the nobles of the land. Saul profited by his associations, gaining leases to the largest salt mines in Poland. The revenues from his various enterprises brought him great wealth, eclipsing the fortune of his rich father-in-law, David Drucker of Brisk.[8]

With Nicholas Radziwill's help, Saul's influence extended to the court of King Stephan Bathory, who became one of Saul's trusting admirers. It was possibly Saul's influence that convinced the king to protect and defend his Jewish subjects. When Stephan Bathory died, the nobles all gathered to elect the next king. The date set for the election was August 18, 1587.

Various noblemen tried to force the election in favor of the candidate of their choice. Through bribery and intrigue, foreign powers vied to place their favored candidate on the Polish throne. August 18th was coming to an end, and no solution had been found. The kingdom seemed ready to split apart, with civil war or foreign domination the apparently inevitable result. The nobles quarreled as the clock pushed toward the ominous deadline. When the tension had reached its peak, Prince

Radziwill stood up to speak. He had to diffuse the situation. To show favoritism toward any of the leading candidates would cause national chaos. The fate of Poland lay in his hands.

"I recommend," he said, "that since we cannot reach a decision about a permanent monarch, we elect in the meantime as a temporary king a man who is not one of the candidates, a man who will agree to serve only until a permanent king can be elected, a man whose wisdom and integrity is known to you all. I nominate for *rex pro tempore*, for interim king, Saul Katzenellenbogen."

Happy to have a respite from the tensions of their deliberations, the noblemen unanimously agreed to Radziwill's suggestion, for what they all feared was civil war. After the royal gowns were draped upon Saul's body, he asked to be shown the royal archives, for it was the right of the king—even a temporary king—to review and even to change decrees of previous kings. Through the night, Saul read and wrote. All previous royal decrees against the Jews were amended. In addition, he endorsed many measures in favor of the Jews of Poland. The following morning Saul was exhausted, but the nobles were rested and calm. Unexpectedly, friendship and collegiality replaced hatred and strife. Within a few hours they elected a new king, Sigismund III (Zygmunt III Waza). But for a single night Saul reigned as the king of Poland.

Saul's service as monarch of Poland is recorded only in legend, but his service to the Polish Crown is noted in a number of archival sources. On February 11, 1588, in a royal decree by Sigismund III, Saul is described as "having advanced the prosperity of the realm by his conscientious efforts . . . during the reigns of our predecessors." In 1589 Sigismund wrote, "We, King of Poland, having convinced ourselves of the rare and distinguished ability of Saul, the Jew, do hereby grant him a place among our royal officials." With this appointment came the personal protection of the king. For his services to the Crown, Saul was given a thick gold chain studded with jewels. In his will Saul ordered that the chain be sold and that proceeds from the sale be distributed to the poor.

Saul had a daughter, Hindele, whom he loved very much. She was as beautiful as she was wise, and many prominent Jewish families sought her hand for their sons in marriage. Among them was the eminent rabbinical family the Heschels, the ancestors of my mentor, Abraham Joshua Heschel. Indeed, it seems to have been agreed that Hindele would marry the young Rabbi Heschel. But when the brilliant young scholar was brought to meet the prospective bride, she apparently spurned him. Members of Saul's family, basking in the prestige of his election as king of Poland, treated members of the scholarly and pious Heschels with scorn and disdain. The marriage was called off, but the rabbi's friends in the town decided to seek revenge against Saul's family and against the unsuspecting young Hindele. An opportunity soon presented itself with the sudden death of the queen of Poland.

While nothing could fulfill a young girl's fantasies more than to become a queen, nothing could be more problematic for a young Jewess than to be forced into marriage with a Christian man—even a king.

Saul's enemies spoke to their friends at court lauding the beauty and wisdom of young Hindele. Since they knew that Saul never would surrender his daughter for such a marriage, they proposed that she be kidnapped and brought to the palace.

When the king himself heard of the idea, he ordered his soldiers to kidnap Hindele and bring her to the palace, where she spent the night in the private chambers of the king.

What happened there is unknown. Perhaps she was seduced by the king, perhaps she was the seducer—perhaps the desire was mutual—or perhaps nothing at all happened. In any case, she was soon released, to her father's relief.

Legend then tells that soon after Hindele's release from the palace, the great, learned, but aged Rabbi Ephraim Zalmen Shor had a vision from heaven. Some years earlier his wife had died. Being nearly seventy years of age, he had no expectation to remarry, but in this vision he was commanded to marry Hindele, the young daughter of Rabbi Saul Wahl of Brisk. The marriage soon took place.[9] Within a year a son, Jacob, was born. Raised by his mother after the death of his father, Jacob excelled in his studies. When it came time for Jacob to be ordained as a rabbi, Hindele brought him to the eminent Rabbi Heschel. But the rabbi, who had neither forgotten nor forgiven Hindele's rejection of him many years earlier, refused to ordain her son.

Ironically, another member of the Katzenellenbogen family married into the Heschel family, and as a consequence one of Saul Wahl's descendants was the famed nineteenth-century Hasidic master Abraham Joshua Heschel of Apt. Nonetheless, Rabbi Jacob eventually received ordination and from 1652 to 1655 he served as the rabbi of Brisk, a post that his father Rabbi Ephraim Zalmen Shor and his grandfather Rabbi Naftali Hirsh Shor had held before him. In the eighteenth century the descendants of Saul Wahl, Abraham and his son Joseph Katzenellenbogen, served as the rabbis of Brisk.[10]

As was already discussed, the first famous Heschel in Poland was Abraham Joshua Heschel, who is buried in the old Jewish cemetery of Cracow. Next to his grave there is a small empty space without a tombstone, indicating that in the post–World War II restoration of the cemetery the identity of the person buried there was forgotten, or merely overlooked. A study of charts of the cemetery from the prewar period, however, shows that this is the grave of Abraham Joshua Heschel's successor to the office of chief rabbi of Cracow, Rabbi Judah Loew Klausner, who served in that position until his death in 1671. Klausner and Heschel were also related by marriage: Klausner's daughter was the wife of Heschel's son Saul.[11]

Judah Loew Klausner was also known as Rabbi Leib Fishels, after his father-in-law, Ephraim Fishel of Lukow. Ephraim Fishel of Lukow was a direct descendant of the Fishels of Cracow. His maternal grandmother, Valentina, was the daughter of Rabbi Solomon Luria of Lublin.[12] Ephraim Fishel of Lukow was also the great-great-great-great-great-great-grandfather of Ephraim Fishel Solomon of Makow—the Makower Ruf, my great-great-great grandfather.

Ephraim Fishel served as rabbi of Lukow—a post previously held by his father and later held by his son— until his death in 1653.[13] The first rabbi of Lukow was Joel Sirkes, whom we met in Cracow. Sirkes also served as rabbi of Brisk, as had Ephraim Fishel's grandfather, Ephraim Fishel of Brisk. Ephraim Fishel of Lukow's wife was named Gitel. She was the daughter of Mordecai Shrenzel. The Shrenzel family, also known as Nachmanowicz after the family patriarch Nahman, was among the mainstays of the Jewish community of Lwow. In the sixteenth century they had close financial ties to a number of Polish kings, including Stephan Bathory. They were among the wealthiest Jewish families of Poland.[14] Mordecai Shrenzel's wife, Rivkah, was the daughter of Rabbi Joseph Katz—the brother-in-law of Moses Isserles, who lies buried next to him in the old Jewish cemetery of Cracow. Though Lwow was a city that boasted of the many distinguished rabbis who had served there—including members of the Shrenzel family—and of the prominent yeshivah that was established there, it was also, by the nineteenth century, a center of the Jewish Enlightenment (Hebrew: Haskalah) in eastern Europe. In the 1880s it already had a Zionist constituency. Before the Holocaust, over a hundred thousand Jews lived in Lwow.[15]

Ephraim Fishel was also the name of the son of Rabbi Judah Loew Klausner and his wife, Yuta. This Ephraim Fishel was apparently named for his grandfather, Rabbi Ephraim Fishel of Lukow. It was this Ephraim Fishel who served as the *parnas*, or elected chief official, of the Council of Lands, the most powerful and prestigious position of lay leadership of Polish Jewry. Like his father, Judah Loew Klausner, he was given the title "servant of the king," which afforded him substantial economic opportunities, and which meant that disputes involving him could be resolved only by the king's court. These privileges were granted him by King Jan Sobieski III in 1679 and reaffirmed by King August II in 1699. He lived most of his adult life in Ludmir (Polish: Wlodzimierz Wolynski), which is located in Vollynia. His son and grandson served as rabbis of Ludmir.[16]

The father of Judah Loew Klausner of Cracow was Zechariah Mendel Klausner, who was known as Zechariah the Prophet. No one seems to know why he was given this unusual title. Zechariah Mendel's family was deeply rooted in Poznan. For Jews fleeing Germany, Poznan, near Poland's western border, was a natural first stop. Zechariah Mendel's grandfather had been a student of Shalom Shakhna of Lublin; Zechariah's wife came from a prominent rabbinic family that had come to Poznan from Worms. This family was related to the Luria family, and like the Luria's it could trace its lineage back to Rashi, the greatest of all Jewish commentators, who lived in eleventh-century France. And through their patriarch, Rabbi Judah the Elder of Prague, who died in 1439, the family traced its roots further back to the great tenth-century Babylonian sage Hai Gaon, and through him to the biblical figure Zerubabel ben Shealtiel, a direct descendant of King David. Zechariah Mendel's wife, whose name is lost to us, was the aunt of two brothers whom we met in a previous chapter, Rabbi Hayyim ben Bezalel of Friedberg and Rabbi Judah Loew of Prague. Hence, Judah Loew of Prague and Judah Loew of Cracow were first cousins. Both had been named after their great-great-grandfather, Judah the Elder of Prague. Like his older and more famous cousin, Judah Loew of Cracow was known by the acronym Maharal, and as the High Rabbi Loew.[17]

Born in Poznan, Judah Loew of Prague served for a while as rabbi of his native city. However, he is known to posterity as the rabbi of Prague. Though he is best known in legend, as the creator of the golem—the artificial human being of Jewish folklore—his most masterful achievements lie in the extraordinary contributions to Jewish thought found in his published works. Among the most profound and prolific writers of his age, he was probably the most important Jewish religious thinker to emerge from sixteenth-century Poland. His writings helped shape Hasidism in its nascent stage in the eighteenth century, and profoundly influenced the particular form it took in the heart of the Polish lands in the nineteenth century. One Hasidic master said of him, "The Maharal of Prague has brains even in his feet."[18]

Judah Loew of Prague's intellectual jousts with Eliezer Ashkenazi over the place of philosophy in Judaism and his opposition to the codification of Jewish law have been discussed above. Whereas Luria and Isserles opposed the popular spread of Jewish mystical ideas, Judah Loew did not. His works offer the most complete Jewish theological system produced by any Ashkenazic Jewish thinker. Though not systematic in the philosophical sense of the term, his writings nonetheless articulated a comprehensive theology of Judaism predicated upon Jewish mystical ideas. Written in a clear, though often repetitious Hebrew style, his works express recondite kabbalistic ideas in a readily accessible manner. According to one Hasidic master, Judah Loew's goal was to "reveal the concealed." From the theological constructs he formulated, Loew goes on to recommend a program for the reformation of Jewish spiritual and intellectual life, including a plan for the restructuring of Jewish education on all levels. For Loew, mystical theology and social action are intertwined. Though during his lifetime many of his ideas fell on deaf ears, they found resonance and implementation in generations to come.

When I went in 1992 to Poznan to deliver a lecture, I tried to find some remnant of the presence of Judah Loew, some trace of more than six hundred years of Jewish life in that Germanic-like city of grace, beauty, and economic expansion.[19] But all that is left is the hull of a building that once was a large synagogue. It was converted into a swimming pool by the Nazis, and remains in use as such today. The main Jewish cemetery was destroyed and is now part of the Poznan fairgrounds. However, though Loew's presence cannot be detected in his native Poznan, it is pervasive in his adopted city, Prague. His tombstone stands prominently in the old Jewish cemetery of Prague and has become a major tourist attraction. In his synagogue in Prague, the gothic Altneuschul where, according to legend, the remains of the golem are stored, his chair remains in place next to the Holy Ark. According to a tradition, since his death in 1609 no one has sat in that chair. A famous statue of Rabbi Loew by the sculptor Saloun still stands in Prague. In Bohemia, Loew is not only a spiritual hero to Jews, but a national hero to all Czechs. In the long history of the Jewish diaspora, Judah Loew of Prague is the only rabbi who is considered a national hero of the people among whom he dwelt.

In Poznan, there is no statue of Rabbi Loew. However, a statue of Adam Mickiewicz, the poet laureate of Poland and a national hero, stands next to the university there that bears his name. Like Czeslaw Milosz, the Nobel Prize–winning Polish poet of our own times, Mickiewicz was from the Lithuanian precincts of Poland. There is evidence that Mickiewicz's wife, Celina, and perhaps Mickiewicz himself, were of Jewish origin. His wife's family, and possibly his own, were descendants of a group of families that, in the late eighteenth century, were followers of the mystical messianic madman Jacob Frank, who along with his followers converted to the Catholic faith.[20]

Regretfully, my lecture itinerary did not take me to Wroclaw, known in German as Breslau, now in the far southwestern corner of Poland. A flicker of Jewish life remains there, but hardly the flame it once was. It was from there that modern forms of Jewish scholarship and thought emanated in the nineteenth century. There, the great Jewish historian Heinrich Graetz wrote his still unsurpassed *History of the Jews*. There the Jewish Theological Seminary of Breslau, where tradition merged with the best of modernity, functioned until the Nazi onslaught. Founded in 1854 by Zechariah Frankel, it was the foundation of the movement now known as Conservative Judaism. Not by coincidence, one of the founders of Reform Judaism, Abraham Geiger, served as a rabbi in Breslau for twenty years in the nineteenth century. Nor did my itinerary take me to the western sectors of the former Soviet Union, once Polish provinces with a substantial Jewish presence.

Until the nineteenth century there really were no *Russian* Jews, except in the far eastern provinces of the Russian empire. They were Polish Jews living in territory occupied by Russia. Only later were Jews permitted to move eastward to populate the cities of the czars and the Soviet commissars. Until then they lived in the historic Polish lands of Ukraine, Lithuania, Byelorussia, and Volhynia. Though my itinerary kept me within the boundaries of the current Republic of Poland, I ventured far to the east within those boundaries to a city where, before World War II, almost half of the population were Jews, namely, Bialystok. I was invited to lecture to faculty and students at the diocesan Catholic seminary, as part of the celebration of the four hundredth anniversary of its founding. Originally, this seminary had been located in Lwow. Yet despite the substantial presence of Jews in pre–World War II Lwow and Bialystok, no rabbi had ever spoken at or visited this seminary. It is ironic that now that Bialystok is largely bereft of Jews, such an invitation has been extended.

The bishop, who is rector of the seminary, greets me warmly. We had met in Warsaw on previous occasions. He introduces me to the "president of the city," that is, the mayor, who has come to hear my lecture. The mayor asks, "Where in America do you live?"

"Chicago," I answer.

"There are many Polish people there?" he asks rhetorically.

"More than in Bialystok," I reply.

"Does the mayor of Chicago come to your lectures?" he asks.

"I'm afraid not," I answer.

"Is he Catholic?" he asks.

"Yes," I reply.

"Then perhaps he should," is his reponse.

After the lecture, lunch is served. Then I am given a tour of Bialystok. At my request, I am taken to the Jewish cemetery. I know that Eliezer Solomon, the father of the Makower Ruf, died and was buried there in 1840. I go in search of his grave.

The cemetery is huge, much larger than I ever imagined, one of the largest Jewish cemeteries in Europe. As in many cities and towns in Poland, it abuts the Catholic cemetery. The Catholic cemetery is well tended. The Jewish cemetery is abandoned, disheveled, overgrown with brush and thistles. In vain, I search for the grave of Eliezer Solomon. Standing prominently in the middle of the cemetery is a monument that dates from the 1920s. The inscription reads, "A gift from the Jews of Bialystok now living in New York." There still exists today an international organization of Jews with roots in Bialystok. Quite a few live in Australia. One of these Australian Jews, Arnold Zable, wrote *Jewels and Ashes*, a memoir of his visit to Bialystok in the 1980s. Zable went to discover the Bialystok of his parents, who lived there before World

War II. Upon his arrival, one of the few remaining Jews tells him in Yiddish, "A Yid derkent nisht zein Bialystok"—a Jew cannot recognize his Bialystok.[21]

Jews first settled in Bialystok in 1548. When, in the nineteenth century, the Industrial Revolution came to Bialystok, the Jews transformed the city into a major industrial center. In the 1930s, a Jewish community in the city of Bialystok of about 50,000, and in the surrounding province of about 350,000, stood on the brink of annihilation. Despite an uprising in the Bialystok Ghetto, the results of the Final Solution remained unaltered. The Jews of Bialystok were massacred by the Germans, mostly in Auschwitz. In July 1944, 114 remained.[22] Like me, Zable senses the presence of Jewish souls in the absence of Jewish life in Poland today. After visiting the spot where the Great Synagogue of Bialystok—burned down by the Germans on "Red Friday," July 27, 1941, with about a thousand of its worshippers still inside—once stood, Zable writes, "More than ever I feel it—this land is possessed. Everywhere, it seems, there are lost souls seeking refuge. See how we once lived, they seem to whisper. . . . Here my ancestors had lived in a vast network of settlements which teemed with a way of life that had evolved for a millennium; they had created a kingdom within kingdoms, a universe pulsating to its own inner rhythms."[23]

On the long drive from Bialystok back to Warsaw, we make a slight detour, to Makow-Mazowiecki, the home of Rabbi Ephraim Fishel Solomon, the Makower Ruf. On the road near Lomza is a sign indicating that the Treblinka death camp is only miles away. Unlike other members of my family from that part of Poland, I bypass Treblinka. I arrive in the town I have heard about since my childhood. I come to Makow.

The town looks as I imagined it would. The brown wooden houses and poorly paved or dirt streets look like they must have looked over a century earlier, in the time of the Makower Ruf. From my research, I recognize the layout of the town. In the center is the city square. On one side, the side with the church, the non-Jews lived. The other side was completely populated by Jews. As I look around the town, everything seems to be as it once was. Only one element is missing—the Jews. It is Friday afternoon. In a matter of hours the sun will set and the Sabbath will begin. Yet no Jews scurry through the marketplace making last-minute purchases for the Sabbath. There are no Jewish children running in the streets. The hum of prayer and study is not heard within the buildings that once were the synagogues and study houses of Makow. There is no aroma of baking challah emanating from the homes once populated by Jews. The Jews of Makow are gone. In autumn 1942 they were taken to Treblinka and murdered. Like the Makower Ruf, they exist only in memory. Perhaps only the dybbuk of Makow survived them.

I ask where the Jewish cemetery is. I am directed through the "Jewish quarter" to its outer precincts. Overlooking a tranquil lake, there is a bus depot. It is here that the Jewish cemetery of Makow once was. The cemetery was destroyed by the Nazis. The tombstones were used for construction. Remnants of these tombstones still pave parts of the road near the bus depot. After the war, the Poles of Makow salvaged what they could of the shattered tombstones and built a monument to the Jews of Makow. The monument stands some twelve feet high in the bus depot. I read the remaining inscriptions, trying to find some remnant of the tombstone of either Rabbi Ephraim Fishel or of his wife, Rivkah. My search is in vain. Like the Jews of Makow, they are gone. I return to Warsaw, and a few days later I fly to Chicago. On the long flight home, pieces of a puzzle begin to take shape.

When I first went to Poland, it had been a voyage of curiosity. Subsequent trips, however, became journeys of self-discovery. During my first stay in Cracow, I came as a tourist. Now I come as an exiled native son. I walk down streets where members of the Fishel family walked five hundred years ago. I visit St. Anne's Street where they probably lived. When I stand in the throne room in Wawel castle, I know that they once stood there before the kings of Poland. In the Old Synagogue in Kazimierz, I listen for echoes of their presence, of their prayers. When I stand in the oldest sections of the Jaggelonian University, I know that the synagogue where they worshipped once occupied that spot. Somewhere, under my feet, they must be buried in the now forgotten first Jewish cemetery of Cracow. In the old Jewish cemetery adjacent to the Rema Synagogue, I visit the remains of my ancestors. I pause over the grave of Abraham Joshua Heschel of Cracow, now knowing that he was the ancestor of my mentor, and knowing as well that in the grave next to his, unmarked by a tombstone, are the remains of my ancestor, Rabbi Judah Loew Klausner. I can now reflect on the fact that they were related by marriage, that almost three hundred years before I met Abraham Joshua Heschel in New York and became his disciple, our families were linked in Cracow, and that we are both descendants of Rabbi Saul Wahl of Brisk. After spending many years in research and writing about Rabbi Judah Loew of Prague, I now know that he is part of my family history. No longer merely a subject of academic curiosity, he is a leaf on my family tree.

When I visit Lublin, I now know that Shalom Shakhna and the Maharam of Lublin are not simply abstract figures in the history of Polish Jewry, but part of my personal legacy; that theirs is not simply an intellectual inheritance, but a family bequest for me to preserve and to cherish. When I stand at the grave of Solomon Luria, it is not enough to reflect in awe about his spiritual and intellectual accomplishments. I now am also obliged to express filial reverence to a direct ancestor. And as I travel across the Polish landscape, I am now intensely aware that I literally walk in the footsteps of my ancestors, that the sparks of the souls that I try to elevate there are theirs as well as my own.

My genealogical research is not simply a scholarly exercise in historical research. Rather, it has become an adventure in self-understanding. The more I discover about the past, the more I understand the present. The more I know about my forebears, the better I understand myself.

Now I understand that what originally seemed matters of chance were perhaps destined. Many episodes in my life that seemed unrelated and random now have a cohesive plot. Questions long unanswered, commitments long unexplained, activities that seemed unconnected suddenly appear part of a pattern deriving from a past obscured until recently.

Why did I become the protégé of Abraham Joshua Heschel? What was the attraction that drove me to become his disciple? Why did I spend so many years studying the history and the heritage of Polish Jews? Why did my grandmother's stories about her ancestors make such a huge and lasting impression upon me? Why do I feel strangely at home in Poland though I do not speak Polish and though it is so radically different from America? Why did I prepare myself to engage in interfaith dialogue? Why did I become so intensely involved in Polish-Jewish dialogue?

It is as though what I have discovered about my family's distant past serves to explain many of the things I do in the present. In unlocking the portals to the history of my ancestors in Poland, I have found explanations for much of the story of my own life in America.

My family history may be unusual only in the sense that the effort has been taken to retrieve it. In all likelihood, it is probably similar to that of many Jews with Polish roots, that is, most Jews in America and about half in Israel. When I envision the lives of my ancestors in Poland, I am drawn to ask: Who were they? And who am I because of who they were? These questions are not mine alone to ask. They are questions that might be posed by the present diaspora of Polish Jewry. But for most Jews, especially those in the United States, the spiritual heritage of Polish Jewry is overshadowed by a vague nostalgia for a vanished world they know little about. The touchstone for Jewish life, meaning, and identity for the past few decades has not been the spiritual heritage of Polish Jewry. Instead, a "civil religion" has dominated Jewish life in its two largest communities: America and Israel. At the ideological core of this civil religion is a fundamental dogma, often referred to as "Jewish survival," often described as the "myth" of destruction and rebirth, of death and resurrection, of the Holocaust and Israel, Auschwitz and the Jewish State. This dogmatic pillar that has shaped the consciousness of contemporary Jewry bypasses the spiritual heritage of Polish Jewry. Its point of departure is the name of a place that has come to symbolize the Holocaust, a place called Auschwitz.

Auschwitz

It was a Jewish custom for individuals to learn humility by wandering for a year from town to town as a beggar. One never could spend less than a single day in any town, despite the humiliation one might suffer there. Nor could an individual spend more than two consecutive nights in any town, despite the hospitality received there.

In 1777 Rabbi Elimelekh established his Hasidic court in Lizensk, making it the capital of Hasidism in Polish Galicia. In his earlier years, he undertook the task of learning humility by posing as a beggar. With his brother, Rabbi Zusya, Elimelekh wandered from town to town. One afternoon, the two brothers arrived exhausted in a small Galician village. Despite their hunger, they could not eat. Despite their fatigue, they could not sleep. They felt something they never had felt before. A feeling of unspeakable dread came over them. A most profound sense of sadness overwhelmed them. In the middle of the night they left the town, never to return. The name of this town was Oswiecim—Auschwitz.[1]

There is a sense in that place both of the surreal and of the all-too-real. There, on the spot where hell dwelt on earth, all pretensions evaporate, all certainties collapse. Your legs feel weak. You begin to feel faint, nauseous, stricken by terror and fear. There is a natural tendency to run away, an instinctive sense of avoidance, but the pull of the past is too powerful. One wanders the grounds wondering "Why?"

It's difficult to absorb, hard to think. The mind goes blank. There are tears in your eyes, anguish grips your soul. Standing with small remnants of human ash and bone scattered on the ground at your feet, surrounded by the remains of prisoners' barracks, torture chambers, execution walls, railway tracks, and crematoria, your head tilts upward toward a silent gray sky, and one word comes to the mind, the heart, the mouth: "Why?"

When you stand there, the Holocaust is no longer an abstraction. Unintentionally, you step on white pieces of bone that litter the ground near the crematoria. "I see my relatives in each handful of ashes," the poet had written. Whose bones and ashes do I place in my hand when I scoop up a handful of dirt from the ground?

The death of millions of people is a statistic, but the death of a single person is a tragedy. During the Holocaust, people usually perished in groups; yet they died one by one. Each bore his or her own particular dreams, loves, and aspirations. Each face was different, unique. Each a world, a universe of thoughts and emotions abruptly snuffed out.

Robbed of their possessions, their identity, their future, each went to his or her death with a last thought, prayer, song, scream. Each was a person, much like us, until they became citizens of a domain of no escape, no return, no hope—a domain where they were condemned to death for the "crime" of being alive. While we may know neither their names nor anything about how they lived, we can be quite certain of how and where they died. Their passports to the future were suddenly revoked in the capital city of the Holocaust kingdom: Auschwitz-Birkenau.

Fettered, enslaved, subjugated, they were caught in a net that stretched throughout Nazi-occupied Europe. Their humanity crushed by their harsh overlords, they became preoccupied with daily survival. Trapped in a nightmare without respite, they faced death as usually the only available means of escape.

Driven by dogs and beatings to cattle cars, they heard the sealing of the doors that was also the sealing of their fate. The barbed wire that encompassed these places stood as an impenetrable border between the life they once had known and the deprivation they would experience. Huddled in barracks, devoid of the necessities of life, they became the living dead—until they became simply the dead.

To be shot, hanged, or beaten to death at least meant an individualized murder. But the fate of most was mass murder. From the gas chambers, there was no return. In the crematoria, ashes of the victims mingled—like their common fate. The insatiable appetite of the fire-breathing dragon turned people into ashes. Lives went up in smoke. An assembly line of death, the Nazi killing centers manufactured mass murder on an unprecedented scale.

The screams of the dying, the sounds of parents trying to comfort children destined for imminent death, are now silent. Only the memory of murder and the murder of memory remain. That which has survived and has been preserved—like mounds of human hair and piles of shoes—offers grim reminders of what happened there. In a more tranquil moment than standing there viewing what remained of the 1.5 million people murdered in Auschwitz, of whom over 1.1 million were Jews, I recall a poem of Abraham Sutzkever:

> I need not ask whose,
> but it pains me in my heart.
> O shoes, tell me the truth,
> Where are they—the feet?[2]

I think of the Auschwitz memoir of Primo Levi:

> [O]ur language lacks words to express this offense, the demolition of a man. . . .
> Nothing belongs to us anymore; they have taken away our clothes, our shoes, even
> our hair. . . . They will next take away our name.[3]

Upon leaving the grounds of Auschwitz-Birkenau, I open a book I am carrying, *A Prayer for Katerina Horovitzova*, by my friend Arnošt Lustig, the Czech-Jewish novelist who wrote about his experiences in Auschwitz.

His eyes reiterated . . . that these ashes would be indestructible and immutable, they would not burn up into nothingness because they themselves were remnants of fire. They would not freeze, but simply mingle with the snow and ice, never drying under the sun's hot glare because there's nothing more to dry out of ashes. No one living would ever be able to escape them; these ashes would be contained in the milk that will be drunk by babies yet unborn and in the breasts their mothers offer them; the ashes will linger in the flowers which will grow out of them and in the pollen with which they will be fertilized by bees; they will be in the depths of the earth too, where rotted woodlands transform themselves into coal, and in the heights of heaven, where every human gaze, equipped with a telescope, encounters the invisible layers which envelop this wormy terrestrial apple of ours. These ashes will be contained in the breath and expression of every one of us and the next time anybody asks what the air he breathes is made of, he will have to think about these ashes; they will be contained in books which haven't yet been written and will be found in the remotest regions of the earth where no human foot has ever trod; no one will be able to get rid of them, for they will be the fond, nagging ashes of the dead who died in innocence.[4]

In recent decades, the name "Auschwitz" has come to signify more than the name of a place where over a million Jews were turned into smoke and ashes. For Jews, the name "Auschwitz" has come to signify the Holocaust itself.[5] What took place there came to signify what took place in much of Nazi-occupied Europe. In the Jewish psyche, "Auschwitz" includes everything that the Nazis and their allies did to the Jews; everything that those in the occupied countries watched being done to the Jews; everything that the eventually victorious Allies did not prevent from happening to the Jews. For Jews, "Auschwitz" includes Treblinka and the Warsaw Ghetto, Mauthausen and Bergen-Belsen, and the activities of the Iron Guard in Romania, the Arrow Cross in Hungary, and the Vichy government in occupied France. It includes the actions of the SS and the action of their Lithuanian and Ukrainian collaborators; the inaction of many people in occupied Europe who did not help Jews — either out of fear of the Nazis, hatred of Jews, or apathy; the Vatican that did not adequately denounce the Nazis; President Franklin Delano Roosevelt's failure to authorize any sort of meaningful rescue effort. "Auschwitz" refers to a nexus that binds all perpetrators, victims, and bystanders who were involved in the destruction of two-thirds of European Jewry.

This use of the name of one place to signify events that happened in many places is not accurate historically or geographically. But, as often happens, an event that happened at a single place at a particular time comes to represent much more. For Jews, Auschwitz signifies an event, an experience, that threatened the very survival of the Jewish people, the very existence of Judaism, the very meaning of Jewish existence.

For both Israeli and American Jews, just as "Auschwitz" has come to signify what must never happen again, so the State of Israel has come to symbolize Jewish survival in the post-Auschwitz world. "Auschwitz" represents death and destruction; Israel represents survival and rebirth. This idea has become the most fundamental dogma of Jewish communal life today.

In May 1990, when I visited Auschwitz for the first time, a group of Israeli high school students were there. They stood near where the crematoria had once devoured Jews. They carried Israeli flags, listening somberly to their teachers, singing patriotic

Israeli songs. The teachers explained that Jewish life in the diaspora was doomed to disappear, either by assimilation or annihilation, that diasporan Jews were dependent upon non-Jews for their very survival, that the only viable alternative for a Jew is to live in Israel.[6] The teachers told their students that non-Jews were anti-Semitic. They could not be trusted. The Holocaust proves this. What happened on the ground on which they stood demonstrates why Israel is critical to Jewish survival, why the Zionist ideology is right, why Israel must remain self-reliant.[7] The teachers pointed out that although it was Germany that launched and vigorously pursued the Holocaust, the Poles helped the Nazis carry out their murderous aims. Some of the girls wept. Many of the boys cast an angry, defiant gaze. The students were hearing a chronicle that one could hear in Israel or in America, a chronicle that makes any rapprochement between Jews and Poles impossible, that obfuscates the spiritual achievements of Polish Jewry. The Holocaust story was being told not to denigrate or to stereotype Poles—that was a by-product[8]—but to forge the foundation for a post-Holocaust Jewish identity, to give Jews a way of viewing the world in a post-Auschwitz era, of finding meaning in an event bereft of meaning.

An understanding of how Jews have told the story of the Holocaust offers insights into how Jews understand themselves in the post-Holocaust world. Though the story is complex, we can nonetheless see some of its basic components.

American Jews were virtually untouched by the storm of fire that engulfed Europe during the war years. Theirs was a country of unprecedented power and wealth, a country that had never known foreign occupation, and where it was believed that all obstacles could be overcome. Theirs was a mentality where martyrs were viewed as cowards; where heroes may die, but they die fighting. And if some of these claims are not totally factual, they nevertheless are widely believed.

For most Americans, the United States is a "promised land," a "new world." Europe is the old world, a world left behind. Americans understand themselves to be a new kind of people in a new world.[9] And American Jews see themselves as a new kind of Jew, with Europe and its memories of persecutions, poverty, massacres, and oppression left behind.[10] Israeli Jews, too, understand themselves to be a new type of Jew: free, independent, and self-reliant. For the Israelis, self-reliant survival became the essential characteristic and imperative of post-Holocaust Jewish existence. According to Zionist ideology, the Holocaust represents the inevitable fate of Jews in the diaspora, the inevitable history of the Jews when they permit themselves to depend upon others for their security and survival. The American Jew has the story of the Alamo and the Israeli Jew has the similar story of Masada: better to die fighting than to accept a passive death. Better to die a fighting hero than a praying martyr.

Because of this mentality of American and Israeli Jews, relating the story of the Holocaust became a problem. They could not identify with the fate of those who perished, or more precisely, with the way in which most actually died. But, being Jews, they somehow had to identify with what had happened to other Jews. This, it would seem, led to a logically inconsistent but psychologically coherent response to the Holocaust. On the one hand, they *accepted* what had occurred, though without *identifying* with it. On the other hand, they *rejected* what had occurred, and *identified* with it.

How was this possible? American and Israeli Jews, each in their own manner, came to the conclusion that accepting what happened meant accepting the responsibility of assuring that it never would happen again. The primary Jewish response to the Holocaust is expressed by the motto "Never Again," which means that Jews would not and could not allow what happened to "them" (i.e., to the European Jews) to happen to "us" (i.e., American and Israeli Jews).

By becoming aware of what happened and by committing themselves to preventing its reoccurrence, American and Israeli Jews demonstrated that as "new" kinds of Jews, they could not identify psychologically or experientially with the Holocaust experience of European Jews, that is, with how Jews lived or died in Europe before or during the Holocaust. And so, rather than tell a story of martyrdom as they had about previous persecutions, Jews began to emphasize another side of the Holocaust story—resistance and heroism. Israeli and American histories of the Holocaust began to stress the story of armed resistance rather than the story of pious Hasidic Jews martyring themselves, or of Jews who relied on others for their survival.[11] The Warsaw Ghetto uprising in 1943 became a model. Indeed, some Jewish historians and journalists see the Warsaw Ghetto uprising as the first chapter in the history of *zahal*, the Israeli Defense Forces.[12] By making the fighting resisters the paradigm of the Jewish experience during the Holocaust, American and Israeli Jews now had a way of identifying with the Holocaust story, a way of making it their story. By rejecting identification with those who went to their deaths passively, and by affirming identity with those engaged in armed resistance, Israeli and American Jews arrived at the agenda that dominates Jewish life today—the paramount importance of Jewish survival, expressed by the motto "Never Again."

The view that Jewish survival is better assured by complete self-reliance led to the need to recast the Holocaust as a history of the betrayal of the Jews by others. There was a need to demonstrate that the history of anti-Semitism in Europe made the Holocaust inevitable and that the betrayal of the Jews by their non-Jewish neighbors in the European lands in which they lived made the tragic result of Nazi oppression possible. Both Israeli and American Jews affirmed the same premise, namely the nonviability of Jewish life in Europe.

This recasting of Jewish history during the Holocaust led to a recasting of Jewish history *before* the Holocaust. For example, the Jewish festival of Hanukkah is understood by the Talmud and by classical Jewish religious tradition to be the story of the *spiritual* victory of Judaism over Hellenism. The story centered on the rededication of the Temple after its defilement by the Greeks, on the one bottle of holy oil that was only supposed to last for one day but that miraculously burned for eight days, and on the miracle wrought by God. Now the story is less a spiritual one than a *military* saga of the triumph of the Maccabees.[13]

For the most part, however, recasting the story of the Jewish past came to embody what Salo Baron called the "lachrymose conception of Jewish history." Reducing Jewish historical experience to a chronicle of persecution and pogroms marginalizes the political, spiritual, social, and economic achievements of the Jews of past centuries. Jewish history is described as one long vale of tears that finally experienced relief with the settlement of Jews in America and with the establishment in 1948 of the

Jewish State. The achievements of the Jewish people throughout their history are eclipsed by a tale of perpetual woe, a stream of relentless catastrophe.

Following this lachrymose theory of Jewish history, the Holocaust emerges as the almost inevitable climax of centuries of persecution. As the Israeli novelist Aharon Appelfeld put it, "Jewish history is a series of holocausts, with only some improvement in technique."[14] Furthermore, the story of a formidable diasporan community such as Polish Jewry may be told according to a narrative rooted in the underlying historical determinism of Zionist ideology. Despite assimilationist trends in modern Polish Jewry, it was unlikely that the Jews of Poland would disappear through assimilation. Therefore, their inevitable fate had to be physical annihilation. The Holocaust is invoked as the demonstration of the validity of this inevitable "law" of Jewish history.

That the Nazi death camps were located in Poland, it is further argued, was not by chance, since the Poles — either actively or through passivity — collaborated with the Germans in the annihilation of the Jews. Those who espouse this view see the Holocaust, in part, as the story of Polish complicity with the Germans in the destruction of Polish Jewry. The pre-Holocaust history of the Jewish experience in Poland is thus recast as a chronicle of anti-Semitism that reached its natural and inevitable result during the years of World War II. While the more dispassionate theory that history is the result of an inevitable unfolding of events would seem — like any form of determinism — to free the actors from moral responsibility, this approach places substantial responsibility for the Holocaust on the Poles. In the popular American and Israeli understanding of the Holocaust, the Poles all but replace the Germans as the perpetrators of the Holocaust, as the archenemies of the Jews throughout the thousand-year Jewish presence in Poland.[15] Indeed, just as this narrative fits available facts into a Zionistic ideological overlay, it is also correlative with cultural assumptions characteristic of the American Jewish mentality. For American Jews, the Europe that their immigrant ancestors had left had to be envisaged as being so intolerable to Jewish life as to have compelled them to forsake it for America. The more inhospitable to Jews Poland (the place of origin of most American Jews) could be portrayed to be, the greater the justification for emigrating to America. Thus, both American and Israeli Jews had a vested interest in depicting the Jewish experience in Poland as a history of persecutions, pogroms, and perpetual anti-Semitic outbreaks.

The focus of Jewish history is shifted from what Jews *did* to what was *done* to them. Jews are portrayed as the victims of history, rather than creative actors in their own historical drama. The lachrymose historiography of Jewish experience pervades. Ironically, both Jews and Poles arrived at a similar reading of their own histories. Jews saw themselves as the perennial biblical "suffering servant." Poles saw Poland as "the Christ of the nations." Many Poles tended to blame their historical misfortunes on the Jews, while many Jews blamed theirs on the Poles. How the story of Polish-Jewish relations during the twentieth century, and especially during and since the Holocaust, came to be told stimulated a recasting of Polish-Jewish relations throughout the past centuries in a similar light.

Not only was the telling of the story of the Jewish past revisaged, but the agenda of the Jewish present and future also was changed. In past generations, the most important thing for Jews was the survival and perpetuation of Judaism. Now, the basis for action and policy in the Jewish world is the survival of the Jews as an end in itself. This is the meaning of the motto "Never Again." And, just as "Auschwitz" has become for Jews the symbol of the Holocaust—the paradigm of what must never happen again—so the State of Israel has become for most Jews the symbol of Jewish survival, the necessary condition for the continued survival of the Jewish people. The enormous political, ideological, and economic support given Israel by world Jewry, particularly by American Jews, is precisely because most Jews view Israel as the incarnation of Jewish survival. Accordingly, Jews tend to perceive—rightly or wrongly—any act of anti-Semitism, or any threat to Israel, as a threat to Jewish survival. The affirmation of the motto "Never Again" means to fight, in every possible way, any perceived threat to Jewish survival because a threat represents a potential Holocaust. This is why, when foreign dignitaries come to Israel, they are always brought to Yad Va-Shem, Israel's memorial to the Holocaust. And, not surprisingly, the rallying cry of the Jewish effort to save Soviet Jews by bringing them to Israel and the United States has been "Never Again, is now!"

Jewish survival has become the fundamental dogma of the creed of the "civil religion" of American and Israeli Jewry. Civil religion articulates the self-conception, mission, values, and beliefs of a sociopolitical group. It formulates that entity's vision of the nature and meaning of its existence. It serves as a cohesive force binding together individuals of various religious, social, economic, and cultural perspectives. To a substantial degree, much of the civil religion of American Jewry and of Israel can be understood as a response to the Holocaust.[16] The civil religion of American Jews, in effect, allows for American Jews to affirm their identity as Jews without being committed to Jewish theological belief or religious practice. For example, an American Jew can hold positions of Jewish communal leadership though he or she is an atheist, is married to a non-Jew, and does not observe Jewish religious practices. Conversely, were such an individual committed to Jewish belief and practice, but not to the beliefs and rituals of the "civil religion" of American Jews, he or she would be a persona non grata in Jewish communal life. Such an individual would be virtually shunned by the Jewish establishment.

A faith without a theology, civil religion, subordinates the continuity of Jewish religious faith to the survival of the Jewish people. The claim that Jewish survival is of paramount importance leads to the view that the Jewish religion is of value primarily because it helps ensure Jewish group survival. The "myth" of death/rebirth, Holocaust/Israel tends to replace belief in God as the foundation of Jewish faith. For example, the idea that the survival of the Jewish people has replaced faith in God as the ultimate Jewish value is evident in the song introduced by secular Zionists to celebrate Hanukkah. This song, sung today in many synagogues, contains the lyric "Who can retell the victories of Israel?" The original lyric, quoting the Psalms, is: "Who can retell the victories of God?" (Psalms 106:2). Here, the people of Israel not only have replaced God, but have become the sole instrument of Jewish redemption as well.

One of the many other examples that may be offered relates to the famous group of Zionists founded in Russia in 1882 who called themselves BYLU, an acronym for Beit Yaakov Lehu V'Nelkha (House of Jacob, come let us go). This phrase is from Isaiah 2:5. Significantly, the final words of the phrase—"in the light of God"—were excluded. Another example is Vladimir Jabotinsky's description of his Zionist activity as "the work of one of the builders of a new Temple to a single God whose name is—the people of Israel."[17] A more recent example comes from a 1995 fundraising letter sent out by AIPAC (American Israel Public Affairs Committee), also known as the "Israel lobby." It reads, "For Americans of conscience, Israel is a solemn pledge to six million Jews who perished during the Holocaust. . . . Defending Israel is a matter of honor. If you're Jewish, Israel is much more. It is the living manifestation of our belief—our past, present and future rolled up into one. Defending Israel is not just a matter of honor, it is a matter of faith. . . . Israel's reality is central to my religious faith."[18]

Concerning American Jews, a number of Jewish scholars have observed that faith in Israel and in the Jewish people has replaced or superseded faith in God. "Zionism . . . has become American Jewry's religion," writes Jewish historian Arthur Hertzberg.[19] Similarly, Leonard Fein observes, "In a very precise way, Israel had now become the faith of the American Jew."[20] Consequently, as Hertzberg notes, one cannot be ostracized from American Jewish communal life for being an atheist, but one can be virtually excommunicated for not affirming the dogmas of the civil religion.[21]

In a similar vein, the eminent British Jewish theologian Louis Jacobs has written,

> There is a tendency nowadays, even among religious Jews, to argue that Judaism is of value because it ensures Jewish survival. But this makes Jewish survival the ultimate instead of God and His service. . . . The religious believer will struggle as hard for the right of his people to survive . . . as his non-believing fellow-Jew. . . . He will see in the survival of the Jews a means to an end and not the end in itself. . . . Religion is sui generis. It is not "for" something else. Its aim is the worship of God.[22]

Leonard Fein similarly observes, "The Holocaust and Israel . . . give us both a motto—'Never Again!'—and a method—the nation state. . . . 'Never Again!' tells us only what to avoid, not what to embrace . . . And the nation state? Its defense points to a politics, not to a value system." And, further, "I am inclined to think that most Jewish survivalists would be hard-pressed to name the Jewish values our survival is meant to ensure. Instead, the means have become the end. . . . My purpose is to suggest that the preoccupation with survival for its own sake is not merely redundant, but self-defeating. . . . Far from assuring the Jewish future, the survivalist betrays it."[23] And, as Abraham Joshua Heschel wrote, "'To be or not to be' is not the question. . . . How to be and how not to be is the question. The true problem is *how* to survive, what sort of future to strive for. . . . It is more urgent to be concerned with revival than about survival."[24]

The ideology of survivalism, coupled with the dual dogmatic pillars of Jewish civil religion of Holocaust-destruction and Israel-rebirth, folded nicely into an increasingly secularized Jewish self-identity. In Israel, the form it took was secular nationalism; in America, Jewish ethnicity. American Jews departed from their earlier practice, prevalent in the 1950s, of identifying themselves as adherents to one of the three American religions (Protestantism, Catholicism, Judaism) and adapted the ethnic approach of becoming hyphenated Americans, that is, Jewish-Americans. As an American ethnic group, a homeland was required and Israel had become available. Eastern Europe, which did not bear fond memories for Jewish immigrants, was discarded. Jews reveled in their ethnicity, in "Jewish power," in Israel.

In 1990 a major demographic study sent shock waves through the American Jewish community.[25] Intermarriage between Jews and non-Jews was over 50 percent. Jews were culturally illiterate about Judaism. Jewish identity was in sharp decline. Over two hundred thousand American Jews had formally joined another faith-community. Something had gone wrong! However, compared to intermarriage between other ethnic groups, the figure for American Jews was not unusual. The figure for Jews also was similar to statistics measuring ethnic identity among other third- and fourth-generation Americans. Why the panic? Why the concern? Perhaps because American Jews began to realize that ethnicity and survivalism had backfired. Now the slogan was no longer "Jewish survival" but "Jewish continuity." Yet a critical question remained: Continuity with what? The spiritual heritage of east European Jewry provides a promising answer.

What is being suggested here are the following four points:

1. The lachrymose historiography of the Jewish experience should be rejected.

2. The civil religion of American Jewry should be replaced.

3. Jews—particularly American Jews—should realize that their calls for "Jewish continuity" are specious unless Jewish continuity means continuity with the spiritual tradition of the Jewish past, and particularly with the spiritual heritage of Polish Jewry.

4. The spiritual heritage of Polish Jewry can provide a foundation for an authentic Jewish continuity, an alternative to obsolete forms of Jewish secularism, and a conceptual framework and a value system for the re-creation of Judaism in the future.

By permitting the legacy of Polish Jewry to fade into oblivion, American Jewry is, as Abraham Heschel claimed, making a second Holocaust upon itself. It is exterminating the spiritual resources required for Jewish continuity, creativity, and renewal. By making a culture of death, contemporary Jewry is bringing about the death of a culture. By being obsessed with a lachrymose view of Jewish experience in Poland, by focusing on past martyrdom alone, Jews are forgetting for what and why those individuals became martyrs. Reclaiming the spiritual heritage of Polish Jewry can provide a foundation for an authentic and vital Jewish future. By holding on to the coattails of their ancestors, Jews can jump over the abyss of meaninglessness, despondency, and absurdity that are the real threats they face.

Near Lwow was the infamous Janowska Road concentration camp. Terrorized inmates were awakened in the middle of the night and forced into a field near the camp. In the midst of the field were two huge pits caused by bombs exploded during the last war. The sentry told the inmates that each of them must jump over one of the pits and land on the other side. Failure meant death. Sick, starving, exhausted inmates stood in line waiting for their fate to be sealed in this macabre game played by their Ukrainian guards. Among the thousands of Jews imprisoned there was Israel Spira, the Grand Rabbi of Bluzhov.

Rabbi Israel Spira awaited his turn. Standing next to him was a Jewish "freethinker" with whom he had become friendly in the camp. Seeing the size of the pit, the freethinker was ready to give up and be shot. But the rabbi insisted that they try.

The rabbi was then fifty-three years old, and weak from slave labor and malnutrition. When they reached the pit, each closed his eyes and jumped. The freethinker was amazed to be alive.

"How did you do it?" he asked the rabbi.

"I held on to the coattails of my ancestors," said the rabbi. "And how did you make it?" he asked his friend.

"I was holding on to your coattails," said the freethinker.[26]

Jewish Continuity

Once there lived in Cracow a rabbi named Isaac. He was very poor. Isaac lived with his wife and children in a house with only one room. In the middle of the room there was a stove. During winter, when they had money for wood, the heat of the stove would offer warmth and would cook the meager food that barely sustained them from day to day.

One night, the rabbi had a dream. He dreamed that in a land called Bohemia, in a city called Prague, there was a bridge under which a river flowed. The bridge was near a large castle. Under the bridge, on the bank of the river, an enormous treasure was buried.

When the rabbi awoke the next morning, he remembered his dream in vivid detail. But the needs of his congregants were pressing, and off he went to the synagogue. Yet, throughout the day, all he could think of was his dream. That night he went to sleep, hoping that in his sleep he might be free of the dream from the previous night. But once again the dream returned, and it was identical to the dream he had had the night before. In the morning he awoke and the dream, once again, preoccupied him throughout the day.

When the same dream came again that night, he knew it was not simply a dream, but a message, for tradition taught that a dream that occurs three consecutive times must be taken seriously. He awoke and looked at his exhausted wife and hungry children shivering in their sleep near the cold stove. The rabbi dressed quietly and left a note that he had gone to Prague to find his dream.

The rabbi traveled the cold and dangerous roads from Cracow to Prague for three days and three nights. On the morning of the fourth day he entered Prague. It was not long before he saw the river, and it was exactly as it had been in his dream. He followed the river until he came to a bridge near a huge castle. Both were so reminiscent of what he had seen in his dream that he thought he was in his bed in Cracow, asleep.

He looked down from the bridge at the spot where the treasure was supposed to be buried. But because the nearby castle was the home of the king, royal guards stood watch on the bridge all day. The rabbi waited for the guards to leave so that he could dig up the treasure under the bridge. But when the sun set and the guards began to leave, a new group of guards immediately replaced them. And so, day after day, night after night, the rabbi stayed near the bridge, hoping for an hour when the bridge would remain unguarded, allowing him to claim the treasure he was sure was buried there.

As time passed, the rabbi became friendly with one of the guards who stood post on the bridge. The guard was grateful to have a person of culture and learning with whom to converse during the long lonely hours of standing watch at the bridge. One day, the guard told the rabbi that he had had a strange dream the night before. The guard dreamed that in a land called Poland, in a city called Cracow, there lived a pious but poor man with his wife and many children. They lived in a one-room house, and in the middle of the room there was a stove, and under the stove a great treasure was buried.

Rabbi Isaac immediately returned home. He moved the heavy stove and began to dig. There, in a large iron trunk, he found a great treasure. With half of the money he built a great synagogue. That synagogue still stands today in Cracow; it is called Rabbi Isaac's Synagogue.[1]

The message of this story is that the treasure we seek is right beneath our feet, though we are not always aware of it. What we need to do is dig to uncover it. A dominant feature of Jewish communal life since the Holocaust, particularly in America, has been a tendency to ignore the treasure, to consider the Jewish spiritual heritage — particularly that which derives from eastern Europe — as a nostalgic curiosity at best and an irrelevant obsolescence at worst. The precious legacy of the Jewish past has largely been replaced and eclipsed by the "civil religion" developed both by American and Israeli Jewry. This civil religion is, in effect, subversive of the continuity of the spiritual heritage of Judaism.

Despite the clarion calls for continuity echoing throughout its communal structure, American Jewry has failed to recognize that the only tradition it embraces is one of discontinuity, especially with regard to the spiritual heritage of its largely east European forebears. By neglecting its legacy, by leaving the spiritual treasure of east European Jewry buried, contemporary Jewry has allowed itself to become a conclusion without a premise, a fallacy. As Abraham Heschel observed, by neglecting the very tradition and heritage that the Nazis attempted to expunge, contemporary Jewry is bringing about a "second Holocaust." While during the Holocaust others sought to annihilate Judaism, this second Holocaust is being brought by the Jews upon themselves.

In 1907, in an essay entitled "The Problem of Judaism in America," Professor Israel Friedlaender of the Jewish Theological Seminary of America diagnosed the spiritual atrophy that even then was characteristic of the American Jewish community. In 1920 Friedlaender was murdered at the age of forty-three while on a fact-finding mission for the Joint Distribution Committee in Ukraine. Eulogized at Carnegie Hall as a modern Jewish martyr, Friedlaender had commented on attitudes toward martyrdom in that essay:

> The problem of the *Jews*, of the physical misery of our nation engages the heart and hand of every Jew with a spark of Jewish consciousness or sentiment in him. Powerful organizations grapple energetically, and more or less successfully, with

this problem. But most of us utterly ignore the problem of *Judaism*, the problem of our spiritual misery. . . . And, while our heart is aroused over the martyrs that fell by the hands of violent mobs, we witness with indifference the disappearance of that for which they became martyrs.[2]

Friedlaender previsaged what experience has demonstrated. He knew that a Jewish communal agenda rooted in survivalism ironically posed an ultimate danger to both the physical and the spiritual survival of the Jewish people. He realized that without spiritual substance, "Judaism is no more than a body without a spirit, a dead inanimate mechanism, which may, by sheer mechanical momentum, move on for a little while, but must in the end come to a complete standstill. The problem of Judaism would then consist in the fact that the soul, or spirit, of the Jewish people, as manifested in our culture, has in modern times shown symptoms of decay so alarming in nature as to make us fear for its continued existence."[3] Without the body, the soul is a vagabond spirit. But without the soul, the body becomes a corpse. The spiritual is the vitalizing force that is essential to physical survival. Survival for the sake of survival is a tautology, a redundancy bereft of a referent of meaning. In the final analysis, Jewish survivalism brings about the very situation it was devised to prevent.

In a similar vein, Abraham Heschel points out that Jewish survivalism is not only counterproductive, but that it rests upon a conceptual fallacy. Heschel has written: "Such a doctrine is built on the myth that all creativity is the product of the biological will to live. However, a doctrine that regards Judaism as a contrivance is itself a contrivance and can therefore not entertain the claim to be true."[4]

With all of its affluence, influence, know-how, and power, the highly organized Jewish communal structure has not been able to produce a single generation of Jewishly culturally literate Jews. American Jews have been spectacularly successful as Americans but not as Jews. As Steven Bayme has put it, "We are very good at telling the State Department what to do about Israel, but in the privacy of our homes, we cannot find words to tell our children why they should be Jewish."[5]

Upon his arrival, in 1902, from England, to head the Jewish Theological Seminary of America, Solomon Schechter quipped that the Jews of America seemed to him as little more than "amateur Christians." Schechter observed that it was not so much the *galut*—the exile of the Jews—that he feared, as much as "the *Galut* of Judaism, the *Galut* of the Jewish soul wasting away before our very eyes."[6] Rabbi Mendel of Kotzk once said that it is bad enough to be in a state of *galut*, that is, exile, alienation from one's authentic self. Even worse, however, is being in *galut* and not even being aware of it. American Jewry is in *galut*, not simply in the sense of being geographically dislocated from the Land of Israel. But, more significantly, it is in a state of *galut* because it largely fails to recognize how alienated it has become from the wellsprings of its own spiritual foundations, particularly those that derive from eastern Europe. Indeed, much of American Jewry mistakenly identifies the belief structure of the civil religion it has embraced, such as the dogma of Jewish survivalism, with the very spiritual heritage it has jettisoned. For the overwhelming majority of American Jews, Judaism is a "second language" that they speak poorly, if at all. What is even more disheartening is that they confuse a foreign idiom such as the civil religion with authentic Jewish thought and expression. Both Heschel and Schechter taught that Judaism is not only a way of living but a way of thinking. American Jewry not only thinks about everyday subjects in non-Jewish categories, but it thinks and speaks about Judaism in non-Jewish categories that it then equates with Judaism. It is not only a community in spiritual *galut*, but one that is in spiritual *galut* and does not even know it is there.

The continuity of a tradition assumes that the wisdom of the past can be applied to the perplexities of the present, that the experiences of the present may be encountered and interpreted in the framework of archetypes inherited from the past, that, in the rabbinic parlance, "the experiences of our ancestors are signs to their descendants" *(ma'aseh avot siman le-vanim)*. For Jews, memory is a crucial element of faith. Memory both recalls the past, defines the present, and hopefully shapes the future. For Judaism, amnesia is the most deadly disease. Without memory, the past is forsaken. Continuity is annihilated. The future is jettisoned.

While the American experience has been one of unprecedented blessings for Jews, it has been one of unprecedented catastrophe for Jewish continuity and spirituality. Starting life afresh in the "new world," American Jewry severed its lifeline with its past. Like messengers who forgot the message, Jews have excommunicated themselves from their own religious tradition.

A land of economic opportunities and a safe haven for Jews, America also offered an environment of spiritual peril. In Europe, the danger was concrete and embodied. In America, it was subtle and elusive—slowly corroding the Jewish soul rather than hacking apart the Jewish body. For the "new Jews" of America, they had come to the *goldene medinah*, "the golden land," but to those who remained in eastern Europe, America was a *treifa medinah*, an "impure land" replete with spiritual ambushes. For American Jews it was a promised land; for those in Europe it was a promising land, that is, promising the dissolution of an enduring tradition. For example, in 1889 a Jewish journal published in Polish Galicia carried this report from its New York correspondent: "There is no faith and no knowledge of the Lord among most of our brethren who live in this land. . . . [T]he younger generation has inherited nothing from their parents except what they need to make their way in the world; every spiritual teaching is foreign to them."[7] Given the fate of European Jewry during the Holocaust years, it would be foolish to contend that the Jews who came to America and their descendants would have been better off had they remained in Europe. However, what is being suggested is that American Jews would have been better off if they had allowed more of Europe to remain in them.

Certain aspects of the American mind-set that are intrinsically inimical to the continuity of Jewish tradition have been adapted by much of American Jewry, and have become incorporated into the civil religion of American Jewish communal life. Two prominent paradigmatic characteristics of the American worldview serve to sabotage the possibility for Jewish continuity. The first is the idea that the American experience is new and therefore unrelated to the past. The second is that history—rather than being a guide and a teacher to help us to navigate a path to the future, to prevent us from repeating the mistakes of the past—is an irrelevant exercise in obsolescence. These two ideas are inextricably interlinked, for if our situation is completely new and unprecedented, then the collective experience of the past proves inapplicable to the problems of the present and the challenges of the future.

The proclivity of Jews in the United States to ignore and discard traditions inherited from their European past is particularly American. While Europeans tend to look to the past for direction into the future, Americans tend to rush onward without a backward glance. This attitude was perhaps most succinctly summarized by Henry Ford when he declared, "History is bunk." For a tradition, like Judaism, that is rooted in memory, where continuity is assured only by the perpetuation of collective memories through faith and by the enactment of faith as memory through ritual, an attitude that denies the pervasiveness of the past, that neglects not only its history but how tradition has interpreted that history, threatens to undermine not only that tradition, but the very idea of tradition itself.

When, in 1832, the American statesman Henry Clay coined the term "self-made man," he was expressing a peculiarly American view, for Americans always have tended to see themselves as the creators of a new self in a "new world." Indeed, a fundamental dogma of American civil religion is that America is a new world, a new promised land. For this reason, immigrants coming to America, particularly east European Jewish immigrants, tended to view their arrival in America as a birthday, as the beginning of a new life, severed from their life in the "old world." In this regard, Abraham Cahan, the editor from 1902 to 1951 of the *Jewish Daily Forward* (*Forvitz*), the leading Yiddish newspaper in America, wrote,

> The immigrant's arrival in his new home is like a second birth to him. . . . his entry into a country which is, to him, a new world in the profoundest sense of the term. . . . The day of an immigrant's arrival in his new home is like a birthday to him. Indeed, it is more apt to claim his attention and to warm his heart than his real birthday. Some of our immigrants do not know their birthday. But they all know the day when they came to America.[8]

A similar motif may be found among Israeli Jews. A fundamental premise of Zionism has been the creation of a new species of Jew in a new kind of state. As the Israeli author Amos Elon has observed, "This new [Israeli] society as envisaged by the early pioneers, was to be another Eden, a Utopia never before seen on sea or land. The pioneers looked forward to the creation of a 'new man.' . . . Others claimed that at the very moment they set foot in Palestine they had been 'reborn.'"[9] Already in 1944 David Ben-Gurion, born in Plonsk, Poland, in 1886 and Israel's first prime minister, said in a speech delivered in Haifa, "Not our origin or our past but our mission and our future is what determines our path."[10]

About Clay's term "self-made man," Mark Twain once quipped that "a self-made man is about as likely as a self-laid egg." The idea that a person is "self-made," that each person is a tabula rasa, is foreign to classical Jewish thought. The European Jew defined himself or herself as "X *son of* Y" or as "A *daughter of* B." Who one is, is always related to one's family origins, to *yihus*, to genealogy. But as Hayyim Solomon wrote to his family in Poland in 1783, in America "*yihus* is worth very little."[11] The American tendency is to sever one's genealogical roots, to discard them. This approach, in effect, rejects the most fundamental form of continuity, namely, biological continuity, the continuity of the family. Since a basic claim of Jewish tradition is that the Jewish people derive their identity, their cohesion, and their continuity from being members of an extended family with shared familial roots beginning with the biblical patriarchs, jettisoning the idea of identity through genealogy subverts the very premise of Jewish continuity and identity.

American Jews assimilated, and in doing so accepted the dominant American tendency: to affirm discontinuity with the European experience. Most American Jews perceive the experience of Jews in America as being essentially new and different from all past Jewish experience. As Jonathan Woocher in his definitive study of the civil religion of American Jews puts it, in addition to the myth of destruction and rebirth, "the second great myth of American Jewish civil religion is its story of the American Jewish experience itself: America—and American Jews—are different."[12] From this perspective, that which is new, unprecedented, and unique (not to mention self-reliant) need not turn to the past for wisdom or guidance.

Two approaches to Jewish history have served to fortify the essentially antihistorical attitude of American Jewry and to reinforce the fundamental myths of its civil religion. The first is the lachrymose conception of the history of the Jews. The second is the historiographical reading of Jewish experience, past and present, as a never-ending series of crises. What both have in common is that they undermine any basis for Jewish continuity with the past. The lachrymose conception of Jewish history, which obsesses on the negative aspects of Jewish historical experience, fails to see any value in perpetuating a chronicle of victimization and trauma. The vision of Jewish history as a series of reactive responses to crises does not acknowledge any history at all, first because history is *made* and not reacted to, and second, because a series of unique crises cannot be conceived as features of a continuous tradition.

The lachrymose conception of Jewish history correctly maintains that a history of victimization constitutes an exercise in masochism. One response to the lachrymose reading of Jewish history, rejected even by its strongest advocates, would be for Jews to avoid the suffering endured by their ancestors by abandoning their very identity as Jews. What adherents of this historiographical camp do propose, however, is that Jews forge a new, unprecedented identity as self-reliant, self-created, auto-emancipated (to use Pinsker's phrase) people. This approach has largely been incorporated into the civil religion of Israeli and American Jews.

According to these two historiographical postures, if *having* a history means *making* history, then the Jews have no history, only a chronicle of suffering. If history means being proactive rather than reactive, having heroes rather than being victims, being self-reliant rather than targets of oppression, being self-created rather than molded by the designs of one's enemies, then there is no Jewish history—and thus no point in trying to find a foundation for the future in the past. This historiographical stance was perhaps best summarized and popularized by the Israeli novelist Haim Hazaz in his now classic Hebrew short story, "Ha-Derashah" ("The Sermon"). As Yudka, the major figure in the story, says:

> We didn't make our own history; the goyim made it for us. . . . [T]hey made our history to suit themselves, and we took it from them as it came. But it's not ours. . . . Because we didn't make it, we would have made it differently. . . . In that sense, and in every other sense . . . we have no history of our own. . . . What is there in it? Oppression, deformation, persecution and martyrdom. And, again and again and again without end. That's what's in it and nothing more! . . . Jewish history . . . has

no glory or action, no heroes and conquerors, no rulers and masters of their fate, just a collection of wounded, hungry, groaning and wailing wretches, always begging for mercy. . . . I would simply forbid teaching our children Jewish history. Why the devil teach them about their ancestors' shame? . . . [A] special perverted, fantastic psychology has grown up around us. . . . We love suffering, for through suffering we are able to be Jews; it preserves us and maintains us.[13]

In his magnum opus, *A Social and Religious History of the Jews*, and in his other studies, Salo Baron, the most eminent Jewish historian of the twentieth century, demonstrates the fallacies of the lachrymose conception of Jewish history. While Baron was painfully aware of the traumas and tragedies that punctuated Jewish experience, he marshaled an indisputable mountain of evidence of Jewish achievement in the intellectual, religious, cultural, economic, social, and political spheres. These expressions of Jewish creativity cannot be explained away as simply being reactions to gentile oppression. Baron further demonstrates that the relations of Jews and gentiles cannot be reduced to those of victim and oppressor. Rather, he illuminates elements of mutual and beneficial influence. With specific reference to Poland, he shows how, rather than being passive pawns of Polish overlords, Polish Jews were often able to manipulate the secular authorities to do their bidding. He shows, for example, how Jews were active players in trying to determine who sat on the Polish throne.[14] Subsequent historians, concentrating on the history of the Jews in Poland, have painstakingly documented how a confluence of mutual interests between Jews and non-Jews in Poland forged a marriage of convenience between interdependent parties, of how dependent the Polish nobility often was on the Jews for the economic wherewithal that gave stability to their position of civil power. As Baron wrote in the 1960s, "All my life I have been struggling against the hitherto dominant lachrymose conception of Jewish history—a term which I have been using for more than forty years—because I have felt that an overemphasis on Jewish sufferings distorted the total picture of Jewish historic evolution and, at the same time, badly served a generation which had become impatient with the nightmare of endless persecutions and massacres."[15]

According to Baron, the lachrymose conception of Jewish history not only represents a one-sided, inaccurate, and a "distorted view of the Jews' past," but it is a "non-Jewish" concept introduced by Jewish historians and theologians of the nineteenth century to further their particular sociopolitical agenda. At the root of this agenda was the conception of the European Jew as a pariah, and as such, inferior to the peoples of Europe. The Jewish historians of the modern period wanted to use the lachrymose vision of the Jewish medieval past "as a weapon in the prolonged desire for [Jewish political] equality" by juxtaposing medieval Jewish oppression to the modern freedoms offered by the then emergent democracies of western Europe. In Baron's view, rather than being an objective reading of Jewish history, the lachrymose conception was a tool to further a now obsolete Jewish political agenda. For Baron, despite their awareness of the traumas of history, the Jews of medieval Europe never viewed Jewish history as the "depressing spectacle" described by modern Jewish historians. Nor did the Jews of the Middle Ages see themselves as a pariah people. And "at no time in antiquity or in the Middle Ages did they admit that their sufferings were due to their personal or group inferiority." Baron also attacks Zionistic formulations of the lachrymose conception that "display [the] forthcoming rebirth of the people in Zion against a dark background."[16] By disassociating themselves from the Jewish past, some advocates of the lachrymose conception of Jewish history threw out the baby with the bathwater. The bathwater was the chronicle of tragedy and trauma. The baby was the spiritual heritage of Jewish experience.

One strand of Zionist historiography contrasts the lachrymose rendering of Jewish history with the proactive, self-reliant, heroic portrait of Israeli existence brought about by the realization of the mission of Zionism in the creation of the State of Israel. From this perspective, Zionism represents a radical break with the passive past, with the persecutions characteristic of diasporan Jewish experience. Consequently Zionism is, by its nature, discontinuous with the Jewish past. This position is expressed by Yudka in Hazaz's short story:

> One thing is clear. Zionism is not a continuation, it is no medicine for an ailment. That's nonsense! It's uprooting and destruction, it's the opposite of what has been. . . . The fact is, it turns away from the people, is opposed to it, goes against its will and spirit, undermines it, subverts it and turns off in a different direction, to a distant goal; Zionism, with a small group at its head, is the nucleus of a different people . . . not new or restored but *different*. . . . This community is not continuing anything, it is different, something entirely specific, almost not Jewish, practically not Jewish at all.[17]

Hazaz exposes the fallacy of that aspect of American and Israeli civil religion that sees Zionism and the State of Israel as being the fulfillment of the continuity of the Jewish dream for political and social redemption. For Hazaz, Zionism epitomizes discontinuity with past Jewish traditions.

According to most of the great Lithuanian rabbis of the early twentieth century, the only strand of Jewish tradition that Zionism represents, if any, is the tradition of the false Messiah. The Brisker Rav, Rabbi Joseph Soloveitchik, compared Theodore Herzl and the Zionist movement to Shabbatai Zevi, the false Jewish messiah of the seventeenth century. Indeed, Herzl's diaries indicate that he strongly identified with Shabbatai Zevi.[18] Rabbi Eliezer Hayyim Meisel of Lodz saw Zionism as a worse threat to Jewish continuity than the false messiahs of the past because political Zionism also tried to "force the people away from their belief in the principles of the Torah and the commandments."[19] The fear was that Zionist nationalism would supplant Jewish tradition, that it would undermine the spiritual heritage of Judaism, that Jewish nationalism would become a substitute for Judaism, that Zionism would replace Judaism as the foundation of Jewish identity, and that the Jewish people would replace God as the object of ultimate concern. Similarly, Solomon Schechter, the first eminent Jewish leader in America to embrace Zionism (in 1906), warned that:

> [T]he strong tendency to detach the [Zionist] movement from all religion . . . can only end in spiritual disaster. There is such a thing as the assimilation of Judaism even as there is such a thing as the assimilation of the Jew, and the former is bound to happen when religion is looked upon as a negligible quantity. When Judaism is once assimilated, the Jew will follow in its wake, and Jew and Judaism will perish together. All this is a consequence of preaching an aspect of Nationalism more in harmony with Roman and similar modern models than with Jewish ideas and ideals.[20]

The civil religion has realized these fears. For example, "We are One," the mantra of the Jewish communal structure, has all but replaced the biblical proclamation, "Hear O Israel, the Lord our God, the Lord is One" (Deut. 6:4). None of the dogmas of the civil religion has to do with God. As Jonathan Woocher points out, the role that God plays in civil Judaism is "thoroughly insignificant."[21]

An early opponent of the lachrymose conception of Jewish history was Simon Dubnow, the great late-nineteenth-century Jewish historian. He put forth a secularist, nationalist reading of Jewish history where Jewish national autonomy rather than Jewish religion was portrayed as the basis for Jewish continuity. He focused on the Jews as makers of history, and not merely as a people that subjectively experienced a history imposed upon them by others. Dubnow characterized Jewish history as a succession of changing autonomous geographical centers. For Dubnow, the greatest paradigm of Jewish autonomy was the Council of Lands that governed Jewish life in Poland from the sixteenth to the eighteenth century.[22] While Dubnow saw Jewish autonomy in the diaspora as the defining characteristic of Jewish historical experience, and while he was no advocate of Zionism, many Zionist historians built upon his view of diasporan autonomy and revisaged it to fit the Zionist ideology. For example, they portrayed the Council of Lands and various military initiatives taken by Polish Jews throughout their history, but especially during the Holocaust (particularly the 1943 Warsaw Ghetto uprising), as precedents and as preparations for the political autonomy and the military self-reliance that came to fruition with the establishment in 1948 of the Jewish State. From this perspective the political heritage of Polish Jewry, not its spiritual heritage, offers a basis for Jewish continuity that attained its culmination and fulfillment in the State of Israel. However, this nationalized and secularized reading of Jewish history subverts the whole concept of spiritual continuity by reducing Jewish history to an experiment in political autonomy, the value of which lay only in its conserving the Jewish people throughout the centuries and preparing Jews for the realization of their political destiny with the establishment in 1948 of the Jewish State. In this view, the primary value of Judaism is to serve as a force to preserve the Jewish people in the diaspora until the re-establishment of the Jewish state could be accomplished. Thereafter, Judaism became obsolete since it had no intrinsic value.

The second philosophy of Jewish history that stifles the continuity of Judaism is one that sees Jewish experience as a perpetual chain of crises rather than as a continuous tradition developing in accordance with its own internal dynamic. This approach sees Jewish history as a series of reactive responses to upheavals precipitated by traumatic historical events like the exile from Spain, the encounter with other religions and ideologies, and radical shifts in political, economic, or demographic realities. In this view, Jewish survival has long depended on the ability of the Jewish people to devise a political, social, or theological solution to the crisis of the moment. For example, in his magisterial scholarly work on Jewish mysticism, Gershom Scholem sees various "major trends" as responses to historical crises. More recent scholarship on the development of Jewish mysticism, however, tends to see it as primarily a continuous unfolding of ideas according to its own internal dynamic. Nonetheless, the crisis-oriented approach to Jewish historical experience has had a major impact upon Jewish communal policy and action. Rather than seeing current events as part of a historical continuum, contemporary Jewish communal life stumbles from crisis to crisis, trying to devise new strategies and tactics as if the past can offer no guidance to dealing with new challenges. Both the historiographical and the administrative stance that advocates a crisis-oriented approach to Jewish past and present experience serves to subvert the possibility of tradition and continuity. If Jewish experience is a series of unique crises, then the possibility for the development of a flowing, natural, dynamic, continuous tradition is precluded. The evocation or the contrivance of a state of perpetual crisis and emergency may be effective in community mobilization and in fundraising, but it subverts the very tradition it purports to defend.

In pre–World War II Warsaw, the profound religious thinker Hillel Zeitlin claimed that the only cohesive force Jews have is Judaism. Zeitlin saw a growing proliferation of secularist movements within the Jewish community of interwar Poland as representing an irreparable breach in the continuity of Jewish tradition, especially as it had developed in Poland. Zeitlin perceived the then growing secular Yiddishist movement and secular Hebraist and Zionist movements in Poland as betrayals of Judaism. He referred to their followers as "Hebrew- or Yiddish-speaking gentiles."[23] For Zeitlin, neither the ideologies nor the value systems of any form of secular Judaism—be it socialist, communist, Zionist, or cultural—could be compatible with the inherited religious tradition of Polish Jewry; a secular Judaism or a secular Jew is an oxymoron, an invitation to the spiritual suicide of both Judaism and the Jewish people.

For many American Jews, politics and social activism are confused with Judaism. Jewish messianism has become transformed into and identified with political liberalism. In the words of sociologist Steven M. Cohen, "Many American Jews were raised with the understanding that liberalism or political radicalism constituted the very essence of Judaism, that all the rest—the rituals, liturgy, community organizations—were outdated, vestigial trappings for a religion with a great moral and political message embodied in liberalism." Or as Leonard Fein more succinctly put it, "Politics is our religion; our preferred political denomination is liberalism."[24] The insightful Jewish sociologist Charles Liebman observed in the 1960s that the shift of the self-definition of American Jews from being primarily a religious community to an ethnic community would occasion a change of focus from religious belief and observance to sociopolitical concerns. Liebman writes, "For many Jews, Judaism has meant the fight for social justice, civil rights and civil liberties. The difficulty with this conception of Judaism is that on the surface it has very little to do with what is uniquely Jewish."[25]

Political liberalism, civil Judaism, and Jewish ethnicity serve not only to replace and to circumvent, but also to subvert the spiritual heritage of Polish Jewry. They offer visions of Jewish identity that are incompatible with the continuity of Judaism as a religious faith. The underlying premise of Judaism is the unique spiritual nature of Jewish faith and of the Jewish people. An underlying premise of political liberalism is universalism, which embodies a denial of the claim of Jewish uniqueness.[26] The underlying premise of Zionism is that Jews must become a nation like all other nations. This also negates the claim to Jewish singularity. While Jewish tradition warns against Jewish assimilation, against becoming "like the nations," the Zionist plan is for the Jews to become like all other nations. Both Jewish liberalism and Zionism draw their conceptual sustenance from European ideologies of the modern period rather than from classical Jewish sources. Like the civil religion and like Jewish ethnicity, Jewish liberalism and Zionism offer models of Jewish identity that differ from those developed by Jewish faith. All these modern secular ideologies serve as a basis for a Jewish identity that would find little resonance in Jewish religious tradition. Each perceives Judaism as a means to an end rather than as an end in itself. Each fails to find intrinsic value in Jewish religious faith. Ironically, contemporary Jews find themselves jettisoning authentically Jewish foundations for Jewish identity in order to embrace contrived and inauthentic frameworks for affirming that identity. They are defining themselves as that which they are not while ignoring the very tradition that defines who they are.

Despite its pretensions regarding self-reliance, for much of its history the American Jewish community has been preoccupied with divesting itself of Jewish traits in order to gain acceptance by Gentile society. Similarly, for much of its history Israel has been a client state of the United States. However, for most of its much longer history Polish Jewry was more self-reliant, more authentically Jewish, more compatible with the integrity of Jewish religious belief and practice, than either American or Israeli Jewry.

Contemporary Jewish life represents a fissure with the heritage of Jewish religious faith. It is a break rather than a link with the past. It disposes of more than it retains; it discards rather than restores. Obsessing on survival, it ignores revival. It curses the darkness rather than rekindling the flame. With little doubt, the spiritual magnates of Polish Jewry would stand aghast at the spiritual bankruptcy of contemporary Jewry. The precious legacy that they preserved, maintained, amplified, and conveyed has been either squandered or left unclaimed by their descendants. Their souls, if they could be heard, would undoubtedly make an urgent plea for today's Jews to search in the ashes and ruins of the past to recover the sparks that might rekindle the flickering flame of the Jewish soul, before it's too late, before the sparks in the embers fade into the darkness of oblivion. With all of its resources and technical know-how, contemporary Jewry has failed to learn how to kindle the spark, how to ignite the flame.

> A young man became an apprentice to a blacksmith. He learned how to hold the tongs, how to lift the sledge, how to smite the anvil and how to blow the fire with the bellows. Having finished his apprenticeship, he was chosen to be employed at the smithery of the royal palace. However, the young man's delight came soon to an end, when he discovered that he had failed to learn how to kindle the spark. All his skill and knowledge in handling the tools were to no avail.[27]

Sparks in Ashes

When the Maggid of Mezeritch (Polish: Miedzyrzecz) was asked how to reignite the flame of spiritual exaltation (Hebrew: *hitlahavut*), he said, "To rekindle the flame, search for sparks amidst the ashes."[1]

Within the ashen remains of Polish Jewry, sacred sparks await rescue and reclamation. Like diamonds seared by fire, the luminescence of these nuggets remains undulled. Their recovery may hold forth the promise for the spiritual resuscitation of the contemporary Jewish soul.

While Polish Jewry was physically decimated during the Holocaust, remnants of its spiritual legacy have survived. While American Jewry has grown increasingly robust materially, its spiritual condition has atrophied. A fusion of the resources of the Polish-Jewish soul with the corpus of contemporary Jewry promises to engender a spiritually revitalized Jewish community. By drawing its sustenance from the legacy left by its physical forebears, rather than from the civil religion, contemporary Jewry has the potential to re-create itself in a manner compatible with its inherited traditions. Only then will it be effectively able to further Jewish continuity, and to become an authentic faith-community rather than a mélange of communal organizations. As Franz Rosenzweig, the eminent German-Jewish philosopher, once wrote, "for what is the use of the most perfect organization of Jews if there are no Jews left to be 'organized'?"[2]

Polish Jewry produced an unprecedented and unduplicated storehouse of spiritual treasures. Nonetheless, not everything that is offered by the past can be applied to the present. What is required is not a photocopy of the past, but a distillation of the best that the past has to offer. From a myriad of moments in time during the millennium of Jewish residence in the Polish lands, sacred sparks may be exhumed to illumine a path toward a spiritually enhanced future.

In the schema of the Jewish mystics, sacred sparks are encased in shells and husks of impurity. The challenge is to separate the spark from the shell, the light from the darkness. The legacy of Polish Jewry contains both sparks and husks, light and darkness. In attempting to recover sacred sparks from the past, attention must be focused on the light and not on the darkness, on the wisdom of the past that is pertinent to the existential conditions of the present. As Rabbi Moses Hayyim Efraim of Sudlikow taught, "The Torah must be interpreted in each generation according to that generation's needs and according to the soul-root of those who live at that time."[3] In the recovery of the spiritual treasures of the past, the husks must be identified and discarded in order to allow the sparks to be utilized in illuminating a path through the present and into the future. Undesirable characteristics need to be recognized so that the sparks and not the husks are perpetuated, and so that the past is not reduced to a romanticized reminiscence.

The history of Polish Jewry is populated by the presence of maestros in the art of soul crafting. However, it is also punctuated by the presence of moral scoundrels. There were saints and scholars, but there were also the unsavory and the uncouth. There were the spiritually adept and there were those who spent a lifetime in trivial pursuits. There were the altruistic and there were the schnorrers, always scheming to acquire something for nothing. Some were obsessed with the quest for divine communion while others were thieves, yokels, and vamps. There were moments of spiritual exaltation as well as times of massacres and persecutions. Sometimes there was prosperity, but there also was crippling poverty and naked misery.

While the past cannot be confused with the present, the wisdom of the past can be infused into the present. An attempt to reproduce today the variegated forms that characterized the life of past generations of Polish Jews would yield only a poor facsimile of what once was. For example, some today mistakenly think that if they dress like Polish Hasidim, they have become Polish Hasidim. But donning Hasidic garb does not a Hasid make. Indeed, the garments identified as Hasidic dress are not even of Jewish origin, but are adapted from clothing worn by Polish gentiles of past centuries.[4] Not so much the outer trappings, but the inner life of Polish Jewry is where spiritual resources may be mined.

For the civil religion of contemporary Jewry, the point of departure is the community; the civil religion sees the individual in terms of how he or she can further the communal agenda. Spirituality sees the community as a backdrop for the spiritual development of the individual. By the twelfth century Maimonides had interpreted the well-known rabbinic adage, "Do not separate yourself from the community,"[5] to mean that the relationship between the individual and the community should be determined by the spiritual level of development attained by the community. In Maimonides's view, one may not separate oneself from a community that nurtures individual spiritual development, but one can separate oneself from a community that fails to do so. For Maimonides, one is obliged to be communally engaged, but not at the price of one's spiritual self-development.[6] For all its successes in other areas, contemporary Jewish organizational and communal life largely remains a spiritual wilderness. Nonetheless, available insights from the legacy of Polish Jewry may be gleaned to serve as a foundation for the spiritual development of the individual.

The relationship between the community and the individual is discussed in a variety of Hasidic commentaries to the biblical narrative regarding the experience of the Israelites in Egypt. In these texts, communal redemption is described as the result of individual redemption. Before the community can be free of exile, alienation, and bondage, the individuals who constitute the community must develop themselves spiritually. "Only when each person attains individual redemption will there be universal redemption and the Messiah will arrive," taught the Ba'al Shem Tov.[7] In this view, the challenge of individual spiritual development should be the leading priority of the communal agenda.

Rabbi Menahem Nahum of Chernobyl interprets the biblical story of the Exodus from Egypt as an event occurring on two levels. One level is liberation from "group exile" (Hebrew: *galut kelali*) and the other is redemption from "individual exile" (Hebrew: *galut perati*). Rabbi Menahem Nahum further taught that each individual dwells in his or her own Egypt, and it is only by the spiritual liberation from this personal Egypt that the process of a collective redemption can ensue. For the individual to be able properly to observe Passover, which celebrates the redemption from Egypt, each person must first move from a state of spiritual fragmentation to a state of spiritual integration, from a state of spiritual alienation (Hebrew: *katnut*) to a state of spiritual fulfillment (Hebrew: *gadlut*).[8] Only when the spiritual transformation of each individual has been achieved can the complete physical, social, and political redemption of the people of Israel be realized.

This view, because it perceives the end of the geographical "exile" of the people of Israel and the redemption of the world as events set to occur in a distant future, focuses upon the more immediate task of the spiritual development of the individual, on life as a mission aimed at spiritual self-fulfillment. Unlike Christianity, which considers the Messiah as the agent of an individual's spiritual redemption, this teaching considers the human person as the protagonist in a drama that can lead to his or her own spiritual salvation. As Hillel Zeitlin put it, "Each person is the redeemer of a world that is all his or her own."[9]

The Hasidic masters individualized earlier kabbalistic teachings about the rescue and repair of the sacred sparks (Hebrew: *tikkun*). They taught that the sparks akin to each individual's soul-root await their rescue by that particular individual. For the Hasidic masters, achieving communion with God is the ultimate reason for rescuing the sparks, the main purpose of individual redemption (Hebrew: *geulah perati*). Proximity to the divine is the prerequisite for spiritual self-fulfillment. This was the Hasidic understanding of the biblical verse, "Draw near to my soul and redeem it" (Psalms 69:18).[10]

In Hebrew, Adam is spelled "A-D-M." Rabbi Nathan Shapiro of Cracow explained that this name is an abbreviation for "Adam," "David," "Messiah." These three have the same lineage, the same soul. Adam is thus a messianic figure. He is the first and the last. Adam is the bud; the Messiah is the opened flower.[11] But who is Adam? The Lurianic kabbalists of the sixteenth century, who had a profound influence upon Nathan Shapiro, taught that the soul of every person is a spark of the flame that was the soul of the original Adam. Each person is "Adam," which in Hebrew means "a human being." According to some kabbalistic teachings, the primary mission of each human is to rectify the spark of Adam's soul that is also his or her own individual soul. When that is accomplished, all of the sparks of the flame of the soul of the original Adam will be reunited. Adam will be restored as he was before the fall. This purified soul of Adam will be the soul of the Messiah. Each person bears a spark of the flame which is the messianic soul. Each individual is therefore responsible to repair, to redeem, his or her individual spark of the soul of Adam-Messiah. Were a single person not to fulfill his or her role in the messianic drama, the final and complete redemption of the world could not arrive. Each individual is a kind of miniature messiah whose mission in life is to achieve spiritual self-realization as his or her unique role in the messianic drama.

While Polish Hasidim were not oblivious to contemporary social and political realities, they did not equate Judaism with politics, messianism with social activism. They did not conceive of the people of Israel as an ethnic group. In formulating their teachings regarding individual spiritual development, Polish Jewry drew upon the vast legacy of Jewish tradition as a foundation for implementing its own visions of the nature of the spiritual journey. The Jewish spiritual masters of Poland did not view themselves as innovators, but as guardians and transmitters of the heritage they had received from their forebears. They saw themselves as links in a long chain of tradition, and they understood their mission to be the perpetuation, the continuity, and the enrichment of that tradition. It was their perceived task to employ that tradition in the enhancement of their own lives and of the lives of the members of the community of which they were a part. They evaluated the quality of life not primarily by the attainment of fame, fortune, or social status, but by how much spiritual substance informed their daily existence; by the extent to which inwardness, holiness, and compassion could be detected in their lives; and by the degree of spiritual refinement that they had been able to attain. For them, life was the ultimate art form, and living was a divinely offered opportunity to cultivate that art form.

Like Jews of all generations since the exile began with the destruction of the Temple, the Jews of Poland prayed for messianic redemption and for the restoration of Jewish sovereignty in Israel in the messianic era. Much has been made by Zionist historians, trying to discern a proto-Zionistic motif in Hasidic life and thought, of the comparatively few Polish Hasidim who went to live in Israel.[12] However, the opposite seems to be true. Polish Hasidim tended to assign a substantial significance to life in the Diaspora, particularly in Poland. Only divine intervention and the actual arrival of the Messiah would convince them to leave the Polish lands. Because of "false" messiahs they had known like Shabbatai Zevi and Jacob Frank, they became overly cautious in acknowledging that certain historical phenomena might indicate the dawning of the messianic era. They perceived the dispersion of the Jews throughout the world not as a political catastrophe, but as a spiritual opportunity. Not atypical in this regard is the statement of Menahem Nahum of Chernobyl: "The mystery of the exile, whereby the people of Israel was dispersed among the nations of the world in the four corners of the world, is explained by the fact that only in this way can they liberate the sparks that fell among the nations because of Adam's sin, for these sparks were attached to him before his sin."[13] It even appears that some of the Hasidic masters—including the Ba'al Shem Tov, the founder of Hasidism—considered the felt desire of some rabbinical leaders in Poland to emigrate to the Land of Israel to be a form of escapism, or worse, as a motivation induced by Satan. He is supposed to have forbidden Rabbi Jacob Joseph of Polonnoye, the author of the first Hasidic book, to travel to the Holy Land. "Every time that you feel a desire to travel to the Holy Land," the Ba'al Shem Tov is reputed to have said to Jacob Joseph, "you should realize that your own town is in trouble and Satan is confusing you so that you will not pray for your own town. So every time you feel a desire for the Holy Land, pray for your own town."[14]

Following earlier motifs in Jewish mysticism, the Hasidic masters of Poland taught that while one form of messianic redemption occurs in time (at the end of history) and in space (in the Land of Israel), another form of messianic redemption occurs within the individual soul. In this view, messianic redemption is primarily a spiritual state rather than a social or a political one. Such a form of messianic redemption is attainable anywhere by anyone able to ascend the ladder of spiritual development. It was this form of spiritual or psychological messianism that was prominent in Hasidic thought. Rather than await the coming of the Messiah, each individual could become his or her own messiah, and achieve redemption within the precincts of his or her own soul.

The "Holy Land" and the "messianic era" were interpreted allegorically to denote a high spiritual state of existence rather than a particular geographical place or moment in history. Exile was identified with a state of spiritual alienation rather than with geographical dislocation from a homeland.[15] It is therefore possible to be in the "Holy Land" while in Poland (or elsewhere), and to be in exile while in the Land of Israel. The spiritual life is thus understood as a process of awakening from the exile, from *galut*, from alienation, as the necessary prelude to realizing the true meaning of life—to individual redemption, which is metaphorically described as "being in the land." The physical exile is no longer considered, as it was in previous generations, as an obstacle to the attainment of spiritual fulfillment; on the contrary, the individual in the state of physical *galut* is able to commune with the presence of God in the world (Hebrew: *Shekhinah*), which is also in a state of exile (Hebrew: *Galut ha-Shekhinah*). Physical exile thus is not primarily viewed as a catastrophe, but as an opportunity for closer communion with the divine. Indeed, the redemption of the divine presence in the world, the redemption of God, so to speak, becomes dependent upon the redemption of the soul of each individual. Each person therefore becomes not only his or her own messiah, but each person also plays his or her own distinct role in the rescue and redemption of the divine from the vicissitudes of this world. Here one encounters an authentically Jewish teaching regarding personal salvation. An individual need not and should not await the final redemption of the people of Israel in the messianic era to achieve individual redemption.[16]

For some of the Hasidic masters dwelling "outside the land" takes on a positive connotation. Dwelling in the land (Hebrew: *ba'aretz*) denotes a state of materiality (Hebrew: *artziyut*), while dwelling outside the land refers to a state of detachment from materiality, allowing for an elevated level of spirituality. Some Hasidic sources go a step farther and claim that being physically in the Diaspora affords a greater opportunity for spiritual exaltation, for experiencing a revelation of the divine, and for communion with God, than does dwelling physically in the Land of Israel.[17] Such a view is found, for example, in the teachings of the Maggid of Mezeritch and his disciple Elimelekh of Lizensk. The Maggid taught that "divine inspiration is more readily attained today in the diaspora than at the time of the prophets and the Temple [in the Land of Israel]."[18]

Drawing upon earlier themes in Jewish mysticism and philosophy, Moses Isserles taught that climbing the ladder of spiritual development could lead the individual to the attainment of the prophetic gift. Revelation was now not only available in one place—the Land of Israel, or in one era—biblical times. Instead, revelation is also available in the here and now.

According to the Talmud God spoke only through Moses and the biblical prophets, making them the sole conduits of divine revelation.[19] The Hasidim, however, maintain that the voice of God emanates from Hasidic masters. In the following parable offered by Elimelekh of Lizensk, divine communion and prophetic revelation are described as being perpetually available. The prophetic gift and communion with God are described as being more easily attainable in the Polish Diaspora than in the Land of Israel during the era of biblical prophecy when the Holy Temple in Jerusalem still stood:

> It is like a King who, when he is in his place of glory—in his own house—his courtyard—his palace—is visited by one who loves him—who comes to invite him to dine with him at his house. Surely the King will be angry with him, for it is hardly fitting that a King should leave his palace for the house of another, however generous the proffered feast. Nor is it possible for a man to invite the King to his house before he sees to all the necessary provisions. Moreover, he must choose advocates and adherents to be present when the King comes to dine with him, in order to be sure to please the King.
>
> But when the King is on a journey and desires a resting-place along the way—then, any clean place in any decent inn—even if it be only a village inn—so long as it be clean—this is the place where the King will rest.
>
> The meaning of the parable is evident. In the days of the Temple, when the Shekhinah of the divine Majesty was in the Holy of Holies—in those days, when a person desired the inspiration of the Holy Spirit or prophecy, it was hard work for him. . . . But now—in the bitterness of the Exile into which the Holy Shekhinah has accompanied us—now that she is wandering here and there in the land because of our sins, seeking an abode—*now* if the Shekhinah should find a place to rest, a clean place, a person (but only a person cleansed of sin and transgression) is the place where the Shekhinah [i.e., God's Presence] will rest.[20]

Not all Jews in the eighteenth and nineteenth centuries in Poland were Hasidim. There were Polish Jews who passionately opposed Hasidism. Among the more secularized opponents of the Hasidim were the *maskilim*, or "enlightened."[21] Among the more Jewishly traditional adversaries of the Hasidim were the *mitnagdim* or "opponents." Neither the Makower Ruf nor most of my other forebears in nineteenth-century Poland were Hasidic Jews. Indeed, Makow was a center from which some of the most virulent attacks against Hasidism emanated.[22] It would be too much of a diversion at this point to examine the areas of contention between the Polish Hasidism and their opponents. However, it is important to note that the Hasidic Jews of Poland were not the only people to emphasize individual spiritual development or to advance the idea that prophecy is currently available. Among the adversaries of the Hasidim, there arose a movement in the Lithuanian districts of Poland during the nineteenth century that stressed the spiritual development of the individual self through a rigorous discipline that embraced radical self-analysis as well as the cultivation of the moral virtues. This movement is known as "*Musar*," which denotes "ethics" or "moral instruction." In the period between the two world wars, the influence of the Musar movement moved westward from Lithuania into the heartland of Poland.[23]

The central figure of the Musar movement was Rabbi Israel of Salant.[24] Like the Hasidic masters, he taught that prophetic inspiration was within reach of individuals who achieve the state of realized personhood that comes with mastering the Musar-prescribed process of moral, intellectual, and spiritual self-development. Like some of the Hasidic masters, Israel of Salant understood "exile" to be a spiritual as well as a geographical condition. For him, each person lives in an "individual exile" (Hebrew: *galut ha-perat*). Sin, moral vice, and the failure to succeed in the spiritual quest create a "new exile" (Hebrew: *galut hadash*) that exacerbates both one's "individual exile" and the exilic state of the community. In his view, the path of Musar, especially the attainment of "complete repentance," allows the individual to attain the prophetic state, which is equated with the realization of one's spiritual potential.[25]

The spiritual magnates of Polish Jewry were not systematic thinkers. They did not strive to construct conceptually integrated philosophical systems. Logical consistency was not their métier. Rather, they offer a smorgasbord of ideas, techniques, paths, concepts, and methods for transforming life into a spiritual adventure, into an art form. While they often disagreed on the meaning of different theological ideas, on the preference of one path over another, on the accuracy of the maps in their possession, on the way to navigate the path toward the destination, and on the employment of various spiritual techniques, they nonetheless were united in the conviction that the goal of the journey is an encounter with the divine, and that individual spiritual development is the necessary prerequisite for divine communion. For Polish Jewry, the categorical imperative is the continuity of the tradition that served as their passport to transcendence, their letter of invitation to God.

The spiritual heritage of Polish Jewry offers many blueprints and strategies for propelling a person toward enhanced self-understanding, fulfilled human existence, and communion with God. According to both Israel of Salant and the Ba'al Shem Tov, the individual must find the route best suited to his or her own spiritual nature. The Ba'al Shem Tov was fond of interpreting the biblical verse "In all your ways, know God" (Prov. 3:6) to mean that each person must find his or her own way to spiritual fulfillment.

Inward Journeys

The prominent French novelist André Malraux once said that "either the third millennium will be a spiritual age, or there will be no third millennium." Similarly, Dag Hammarskjold, the first U.N. secretary-general, warned that "Unless the world has a spiritual rebirth, civilization is doomed." As we witness a growing sense of spiritual homelessness among increasing numbers of individuals, who, in the words of Matthew Arnold are "wandering between two worlds, one dead and the other powerless to be born," the admonitions of Hammarskjold and Malraux take on an added sense of urgency and poignancy. In our age of collapsing ideologies, shifting economies, changing politics, moral anarchy, genocidal violence, and displaced populations, many have come to realize that the emperor has no clothes and that the clothes have no emperor. We find ourselves living through an earthquake with its epicenter in the self. What is happening all around us is also happening within us. The shocks and aftershocks that have convulsed the topography of our daily lives inevitably register on the seismograph of our souls, on our innermost selves.

Rabbi Nahman of Bratzlav once said, "Der Velt iz a dreidel" — "The world is a spinning top."[1] Disoriented by continuous ideological, cultural, social, political, and economic shifts, we are hard-pressed to find an anchor. Even finding oneself often becomes an elusive endeavor. In this regard, the nineteenth-century Hasidic master Rabbi Hanokh of Alexander (Polish: Aleksandrow, a town near Lodz), told this story:

> Once there was a man who, like many of us, would wake up in the morning and would forget where he put his clothing when he went to bed the night before.
>
> One night before going to sleep, this man devised a solution to his problem. Before he got into bed, he took paper and a pencil and wrote himself a note. The note said: "The eyeglasses are on the table next to the bed. The pants are on the chair next to the table. The shirt is over the pants. The shoes are under the bed. And I am in the bed."
>
> The next morning he awoke and he took his list, and to his amazement he found everything he was looking for: his eyeglasses, his pants, his shirt and his shoes. But, then he went looking for the last item on this list, i.e., himself. When he went

to find himself in the bed, he was not there. He sighed and said, "I have found everything but myself. So, if I am not in the bed, then where am I?"[2]

The spiritual quest is a forthright confrontation with the fundamental questions of human existence: Where am I? Who am I? Where should I go? What am I doing here? What should I be doing here? The Hasidic master Rabbi Israel of Rhyzen once prayed, "Dear God, I do not ask You to explain to me why the world was created, or why the good suffer and the evil prosper. Only, please tell me: What am I doing in this world of Yours?"[3]

The spiritual legacy of Polish Jewry offers a series of maps and charts for a spiritual rebirth, not only for the Jewish people but for all peoples. As Abraham Heschel wrote, "The significance of Judaism does not lie in its being conducive to the mere survival of a particular people, but rather in its being a source of spiritual wealth, a source of meaning relevant to all peoples."[4]

Among the primary goals of Jewish spirituality are the consummation of a romance with the divine, the creation of one's life as a work of art, encountering a source of meaning in that which transcends us, and deepening the consciousness of our self-understanding. Within Jewish spirituality, four often converging primary paths are envisaged as propelling us toward these goals. They are: the word, the world, the deed, and the self.

The spiritual quest demands candid introspection. It is told, for example, that once Rabbi Yitzhak of Vorki (Polish: Warka) spent the Sabbath with a simple Jewish farmer. The farmer asked the rabbi to teach him some Torah, but the rabbi was curious as to what he could learn from the farmer. That particular week, the Scriptural reading began with the verse, "See I [God] have set before you this day blessing and curse" (Deut. 11:26). The farmer reflected upon the possible meaning of the first two words of the verse, and he said in Polish: "*Patrz Sobie*," meaning "See the I," "Look at yourself." The rabbi of Vorki was so impressed with this insight that he would quote it to his disciples each year when that verse was read in the synagogue. The spiritual pilgrimage commences with an inward gaze, with the individual's encounter with his or her own self.[5]

Following the earlier Jewish mystics, the rabbi of Kotzk taught that in our world, truth is veiled, incomplete. Each grain of truth is surrounded by shells of falsehood. The goal of life is to encounter truth behind the veils of illusion. In his view, the greatest obstacles in the search for truth are self-delusion and self-deception, that is, living a lie and taking it to be the truth. Truth means sincerity, honesty, integrity. It means not simply trying to define or to uncover what is right, but to live it. Truth means doing what we say, living our stated commitments, becoming our convictions. Life, in this view, is a perilous task. One must try to navigate between truth and illusion, appearance and reality, self-realization and self-delusion.[6] Explaining the commandment, "You shall not steal" (Exod. 20:15), the rabbi of Kotzk said, "This means you should not steal from your neighbor. But it also means: Do not steal from yourself."[7] Just as one is forbidden to deceive one's neighbor, one is also forbidden to deceive one's self. Once Rabbi Bunem of Peshisha (Polish: Przysuche) was asked, "Who is a Hasid?" He answered, "One who does more than the law requires." He was asked, "What does the law require?" His answer, "Scripture commands us: You shall not deceive your neighbor" (Lev. 25:17). He was then asked, "What is required of the Hasid?" His answer: "Not to deceive one's own self."[8] To find truth, to attain integrity, to escape self-deception, one had to try to uncover the divine inner nature secreted in each and every created being, but particularly within one's own self.

The Musar movement taught that the most challenging book for a person to understand is the book of his or her own life. Harder than comprehending the most difficult of printed texts is truly understanding the text and context of one's own existence. For the Musar movement, the task of self-understanding is a never-ending, arduous process of lifelong learning, a curriculum that few really master. Rabbi Simha Zisel Ziv Braude, one of the leaders of the Musar movement, put it this way:

> A person lives with his or her body and soul for a lifetime. A person eats, drinks, and sleeps with himself. No one can take a single step without himself. Each individual knows all his or her deeds, all his or her own most private thoughts, joys, and sorrows. . . . And despite all of this, a person does not really know himself on as much as a single point, unless such an individual is very wise, and has toiled and labored at it.[9]

"A person needs to be an individual unto himself," taught Musar. Every individual is a world unto itself. The task of each person is to explore, to try to understand, and to cultivate the development of that world. Life is viewed as a battle against complacency and self-satisfaction. It is a war that can be won because it must be won. A Musar aphorism states that on the battlefield during a war, a private can be advanced to a general, while during times of peace such promotions are unlikely to occur. Another popular Musar aphorism says, "Never ask if something is possible. Rather, ask if it is necessary. If there is no path, then blaze a path."

For the advocates of Musar, a person is born as a potential human being. Only through constant effort can one achieve the status of realizing that potential. "Life is a ladder," teaches Musar. "One either goes up or down; one cannot stop in the middle."[10] Rabbi Israel of Salant taught that spiritual development is like the flight of a bird. If a bird in flight stops flapping its wings, it will fall. Similarly, an individual who does not continuously exert himself spiritually will both fall and fail in the spiritual journey.[11]

Musar prescribed a regimen aimed at curing the maladies of the soul and instilling spiritual health, that is, a program of spiritual therapy. Just as a physician has to know the anatomy of the body in order to effect a medical cure, taught Musar, so the individual desiring spiritual health is required to study and to understand the nature of his or her own self. For Musar, the prognosis is cautiously optimistic. Central to the teachings of Rabbi Israel of Salant is the assumption that every individual is able to alter his or her personality for the good by means of an intensive discipline of introspection and character training. As the teachers of Musar constantly pointed out, if human beings have the ability to domesticate wild animals, they also must have the ability to temper and to channel for goodness the destructive and self-destructive characteristics of human nature.

For Israel of Salant, *yirah* — awe of God and fear of divine punishment for sin — serves as a critical catalyst in stimulating spiritual development. Taking responsibility for what one does, accepting accountability to a transcendent God, acts as a spur to introspection and to the cultivation of the moral life. Israel of Salant also stressed the importance of daily study of the classics of medieval Jewish ethics and pietica. The goal of such study is to become what one reads, to internalize what one studies. Not simply an intellectual endeavor, study of ethics, of *musar*, is meant to stimulate the emotions as well as the mind, to engender moral as well as cerebral edification.

Like the medieval classics of Jewish ethics that he studied, Israel of Salant taught that the contemplation of death need not be an exercise in morbidity, but that it can be a powerful stimulant for taking responsibility for the creation of one's life as a work of art. Spiritual development entails dispelling moral vice and inculcating moral virtue. In this endeavor, one must discipline oneself against expending energy on fleeting passions and momentary pleasures that divert one's attention from achieving spiritual and moral goals. The crucial component in all self-development is taking care to avoid becoming a slave to bad habits that appropriate moral volition and freedom of action, and that inhibit the will.

Since no two people are the same, each individual needs sufficient self-insight to formulate his or her most effective prescription for spiritual therapy. This requires not only constant introspection, but sincere and even brutal self-analysis. In this process, complacency and pride are formidable stumbling blocks that must be overcome.

On this point Hasidism and Musar converge: both consider pride to be inimical to spiritual development for three major reasons. First, pride is self-deceptive, and spiritual development is always sabotaged by self-deception. Pride tricks us into thinking we are more important than we really are. It fools us into believing that we have no faults, no shortcomings. Arrogance stifles the process of self-improvement by convincing us that we have no need to improve. It does not allow us to see ourselves as we really are. Second, pride is dangerous because it stifles relationships. The ego stands as a barrier, restricting our ability to transcend ourselves in order to be able to forge a relationship with someone else, especially with God. Pride is also dangerous because it is self-destructive and destructive of relationships. Third, pride is dangerous because it is a form of the greatest sin — idolatry. Idolatry means treating something other than God as if it were God. Pride is treating one's own ego as if it were God. The arrogant person worships only his own needs, her own self.[12]

What is humility, the opposite of pride? For Musar, humility is often an exercise in self-deprecation that serves as the necessary prelude to moral self-improvement. While some of the Hasidic masters shared this view, others took humility to entail recognizing one's abilities, accepting one's achievements, acknowledging one's accomplishments, but not making too much of them, not using them as a means of lording over others, or as a barrier between others and oneself. Rather than meaning a loss of identity and self-esteem, humility can offer a proper perspective for understanding the nature of reality and the dependence of the human upon the transcendent.[13] As Menahem Nahum of Chernobyl points out, rather than restricting us, humility liberates us from egocentricity, thereby allowing us to expand consciousness and to embrace limitless possibilities made inaccessible by the restraints of the human ego.[14]

The Ba'al Shem Tov considered sadness and depression to be the reverse side of pride. Pride is ego obsession where we inflate ourselves beyond all realistic proportions; depression is another form of ego obsession where we deflate ourselves beyond all realistic proportions. Manifested either as pride or depression, ego obsession is self-deceiving and self-defeating, blocks creativity, and interferes with the formation of meaningful relationships.[15]

A major teaching of many of the Polish masters, such as Mordecai Joseph Leiner of Izbica, related to the need to control one's anger. Leiner considered anger to be inimical to faith.[16] Anger was considered a particularly destructive strain of egocentricity because unlike other expressions of pride, which harm only the self, anger often harms others as well. Within the Musar movement, anger was considered to be a trap that can hamper the individual's journey toward moral cultivation.

Israel of Salant taught that one must master "tricks of the mind" aimed at breaking bad moral habits such as the proclivity toward anger, and at developing beneficial moral habits such as kindness. For Israel of Salant, attitudinal change is the necessary prerequisite for behavioral change. Only once the individual has internalized moral virtue, can moral action become a regular feature of one's daily behavior. Through the constant employment of focused willpower, virtuous action can eventually be performed unconsciously, naturally.[17]

Israel of Salant compares the cultivation of moral virtues to learning how to read. A person who has just learned the alphabet initially has great difficulty combining the letters, though he or she knows their individual sounds. After practicing for some time, the individual becomes able to read fluently, without being conscious of the single letters and their function. Similarly, in moral behavior the task begins slowly and with frustration. But, eventually, moral behavior becomes almost automatic. In the process of moral development, a goal is to make ethical behavior into an almost instinctual trait, where it becomes as natural as breathing.[18]

As has been noted above, Rabbi Asher Lemel of Cracow is often described as the first Polish kabbalist. In the historical lands of Poland that include Ukraine, however, that honor would more appropriately belong to Rabbi Moses ben Jacob of Kiev. In his book *Shoshan Sodot*, compiled at the beginning of the sixteenth century, Moses of Kiev echoes the view of earlier sources that prophecy may be equated with the attainment of true self-understanding. For Moses of Kiev, prophecy is understood to be the individual's encounter with his or her own most realized self. In this experience, the individual is granted a vision of who one is when all of one's own potentialities have been realized. As the result of such an experience, the former self disappears, and the individual is transformed into the person one is meant to be. Once a person reaches this state of transformation from his potential nature to his perfected nature, he gains access to hidden mysteries of wisdom. Subsequently, such an individual can serve as a mentor and guide to the novice taking the first steps on the path toward spiritual self-fulfillment and enlightenment. A similar idea is found in Moses Isserles's *Torat ha-Olah*.[19] As we have seen, the view that the prophetic experience is a contemporary possibility and not simply a characteristic of ancient times was also maintained by the Hasidic masters and by the masters of Musar.

Following earlier trends in Jewish thought, prominent Jewish thinkers from Poland taught that introspection is not only a vehicle to self-understanding, but that it is also an entrée to a rendezvous with God.[20] For example, some of the Polish masters taught that the divine is accessible within the self, that the path to God involves a journey inward to the center of the soul. In the sixteenth century Judah Loew wrote,

"Within the human being dwells the soul which is a spark of God." As is well-known, Scripture describes God as a fire (Deut.. 4:24). In Loew's view, the human soul is a spark of this fire, that is, a part of the divine.[21]

While Loew uses figurative language to describe the human soul as a part of God, other sources are more explicit. For example, the sixteenth-century Jewish mystic Elijah di Vidas was the author of *Reshit Hokhmah*, which became enormously popular in subsequent generations in eastern Europe. In this work, di Vidas comments on the verse in Deuteronomy (32:9), "For the portion [Hebrew: *helek*, lit. part] of the Lord is His people." Di Vidas writes, "The soul of each member of the people of Israel is an actual portion *[helek]* of God."[22] Probably influenced both by Loew and by di Vidas, Rabbi Shabbtai Sheftel Horowitz of Prague comments on the same verse in Deuteronomy and writes, "It is known that the souls of the people of Israel are a part of God above." (The phrase "a part of God above" [Hebrew: *helek elohah mi-ma'al*] derives from Job (31:2).[23]) Horowitz was perhaps the first author to use the phrase "a part of God above" to describe the soul of each member of the Jewish people as embodying a divine element. In Hasidism, however, the use of this phrase in this manner is extremely common. For example, commenting on Leviticus 19:2, "You shall be holy, for I the Lord your God am holy," Rabbi Menachem Nahum of Chernobyl writes, "'I [God] am holy,' and you [i.e., the people of Israel] are a part of God above. The Holy One, blessed be He [i.e., God] and Israel are one."[24] This idea that the human soul is a part of God, that the human soul is divine, means that the divine may be encountered not only by going out into the world, but also by going inward into the self. In this view, self-understanding, knowing one's own self, one's own soul, inevitably entails communion with God.

Even the eclipse of the divine presence, even God's hiding, is considered to be an invitation to divine communion. It is told that the grandson of Rabbi Barukh of Mezbish (Polish: Miedzybórz) was once playing hide and seek with a friend. The boy stayed in his hiding place, assuming that his friend would come and look for him. But after a while it became clear that his friend had decided not to try to find him. The boy ran into the study of his grandfather complaining about his friend, crying about how his own hiding had been in vain. Upon hearing the story, Rabbi Barukh began to cry. "Why are you crying, Grandfather?" asked the boy. "Because," said Rabbi Barukh, "God, too, says 'I hide; will no one come to search for Me?'"[25] Life is an adventure of hiding and seeking, finding and losing, quest and encounter.

Not only the soul, but also the body can serve as a place for a rendezvous with God. While it is indisputable that strong ascetic trends are found throughout Jewish history, including Hasidism and Musar, it is also evident that without the body, one could not serve God.[26] The commandments of the Torah, the requirements of Jewish law, entail physical actions. As the Zohar states, "The soul cannot operate without the body."[27] Without the body, the divine image implanted within the human being could not become manifest. The divine image requires a vehicle to express itself so that it may realize its essence, actualize its potential, and accomplish its divinely ordained mission. The body is this vehicle; without the body, the divine image embedded within the human soul would remain unrealized, dormant, comatose.[28]

The claim that individual spiritual development can and should be cultivated through the body as well as the soul found strong resonance in Hasidism. That the most mundane physical actions could serve as conduits to spiritual self-development is articulated in the Hasidic concept of "divine worship through materiality" (Hebrew: *avodah she-bagashmiut*). The Ba'al Shem Tov taught that a person is able both to further his or her own spiritual development and to bring about unification of the divine forces in this world and in the supernal realm by the performance of every-day actions, such as eating, drinking, sexual relations, business activities, and social interaction with one's friends.[29] In this view, all human experience, no matter how mundane, has the potential of enabling an individual to liberate and to elevate sacred sparks that relate to one's own self, to one's own soul. The most routine act can become a vehicle to the divine, a redemptive deed. The metaphysical can become personal. The most physical deeds can have a profound impact upon the most supernal realms.

Consider the Ba'al Shem Tov's interpretation of the verse in Job 19:26 "From my flesh, I shall see God." He comments: "From the greatest physical pleasure [i.e., the pleasure of the sexual organ], one causes pleasure Above [i.e., to God]. This pleasure comes about when man and woman unite, and this brings about unification above. Through the physical, we perceive the spiritual."[30] Consider further this text from the teachings of Elimelekh of Lizensk:

> The main reason man was created is to rectify his Root in the upper worlds. This is the meaning of the verse in Genesis 9:6, "For in the image of God, God made humans." . . . The main human task is to rectify the divine structure above. . . . Whenever a person sanctifies himself through a certain part of the body, that person rectifies the universes above that correspond to that particular human limb.[31]

Not only the soul, but also the human body was considered a vehicle to self-knowledge, and hence also to the knowledge of God. For example, Judah Loew took the verse "from my flesh, I shall see God" (Job 19:26) to mean that "when a person contemplates the form of the human body, that individual is able to arrive at a knowledge of God."[32]

The great sixteenth-century kabbalist Rabbi Isaiah Horowitz wrote that when he left his master, Rabbi Solomon Leibush of Cracow, to get married, he asked for his blessing and for advice regarding how to conduct himself. Rabbi Solomon replied, "Sanctify yourself in these two matters, in food and in sexual relations. . . . For all the other commandments of the Torah leave no physical impression. But with regard to these two, food sustains the body and sexual relations bring the body into existence so that theirs is a lasting impression."[33]

In food, as in all created entities, there is a material element and a spiritual element, a "holy spark." The purpose of hunger and thirst is to induce us to eat and drink so that these sparks may be elevated to a higher spiritual plane. Gluttony prevents the liberation of the sparks from the husks of materiality in which they are encased. Sanctified meals allow one to benefit not only from the physical energy contained in the food, but from its spiritual force as well. According to the Ba'al Shem Tov, "we are what we eat" not only in a physical sense but in a spiritual sense as well: "There is a divine spark that is part of yourself in everything you eat and drink, and it is your duty to restore it to its proper place."[34] Hence, sparks of holiness can be redeemed not only in one's travels and through one's prayers and virtuous deeds, but through the most natural acts, like eating, drinking, and sexual relations, when these acts are elevated to a sanctified plane.

Another basic idea of earlier Jewish mysticism that became central to Hasidic teaching, particularly in nineteenth-century Poland, and is an important part of the teachings of the Seer of Lublin, is called in Hebrew *ha-shefa ha-elohi.* This is the idea that human deeds not only influence God, but they also influence God's relationship to us. Just as the upward flow of our activities affects God, there is a perpetual downward flow of divine blessing and grace from God toward us. When the flow upward is characterized by acts of goodness, virtue, and unification, it affects the downward flow in a positive way; conversely, when the flow of human deeds upward is characterized by sinful and undesirable acts, it affects the downward flow in a negative way. In this view, the nature and quality of divine grace are directly related to the nature and quality of concrete human deeds, that is, the economic and social well-being of the community are influenced by the spiritual attainments of the members of the community, particularly by the spiritual accomplishments of the communal leadership.

Not only the physical body but the physical world can serve as a path to spiritual fulfillment and as a passageway to the divine. Encountering the natural world is a second path on the spiritual journey. For example, commenting on the verse in Psalms 8:4, "I look at the heaven, the work of God's fingers," the Hasidic master Nahman of Bratzlav, told this parable:

> Once a prince lived far away from his father the king. Each day he longed for the presence of his father. One day he received a letter from his father, and he was overjoyed and treasured the letter. Yet, the joy the letter gave him only increased his longing even more. He would sit and cry, "Oh, if only I could see my father and touch his hand. Merciful father, how I would love to touch and kiss even your little finger." And while he was crying, feeling the longing for a touch of his father, a thought came into his mind, "Do I not have my father's letter, written in his own hand? And, is not the handwriting of the king comparable to his hand?" And, suddenly, a great joy burst forth in the heart of the prince.[35]

The world is a disguise worn by God. Our task is to unmask God, to find the divine beneath its disguise.

As has been discussed, according to a Musar tradition one's own self is a book requiring study and reflection. The Hasidic master Rabbi Zadok of Lublin also likened the natural world to a book.[36] By means of an encounter with this book, one comes into contact with its Author. The self is one path on the spiritual journey; the world is a second. The third path is the encounter with the sacred word. Prayer and study are actions in which the self meets the word. The sacred word is a rendezvous point for the meeting of the human soul and the divine.

For the Polish Jew, God was not an inaccessible monarch, hidden in an impregnable fortress, but a constant companion, easily accessible, always available, sometimes distant but never remote. In Yiddish they called him *Gottenu*—our little God, *Tattenu*—our little Father. Of the Hasidic master Israel of Koznitz (Polish: Kosienice), it is told that when he prayed to God in the solitude of his room, he would address God over and over in the Polish language with the words, *"moi kochanku"* ("my darling"); and of one of the Hasidic masters who perished during the Nazi occupation, it is told that he would cry in his sleep, "God, please do not ever let me become far from You."[37] When a disciple of the Rabbi of Kotzk informed his master that the Rabbi of Lubavitch taught that "*Gott iz in himel arein*" ("God is in heaven") the Rabbi of Kotzk replied, "*Nein, Gott iz in pipuk arein*" — "No, God is in our guts."[38]

Prayer is an experience of intimacy with God. The words of prayer are the vehicles to achieving this intimacy. It should not be surprising, therefore, that the Hasidic masters described prayer and study of sacred texts as "copulation with God" [Hebrew: *zivug im ha-Shekhinah*]. In the words of the Ba'al Shem Tov, "Prayer is copulation with God [Hebrew: *Shekhinah*]. Just as there is swaying when copulation begins, so, too, one must sway at first and then remain immobile and attached to the divine with great attachment."[39] Through prayer, the human breath, the human soul achieves intimacy and union with its divine source. As a Hasidic text puts it:

> When your prayers are pure and untainted,
> then, surely, the holy breath
> that rises from your lips
> will be joined to the breath of Heaven
> that constantly flows
> into you from Above.
> Regarding the verse, "Every breath shall praise God" [Psalm 150:6]
> our masters have taught it to mean that
> with each breath that you breathe
> God is praised.
> And, as each breath leaves you,
> it ascends to God
> and then it returns to you from Above.
> In this way, that part of God
> that is within you
> becomes reunited with its Source.[40]

As was discussed in previous chapters, study of the sacred and classical texts of Jewish tradition was a central preoccupation of the Polish Jew. It is told, for example, that a certain scholar awakened in the middle of the night perplexed by a passage in the Talmud. He mulled the text over in his mind for many hours trying to discern its meaning. Finally, unable to return to sleep, he decided to go to the study-house to see if a solution could be found by studying the commentaries on that passage. He washed, dressed, and went out into the darkness. A bitterly cold wind encouraged him to hasten his steps. He arrived at the study-house, went to the bookshelf, and found a promising commentary on the very text that troubled him. He opened the book and found the relevant passage. Then he went to sit down to study the passage. But, alas, he could not find a seat. Each chair in the study-house was already occupied by people who were themselves studying.

For the Polish Jew there could be no spiritual achievement without intensive study of the tradition. Spiritual development and Jewish cultural illiteracy were mutually exclusive. Both Jewish continuity and Jewish spirituality were inconceivable without an ongoing intensive study of sacred texts. There could be no authentic Jewish existence detached from lifelong study of the sacred literary canon of Jewish religious tradition.

A variety of views may be found among the spiritual magnates of Polish Jewry regarding the value of study of the tradition (Hebrew: *talmud torah*). All agreed that Jewish learning is the most crucial factor for Jewish continuity. A decline of Jewish learning because of ignorance or arrogance was considered to be a more virulent threat to Jewish survival than the disruption of Jewish communal life by pogroms. Ignorance of the tradition was described by the Hasidic masters as a primary cause of physical and spiritual exile. Conversely, assuring the continuity of the tradition through study of the Torah was considered a redemptive deed.[41]

Study was deemed important because it was linked to action. The sacred texts were studied to discover and to clarify how life was to be lived. The study of the Talmud and the works of Jewish law were aimed at elucidating a lifestyle. Observing the precepts of the tradition was not a matter of personal preference, but the governing factor of individual and communal behavior. In Poland, Jewish law and tradition functioned with the authority of both civil and religious law. For much of its history, Polish Jewry was a nomocracy. Thus knowing, studying, and explicating the law were the preludes to applying it to every aspect of the daily lives of the people. Rabbis were not only spiritual leaders, but also teachers, judges, magistrates, and legislators.

Some stressed the mind-sharpening qualities of Talmudic and legal dialectics. Study was considered to be a means to intellectual development, which in turn was a critical component of the spiritual quest. The method of textual analysis called *hilluk*, or *pilpul*, introduced into Poland by Rabbi Jacob Pollack, became a methodological mainstay of Jewish scholarship in Poland. Across the centuries, many prominent scholars, such as Judah Loew, warned that this method of sharpening the mind could also produce undesirable results. *Pilpul* threatened to make the development of the intellect into a goal rather than a means. In the view of Loew and others, mastery of this method often leads to arid and arrogant intellectual exhibitionism. Yet, when properly applied, *pilpul* (literally, "pepper") could act as a condiment, giving the text an added flavor of meaning and poignancy.[42] Particularly in the Lithuanian yeshivot of the nineteenth century, new analytic methods for the study and the clarification of sacred texts were introduced that offered subtle yet effective ways of elucidating their meaning.[43]

Some maintained that study for its own sake (Hebrew: *Torah le-shma*) is more desirable than study aimed at clarifying behavioral norms and requirements. From this perspective, study for pragmatic reasons such as legal decision-making or personal aggrandizement, or in order to secure a rabbinic appointment, was considered penultimate to the study of the sacred texts simply for the sake of study itself. Study with an ulterior motive was held suspect. For this reason, especially in the Lithuanian yeshivot of the nineteenth century, Talmudic texts with little or no applied legal implications became the basis of the curriculum. The goal of such yeshivot was not primarily to produce religious functionaries but to ensure the continuity of the tradition through learning. Three centuries earlier, scholars such as Judah Loew and Solomon Luria noted that only the academically deficient accepted formal rabbinical credentials. For real scholars, their vast knowledge was the only required credential; it spoke for itself.[44]

While the Hasidic leaders were reviled by their opponents for neglecting study, particularly Talmudic study, such charges were often unfounded. For example, it is told that the Hasidic master Rabbi Zadok of Lublin was once challenged by a *mitnaged* (that is, an opponent of Hasidism) regarding how much Talmud he knew. Rabbi Zadok responded by saying that he knew half of the Talmud. "Which half?" asked the scoffer. "Whichever half you wish," responded Rabbi Zadok.

Nonetheless, Hasidic teachings responded to an issue that the Talmudic scholars of Poland and Lithuania found problematic. For Hasidism, the primary goal of life is cohesion to God (Hebrew: *devekut*).[45] Study is but one of a number of paths to achieving it. Therefore, study became for the Hasidim a means to an end, rather than an end in itself. This shift in the hierarchy of values irked the opponents of Hasidism.

Following certain traditions articulated by Judah Loew, the Hasidim considered study of the Torah as a potential obstacle to communion with God. If a person is preoccupied only with study of a sacred text, how could such a person simultaneously concentrate on achieving cohesion with God?[46] In this regard, the Ba'al Shem Tov is said to have admonished certain scholars who were so obsessed with the text of the Torah that they tended to neglect their relationship with the Author of the Torah. For Hasidism, a substantial danger to spiritual development is the tendency to confuse means with ends, paths with destinations. Hasidism attempt to resolve this problem by reconceptualizing the study of the Torah as a means to communion with God, to an intimate encounter with the sacred text, to self-understanding.

For Polish Hasidim, study that does not enhance self-knowledge, learning that does not bring about spiritual self-transformation, is a non sequitur. In this regard, Rabbi Mendel of Kotzk is reputed to have said the following to a scholar who was erudite but nothing more: "What good is understanding a text if one does not thereby attain a better understanding of oneself?" It is also told that an eminent scholar once approached Rabbi Mendel of Kotzk and boasted that he had gone through the entire Talmud. Unimpressed, the rabbi retorted, "So, you have gone through the Talmud, but how much of the Talmud has gone through you?"[47] No passive voyeur, no casual tourist surveying the landscape of learning, the student of the Torah is one committed to *live* what he or she learns.

According to Judah Loew, study of the Torah is not merely an academic exercise, but an experience in which all aspects of the person should be engaged. Not distinct from experience, study *is* experience. Learning can be life's greatest adventure. Through study one can become what one knows; one can build life as a work of art from the raw materials bequeathed by tradition; one can translate classical sacred texts into a contemporary lifestyle.

The purpose of study should not be self-aggrandizement, but love of God, knowledge of self, and spiritual self-development. Learning is to the soul what food is to the body: a source of sustenance and enrichment. As Rabbi Shneur Zalman of Liady wrote:

> Seeing that through the knowledge of the Torah one's soul and mind encompass the Torah and are in turn encompassed by it, the Torah is called food and the sustenance of the soul. For just as material food sustains the body and enters it and is transformed in the body into flesh and blood, by virtue of which one lives and

endures, so it is with regard to knowledge of the Torah and its comprehension by one who studies with concentration until the Torah is grasped by the mind and becomes united with it.[48]

In this view, one must consume and become consumed by the Torah. Commenting on the phrase *"ve-zot torat ha-Adam"* (lit. "and this is the Torah of man" [2 Sam. 7:19]), Rabbi Mordecai of Chernobyl explained it to mean that "one becomes the Torah oneself." The goal is not only to study Torah, but to become Torah.[49] As Rabbi Efraim of Sudlikow observed, "When one studies the Torah for its own sake, to keep it and perform it, then he brings all his limbs closer to their source whence they originated and were generated, namely the Torah . . . and he becomes identical to the Torah like the unification of man and woman."[50] This observation personifies the Torah as a beloved and the one who studies the Torah as a lover. Like many Jewish mystical and Hasidic texts, this text analogizes the intimacy of study of the Torah to the intimacy of sexual relations. Commenting on Exodus 25:8, "They shall make Me [God] a sanctuary so that I can dwell among them," he noted further, "This verse means that we must create a sanctuary within ourselves for God to dwell. But how can we take God and make God dwell within us? The only way is through the Torah, which is God's Name. Since the Torah is God's Name, it is identical with God."[51]

According to the Gospel of John (1:1), "In the beginning there was the word, and the word was with God, and the word was God." According to the Jewish mystics, however, it was the opposite. In the beginning there was God, and God became the word. God infused the divine Name, the divine presence, into the letters and words of the text of the Torah. By entering the word, we encounter God. God, truth, and self-knowledge can be met in the sacred text, in the word of God.

In Hebrew, the word for a letter is *teivah*. But, *teivah* is also the word for ark. The Ba'al Shem Tov interpreted God's command to Noah to enter the ark as a command to each person to enter the sacred word. Through study of the Torah and in prayer, one enters the word.[52] The sacred word is an invitation for a rendezvous with God.

Moses Hayyim Efraim of Sudlikow wrote:

> Everything depends upon the interpretations of the rabbis. . . . Until they interpreted it, the Torah was not considered complete, but only half-finished. It was the rabbis, through interpretation, who made the Torah whole. . . . He who denies this is as one who denies the Torah itself.[53]

The idea expressed in this text has pre-Hasidic roots, particularly in the writings of Judah Loew who taught that "even though the Torah was revealed at Sinai, the scholar provides its perfection [Hebrew: *tikkun*] and its fulfillment [Hebrew: *hashlamah*]." For Loew, what the scholar provides even surpasses what the prophet can offer.[54] It is the task of the scholar not merely to react to the text, but to become a collaborator with God in perpetuating and in augmenting the meaning of its message. In this view, Judaism is a living faith, and its sacred literature is a living body of work, always growing, always expanding. Studying is an ongoing dialogue between the people of Israel and God, between the people of Israel and the texts it holds sacred, a dialogue of each contemporary generation with all those who came before.

For Judah Loew, the Torah is constantly being given, perpetually being revealed. He once pointed out that this is why, in the blessing over the Torah, God is described not as having *given* the Torah, but as *giving* the Torah.[55] The great Jewish mystic Isaiah Horowitz, the disciple of Rabbi Solomon Leibush of Cracow, who was himself a disciple of Solomon Luria, taught that "the scholars produce new words [in the understanding of the Torah] or derive them through the power of their insight. But all of it was contained in the power of that voice heard at the revelation [at Sinai]; and now the time has come for them to bring it from potentiality to actuality. . . . It thus follows that while we say of God that 'God has given the Torah,' God can also be designated in every present time as 'the One who gives the Torah.'"[56]

For the Polish Jew, the revelation of the Torah at Sinai was not only an event that occurred thousands of years earlier in a land far away, but an occurrence that could be experienced every day, everywhere. As Rabbi Abraham Joshua Heschel of Apt said: "Each Jew is told to consider himself to be standing at Mt. Sinai to receive the Torah. For human beings, there are past and future events, but not for God; day in and day out God gives the Torah and day in and day out one may receive it."[57] That which was given at Sinai is continuously given. That which was received is perpetually being received. Reflecting upon the tradition that the souls of all Jews ever to be born stood at Sinai during the revelation of the Torah, Rabbi Eilmelekh of Lizensk said, "I not only remember standing at Sinai. I also remember who I stood next to when there."

Drawing upon and embellishing upon earlier traditions, the Polish Jew perceived the sacred text as a point of convergence between the human and the divine. As far back as thirteenth century Spanish Jewish mysticism we find the name of God equated with the Torah. In the *Zohar*, the Torah, which embodies the name of God, is correlated with the body of the "community of Israel," which in turn is identified with both *Shekhinah* and the people of Israel.[58] This subsequently led to an equation between God, the Torah, and Israel.[59] This equation is often found in Hasidic literature. One popular expression of the relationship of the community of Israel to the Torah is the claim that the soul of each Jew is identified with each of the letters that comprise the Torah and that the totality of the letters of the Torah comprises the name of God. For example, Rabbi Nathan Shapiro of Cracow reiterates other kabbalistic texts when he writes, "Each member of the people of Israel has a soul that is one of the many letters of the Torah."[60] In the sacred text, the soul, the word, and the divine converge. Through the sacred word, the individual encounters God, his or her own soul, self-knowledge, and the wisdom of the past that may then be applied to the perplexities of the present.

The Talmudic rabbis deferred the rebuilding of the Temple and the restoration of the sacrificial cult to the messianic era that would come at the twilight of history. Until then, the Torah serves as the people of Israel's sanctuary. Until the messianic advent, study and prayer replace sacrifice. Study and prayer fulfill the primary function of sacrifice—bringing one closer to God. In the Talmud one already encounters the view that study of the Torah not only equals but surpasses the offering of sacrifices. Reflecting on the etymological relationship between the Hebrew word for "sacrifice" (*korban*) and the Hebrew word for "near" (*karov*), Judah Loew comments that while the sacrifices served to bring those far from God near to God, those who study the sacred word are *already* close to God by virtue of their preoccupation with God's Torah.[61] The text of the Torah is a door to intimacy with its Author. Study of the Torah is an entrée to love of God and to communion with God. Because of the centrality given study of the Torah, the obligation to study could not be restricted to a scholarly elite, but was viewed as a lifelong endeavor, incumbent upon each individual.

From the perspective of Polish Jewry, the Torah is the only authentic and viable foundation of individual and communal Jewish life. Study of the Torah is the only basis for Jewish continuity. Jewish communal life that does not derive its essential sustenance from Jewish scholarship was, for them, a fallacy, a fraud. For Polish Jewry, a Jewishly illiterate communal leadership would pose a dire threat to Jewish survival and continuity. The civil religion of contemporary Jewry would be, for them, a grotesque facsimile of a precious legacy. What Rabbi Jacob Krantz, the greatest Jewish preacher of eighteenth-century Lithuania, said to German Jewry two centuries ago, he might also say today to American Jewry.

On a visit to Germany, Krantz observed that in the German synagogues the Torah was adorned with beautiful ornaments of gold and silver. Yet it was neither studied nor observed with the seriousness or fervor that was the case in Poland-Lithuania. Krantz said:

> You German Jews bedeck the Torah with beautiful ornaments; she lives with you amidst wealth, luxury, and comfort; yet you do not respect the Torah by living in accordance with her precepts. With us Jews of Poland, on the other hand, the Torah lives amidst poverty. We cannot lavish fancy garments and ornaments upon her. We cannot house her in a beautiful edifice. But because we truly love the Torah, we study and observe her precepts. Need it be said that our love excels yours?[62]

For Polish Jewry, not only study of the Torah, but observance of its precepts was a sine qua non for authentic Jewish life. Jewish law (Hebrew: *halakhah*) prescribed, in the most minute detail, how every action could be the expression of faith in the form a of deed. Jewish religious law serves as the skeleton of Jewish faith, giving it stability and structure. Without observance, faith would be ephemeral. Without a continuity of sacred deeds, the tradition would dissipate. For this reason, the continuous clarification and elucidation of the law through study and analysis is crucial.

Especially during the eighteenth and nineteenth centuries, some Polish Jews, both among the Hasidim and the followers of Musar, taught that while religious observance is necessary, it is not sufficient. Musar taught that ethical and moral virtue needed to be cultivated along with observance, that mechanical obedience is a crippled form of religious life. Musar further insisted that while ritual practices were observed at that time, ethical practices, especially in business, were often neglected. Both for Musar and for Hasidism, the intention when performing a deed became a critical criterion for determining the propriety of the deed. Quality of observance, and not only quantity of observance, became a significant factor in spiritual life. Both Hasidism and Musar taught that a person could all too easily fall into the trap of believing that he or she had attained righteousness through religious observance and involvement in communal affairs. But even externally holy behavior could be tainted.

For instance, commenting on Leviticus 7:1, "This is the law of the guilt offering, it is most holy," Rabbi Mendel of Kotzk observed, "Where is guilt to be found? In the most holy."[63] From this perspective, observance with ulterior motives, observance that does not lead to God, may be compared to a body without a soul. Indeed, for some Hasidic masters, treating the observance of Jewish law as the ultimate goal of the religious life of the Jew was potentially a form of idolatry. For example, Rabbi Mordecai Leiner of Izbica commented on the verse in the Ten Commandments, "You shall not make unto yourself a graven image" (Exod. 20:4). He said, "This means you must not endow the commandments of the Torah with any real existence in their own right, for they are only instruments of God"; that is, the commandments are ways of bringing the person toward God, but they should not be considered as ends in themselves.[64]

For the Jewish mystics, the sacred deed helps redeem not only ourselves but also the divine presence in the world. The human partnership with God is articulated through the performance of sacred deeds. These deeds, defined by the Torah and its commandments, can lead not only to a transformation of the human self, but to a transformation of the divine. Sin brings about and increases disunity and fragmentation within the manifested Godhead (Hebrew: *sefirot*). The performance of sacred deeds brings about unity and harmony within the life of the divine. The effect of good deeds leads to the world being showered with blessings by the upper worlds. This idea is expressed by Levi Yitzhak of Berditchev in his commentary on the verse "The Lord is your shadow" (Psalms 121:5). He writes, "Just as a person's shadow does whatever the person does, so does God, as it were, do whatever a person does. Consequently, a person should perform sacred and good deeds such as showing compassion to those in need, so that God will likewise bestow divine grace upon creation."[65]

In this radical theological claim, the performance of the commandments of the Torah help not only human beings but God as well to move from potentiality to actuality, from exile to redemption. As Rabbi Abraham Joshua Heschel of Apt boldly stated, "By means of the Torah and its commandments, it is as if we make God."[66]

Deeds articulate commitments; sacred deeds express faith and engender communion with God (Hebrew: *devekut*). According to Judah Loew, faith is communion with God.[67] Through faith, one is elevated beyond the realm of the senses. Faith allows us to perceive more than the eyes can see, more than the mind can grasp. For Loew, through faith one becomes able to penetrate the veils of illusion. Faith offers the ability to perceive the light buried in the darkness, to see the truth behind illusion. Faith thereby becomes an act of liberation, of redemption, of revelation. Faith means revealing the concealed.

On verse 14:31 in Exodus—"And Israel saw the great work that God did upon the Egyptians, and the people feared God, and they had faith in God and in His servant Moses"—Rabbi Isaac Meir of Ger commented: "Although they saw the miracles of God with their own eyes, they still were in need of faith, because faith is superior to sight; with faith you see more than with your own eyes."[68] In one sense, to see is to believe. For Rabbi Isaac Meir, to believe is to truly see.

Faith embraces a polarity between words and deeds, beliefs and actions. Faith also combines mind and emotion, intellectual assent and existential commitment. Faith never demands an abrogation of the intellect, a surrendering of the mind.

Intellectual affirmation is a necessary but not a sufficient feature of faith. Verse 14:2 in Psalms reads, "Is there a man of reason who seeks God?" The Rabbi of Kotzk took it to mean, "A man who has nothing but his own reason is incapable of seeking God."[69] Faith is not only something one believes, but something one does. One might consider the word "faith" as a verb rather than an abstract noun. Observing the will of God is how one verifies what one claims to believe in. Faith is verified not by logic but by life, that is, by living a life compatible with one's stated beliefs, by living a life compatible with the will of God. To observe God's commandments is to express faith in the form of a deed. When one person says "I love you" to another person, the proof of the statement's truth is not its logical validity, but the performance of deeds that are consistent with that claim. In prayer, we state our faith commitment. How we act, how we live, demonstrates whether we are what we pray, whether we do what we say.

Faith is an inheritance, a legacy given to the present from the past. But to be complete faith must be renewed. It must be reaffirmed by each person, in each generation. The Jewish liturgy often uses the phrase "our God and the God of our fathers, the God of Abraham, the God of Isaac, the God of Jacob." It was asked, "Why is it necessary to specify each name after already saying 'the God of our fathers'?" The reason given is that neither Isaac nor Jacob relied entirely upon their father's faith. Each sought God, each expressed faith in his own particular way." Of verse 6:5 in Deuteronomy—"You shall love the Lord your God with all your heart"— a Jewish commentator said, "You must love God with all your *own* heart, not only with the heart of your ancestors." In matters of faith, one should try to be a pioneer. But before one can be a pioneer, one must first become an heir.[70]

Rabbi Samuel Edels was the greatest Talmudic commentator in seventeenth-century Poland. Born in Cracow in 1575, he was a great-grandson of Judah Loew. He served as rabbi of Ostraha until his death in 1632. Undoubtedly influenced by Judah Loew, Edels reformulated Loew's view that the life of piety, the spiritual life, has three fundamental components: the individual's relationship with God, with his or her self, and with others.[71] Jewish spirituality thus has a theological, a personal, and an interpersonal or social dimension. There is no basis to the popular view that spirituality focuses only upon spiritual self-development and neglects the dimensions of interpersonal relations or social ethics. Both nineteenth-century Hasidism and Musar stressed communal responsibility and interpersonal relations. For example, the following story is told both of the Hasidic master Rabbi Moses of Sasov and of the master of Musar, Rabbi Israel of Salant:

> It was the eve of Yom Kippur, the most sacred day of the Jewish liturgical year. The people of the town had gathered together in the synagogue waiting for the prayer-service to begin. Only one seat was empty—that of the rabbi. Without him, how could the service begin? The people waited, but still he did not come.
>
> In the synagogue, a young mother sat and she worried—not about the rabbi, but about her sleeping child, left alone in the house nearby. What if the child awoke and found itself alone? The child would be frightened. The mother could no longer wait for the rabbi. She left her seat in the synagogue and ran toward her house. Entering the room where the child slept, her eyes automatically gazed at the crib. But the crib was empty. The child was gone. Her thoughts immediately raced with

ideas about what terrible fate her child had met. Stricken with panic, she was about to scream when she heard a familiar voice say,

"Do not scream, my child, for you will awaken the baby."

The voice came from an old thin man with a long white beard. The man was none other than the rabbi.

"I was on my way to the synagogue when I heard the sound of a child crying in your house. I entered the house, but no one was there. The child had awoken, and not finding you there, began to cry. I played with the child for a while, and then I sang the child to sleep. I have been holding the sleeping child and waiting for you, so that I can go to the synagogue to begin the prayers.[72]

Both the Hasidic masters and those of Musar encouraged the study of the medieval classics of Jewish ethical literature as a required supplement to Talmudic dialectics. Both stressed the cultivation of the moral virtues, especially humility, and the suppression or elimination of the moral vices, such as anger, arrogance, avarice, and envy. Both emphasized the absolute commitment owed by each Jew to the Jewish people. This notion of communal loyalty was, however, vertical as well as horizontal. From a horizontal vantage point, each Jewish person is responsible for the other members of the Jewish community of which he or she is a part. From the vertical perspective, the primary mission is the transmission of the tradition and the spiritual development of the individual members of the community. In this view, it is not the contemporary communal agenda that defines the tradition, but the tradition that defines the authenticity, the viability, and the propriety of various forms of Jewish communal life. Seen from the vertical perspective, communal loyalty extends to the Jewish people of past generations who have bequeathed a heritage for the present. The Jews of the present are further obliged to future generations of Jews to whom they are required to bequeath the tradition that they have inherited from those who came before.

When the Ba'al Shem Tov was challenged by a seemingly insurmountable task, he would go to a certain place in the forest, light a fire, and meditate in prayer— and what he had set out to perform would be accomplished. A generation later, when the Maggid of Mezeritch encountered a similar challenge, he would journey to the same place in the forest, and he would say: "We can no longer light the fire, but we can recite the same prayers," and what he wanted to be done was accomplished. In the next generation, Moses of Sasov went to that very spot in the forest and he said: "We can no longer know how to light the fire. We no longer know the correct meditations on the prayers, but we still know the place in the forest to which it all belongs, and that must be enough." Finally, in the following generation, when Rabbi Israel of Rhyzen was called upon to perform the task, he sat in his home and he said: "We cannot light the fire, nor can we recite the prayers. We do not now even know the location of the place. All we can do is to retell the tale of how it was done. And, that must suffice for us."[73]

Jews no longer dwell in any numbers in the place where the spiritual heritage of Polish Jewry was created. Most of Polish Jewry was consumed by a pillar of fire and smoke. We do not know their resting place. Most of their physical remains have been obliterated. We no longer embody the flame of their religious fervor, of their spiritual achievements. We no longer can perform many forms of their sacred worship.

Yet we can still tell what we know of their tale. We can still convey what we have of their teachings. We can still employ what has been preserved of their wisdom. Perhaps in telling that tale, in reclaiming that legacy, in transmitting that wisdom, and in applying those teachings we can yet recover some sacred sparks from the ashes that remain.

Perhaps in the lands where the descendants of Polish Jewry now dwell we may discover new sacred spots, new sanctified moments. Perhaps by applying the remnants of their treasure trove of spiritual insight to our situation, their legacy may be transmigrated to live yet again, and thereby to acquire a life after death. As Abraham Joshua Heschel wrote soon after the Holocaust in his elegy to Polish Jewry, "A day may come when the hidden light of the East European era may be revealed."[74] And as the Ba'al Shem Tov taught, "The spiritual life is like a bed of coals. As long as a single spark remains, a great fire may be rekindled. However, without that spark, it is impossible to rekindle the flame."[75]

The Land We Shared

The love story of the fourteenth-century Polish king Casimir the Great (Kazimierz III Wielki) and his Jewish consort Esterka is simple and beautiful, as love stories ought to be. The events that gave rise to the legend of their love, however, and the interpretation of those events are controversial and disputed.

Although medieval chroniclers treated the story as historical fact, most modern historians treat it as mere legend. From the fifteenth century onward, Polish and Jewish chronicles and literary sources speak of the liaison between the beautiful Jewess and the powerful king. The earliest known record, less than a century after Casimir's death, appears in the writings of the first important historian of Poland, Jan Dlugosz, who noted that King Casimir the Great maintained an extramarital relationship with a Jewess named Esterka, the daughter of a tailor from the town of Opoczno. According to subsequent embellishments, the love affair blossomed during the king's unhappy marriage to Adelaja of Hesse, and intensified after his subsequent, ill-fated marriage to Krystyna Rokiczonska the Czech.[1] Four children were born to Casimir and Esterka, two boys and two girls. The boys, Niemira and Pelka, were raised as Catholics at the royal court. The girls were raised with the Jews as Jews, with Casimir's approval.

Specific places in Poland have been identified with Esterka. A street in Cracow is named after her. Remnants of palaces that Casimir allegedly built for her near Cracow and Lublin are identified with her. A house in her native town of Opoczno was believed to have been hers. In Kalisz there is a wall, still known as "Esterka's wall," that remains from a castle built by Casimir. Polish folklore tells that each night the ghost of Esterka comes to the wall in search of her royal lover.[2]

The first known Jewish report is found in a historical chronicle by David Ganz, first published in Prague in 1591. In Ganz's view, derived both from Jewish and non-Jewish sources, Esterka was not a mere romantic dalliance of the king. Rather, she lived with him as his wife, as his consort—though obviously without the sanction of the church and without the "official" status of queen. According to Ganz, as well as other Jewish and Polish sources, the renewal and the expansion of the privileges of the Jews of Poland by Casimir can be attributed to his liaison with Esterka.

In many Polish sources, Esterka is described as a temptress who uses her wiles to seduce the king into helping her people. Jewish sources are ambivalent. For some, Esterka—like her biblical namesake, Esther—is a heroine who sacrifices herself for her people's security. For others, Esterka is an embarrassment. Yet in no version of the legend does Esterka repudiate her Jewish faith. In no version does she join the church.

David Ganz's precise version states:

> 1370. Casimir, the king of Poland took for himself a concubine—a young Jewess named Esther. Of all the maidens of the land, none compared to her in beauty. She was his wife for many years. For her sake, the king extended many privileges to the Jews of his kingdom. She persuaded the king to issue documents of freedom and beneficence. [The source of this information is the chronicle of the German physician Heinrich Rattel]. . . . King Casimir died in 1370, and with his death ended the line of Boleslaw the first king of Poland. Then Ludwig of Hungary ruled as king of Poland.[3]

Neither Poles nor Jews accepted Esterka, in legend or in fact, as the queen of Poland. With Casimir's death in 1370 the first royal Polish dynasty came to an end. Had one of the sons born of his love for Esterka ascended the throne of Poland, the son of a Jewish mother, and hence a Jew (at least according to Jewish law), might have ruled as king of Poland. But, according to a legend, he would not have been the first nor the last Jewish king of Poland. There is, in addition to the legend of Saul Wahl's one-night reign, the legend that the first king of Poland was a Jew.

According to Polish tradition, Piast was the first king of Poland and founder of the Piast dynasty that ended with the reign of Casimir the Great. But, according to a legend preserved both in Polish and in Jewish sources, when the earliest Polish tribes assembled to choose their first king, it was decided that the first man entering the town where the electors met, would be the king. As it happened, Abraham Prochownik, a Jew, was that man. For reasons that remain obscure, Abraham abdicated in favor of a native peasant named Piast.[4]

While Piast was the first legendary king of Poland, the first historical king of the Piast dynasty was Mieszko, who assumed the throne in the mid-tenth century. And the first outsider to mention his kingdom, hence the first chronicler to bring an awareness of Poland to the outside world, was the tenth-century Jew Ibrahim ibn Yakov.[5] Furthermore, it was the Jewish minters in Poland who struck the earliest coins attesting to the reign of "Mieszko, King of Poland."[6] Because the minters did not know Polish, this inscription first appeared in Hebrew letters. Perhaps in his treasure-house Casimir kept some of these coins.

When Casimir reaffirmed and expanded the Jewish privileges granted by his ancestor Boleslaw the Pious a century earlier, he may have known that Jewish roots were already well planted in the time of Mieszko. Perhaps this was Boleslaw's way of thanking Abraham Prochownik for handing the Piasts the throne of Poland. Perhaps Casimir's beneficence toward the Jews was his way of perpetuating the gratitude of his ancestors.

Like Ganz, many chroniclers and storytellers of the legend of Casimir and Esterka assume that Esterka was instrumental in persuading Casimir to reaffirm the rights and privileges of the Jews. But it is equally probable that Casimir was motivated by events in his own family's past. It may be that Casimir's interest in the Jews was inspired by Esterka. But, perhaps, it is the other way around, i.e., that Casimir's interest in the Jews, his fascination with them, his feeling of indebtedness toward them, led him inevitably to the lovely young Jewish maiden — to Esterka.

Seeking to deride Casimir's relationship with Esterka, some Polish works describe Casimir as a "great" king made "small" by his love for Esterka. But the opposite may have been true. In the eyes of history, Casimir was great because of his extraordinary accomplishments as king; in his own eyes, Casimir's most fulfilling experience may have been his relationship with Esterka.

Casimir's place as one of the greatest kings of Poland was secured by his deeds during his lifetime. He is the only Polish king known as "the Great." Of him it was later said, "Casimir found a Poland built of wood and left a Poland built of stone." During his reign Poland emerged from obscurity to splendor. The capital city of Cracow gleamed with imposing architectural triumphs: the magnificent St. Mary's Church and the towering Royal Castle on Wawel. The Cracowian Academy (later named the Jagiellonian University) was established. Both builder and lawgiver, Casimir initiated the first codification of Polish law. A new standard silver currency greatly facilitated trade and economic growth. A new system of centralized royal government gave Poland much needed political stability. Casimir's military triumphs and expansion of his country's borders made Poland a power to be reckoned with.[7] For Jews fleeing the scourge of the Black Death in western Europe and the correlative persecution it brought them, Casimir's expansion of the rights of Jews made Poland a land of Jewish refuge, relief, and boundless opportunity.

The Casimir we meet in the legend of Esterka is not the architect of a nation, but a lonely man. Imprisoned in a marriage without love, in a castle with high walls, the great king remained alone — with no one to love and without a male heir. At least three wives shared his bed, but none shared his love. His daughters brought him little joy, for they reminded him of his queens whom he grew to despise. His life in ruins, Casimir concentrated upon building his nation.

Then, suddenly, like the sun bursting out from behind the clouds after a storm, Esterka came into his life. According to one version of the legend, he saw her first as a young girl during the early years of his reign. On a hunting expedition he had stopped for water at the home of her father, a tailor, in a small town near Cracow. The vision of her beauty never left him. And when by chance he met her again when she had blossomed into womanhood, he knew that it was not by chance that he had longed for her all those years. Despite the protests of her parents, she traveled to the palace to consummate their love.

A second version of the story of Casimir and Esterka describes her as the daughter of a prominent Jewish physician who teaches her the art of curing before he dies. When the king falls deathly ill, and when the medical ministrations of all the court physicians have failed, she is called to the palace to try to cure the king. As she nurses him back to health, they fall passionately in love. Here was the lover the king had dreamed about each night of his life. Here was the soul with whom he would become one. Though they had little in common, they were alike in every way. A life of love restored his love of life.

In the depths of their hearts, Casimir and Esterka must have known that while they could remain perfect lovers, and though they felt a bond stronger than any marriage vow could forge, they never could be accepted as husband and wife. Though they most certainly believed *amor vincit omnia* — love conquers all — they must also have known that the devotion each affirmed for the other would be rejected by society at large. In life, their love persisted until their deaths; in legend, their love continues forever. And yet, while all of the interpretations and refractions of the legend of Casimir and Esterka may convey their own kernel of the truth, I prefer to understand the saga as a story of love, rooted in historical fact, with meanings yet to unfold. For as with all tellings of a legend, no telling can claim to be the final word. Legend, unlike life, can be lived again.

Scholars interpret the legend of Casimir and Esterka, as it has been developed and retold over the centuries, as a lens refracting various visions of the place of the Jews in Poland throughout Polish history.[8] How the legend is told may reveal more about the teller than about the legend itself. Poles who perceive Jews as unwelcome, exploitative, ungracious, and devious intruders speak of Esterka as a temptress who through her wiles and intrigue seduced the great king into building her palaces and into bestowing undeserved privileges upon her coreligionists. Jews who understand their experience in Poland to have been characterized by oppression, exploitation, and persecution portray Casimir as a capricious monarch, imposing his power upon a naive Jewish maiden, treating her well only as long as he could exploit her, and then casting her away. For some the legend demonstrates the dangerous dimensions of piercing the social and cultural wall separating Jews and non-Jews in Poland. It portrays the heroism, martyrdom, and self-sacrifice that Polish Jews had to endure in a land where they lived a precarious existence as sojourners. For others, however, the legend indicates the possibilities of a fruitful liaison between Jews and Poles. It depicts the possibility of Jewish acculturation without assimilation — for Esterka never surrenders her identity as a Jewess. It reveals the relationship between Poles and Jews to be more than a marriage of convenience, but a shared life, a fruitful association, a common history and destiny thwarted by historical and social circumstances.

While the legend epitomizes the complex problem of Polish-Jewish relations, it may also offer a vehicle for getting beyond the impasse caused by the perpetuation of seemingly insurmountable walls of mutual prejudice and stereotyping. Perhaps one should consider what might happen if the Jewish and Catholic descendants of Casimir and Esterka were somehow reunited today. Would such a reunion begin with a stalemate? Would it evolve into a dialogue? Would an alternative to rigid stereotyping emerge? Would the participants overcome their enmity long enough to gain an entrée to their own spiritual legacy, and to an alternative view of the Jewish experience in Poland? In reflecting on my own family history in Poland, I am drawn to speculate on how I might react to meeting the descendants of the Ephraim Fishel of Cracow who converted to Christianity and who became Stephan Powidski over four centuries ago. What would we have to say to one another about life in the land our ancestors once shared?

When the famed Nazi hunter Simon Wiesenthal wrote that "throughout the history of Poland, the relationship between Poles and Jews has always been complex," he was grossly understating the case.[9] Throughout the centuries, and particularly in modern times, Polish-Jewish relations have been inordinately complicated, paradoxical, and difficult to define. The historical record is often either obscure, uncertain, or distorted by an overlay of ideological and stereotypic prisms. Paradox is more characteristic of Polish-Jewish relations than is precision and clarity. In reconstructing and analyzing the history of Polish-Jewish relations, the validity of simple, logical, and one-dimensional views are suspect, while paradoxical and internally inconsistent perspectives often ring true. A case in point relates to Poles who tried to save Jews during World War II.

It would be logical to assume that Poles who disliked Jews would not help Jews, especially considering the enormous personal risks Poles ran in aiding Jews. Indeed, of all Nazi-occupied countries, only in Poland did any form of aid to Jews bring with it a penalty of death, not only for oneself but for one's family and associates as well. However, documented records of Poles who did help Jews reveal that an individual's prewar attitudes toward Jews were not a reliable indicator of that person's behavior during the war years. There are numerous examples of Poles with Jewish friends who were apathetic to the Jews' plight after the Nazi invasion.[10] There are also numerous examples of unabashed anti-Semites who helped Jews during the war. Of these, many felt that their Catholic faith obliged them to defend the Jews. For instance, one of the founders of Zegota—an organization of Poles formed to help save Jews during the Nazi occupation—was Zofia Kossak-Szczucka, a Catholic intellectual who thought of Jews as "Christ-killers" and who shared the widespread conviction in interwar Poland that the Jews belonged not in Poland but in their own homeland. Yet Kossak-Szczucka risked her life to save Jews. Despite her personal views she wrote in 1942 that Jews and Poles could resume their political and ideological battles after the war; until then, "Whoever remains silent in the face of [the] murder [of Jews] becomes an accomplice to the murder. He who does not condemn, condones."[11] The contradictions in the behavior of Poles during World War II was thus summarized by an SS officer: "Nowhere in the world is there another nation which has so many heroes and so many denouncers."[12]

There were Poles who saved Jews and there were Poles who murdered Jews. There were Poles who killed Jews not out of any particular animosity, but simply for the purpose of expropriating their property. There were Poles who protected Jews, not because they were philo-Semites, but because they felt morally obliged to do so. There were Poles who saw Jews as fellow victims of Nazi persecution, and there were Poles who saw Jews, Germans, and Russians as the enemies of Poland. There were Poles who helped to rescue Jews from transports and ghettos, and there were Poles who interfered with rescue efforts. There are rescuers like Wladyslaw Bartoszewski, who claimed that the only Poles who helped enough were the ones who died trying, and there are those who perceive as anti-Polonism every accusation against those Poles who either helped make the Holocaust happen or who did nothing to prevent it.

Precisely because of the complexities surrounding Polish-Jewish relations both during and before the Holocaust, there is a tendency to fall back on the simplicity and apparent clarity provided by persistent stereotypes. In Poland today, though few Jews remain, stereotypes of Jews persist. In North America and Israel, Jews of Polish origin, who have largely failed to convey the spiritual heritage of their forebears, have nonetheless managed to successfully perpetuate stereotypes about Poles. Similarly, in American Polonia (people of Polish descent living in America), stereotypes of Jews abound.

During the last decades of the nineteenth century and the early decades of the twentieth century, relationships between Jews and non-Jews in Poland greatly deteriorated.[13] As it happened, it was precisely during this time that waves of Jewish and non-Jewish immigrants from Poland came to the United States, bringing with them heightened prejudices, often grounded in personal experience and reflecting stereotypes then pervasive in Poland. These prejudices became frozen in time and were transmitted to the children, grandchildren, and great-grandchildren of these immigrants.

Progeny of Jewish immigrants from Poland may never have seen Poland nor met any Poles, but they nonetheless learned stereotypes that provided a foundation for interpreting current events in a manner that served both to perpetuate and to fortify animosity toward Poles. The popular Jewish view that Poles are indigenously anti-Semitic served as the basis for the pervasive view—found both popularly and historiographically—that pre–World War II Poland was a disaster area for the Jews and a prelude to the Holocaust. The Polish view that Jews were a "fifth column" in Poland found popular and historiographical expression in the claim that the Jews were atheists and communists who "sold out" Poland by acting in the interests of the foreign powers who occupied Poland during much of its modern history. In this Polish view, the persecution of and discrimination against Jews in the post–World War II era was a justifiable reprisal for the historical proclivity of Jews to serve the anti-Polish policies of the foreign powers, especially Russia, the historic enemy of the Polish people. Some Poles further contend that international Jewish influence during the post–World War II period convinced the western democracies, especially the United States, to betray the promises of support made to Poland by the Allies during World War II. They also claim that Jewish novelists, filmmakers, and comedians perpetuate negative stereotypes of Poles in their writings, movies, and Polish jokes, thereby increasing discrimination against Poland and against Poles in the West.

For Jews, the persecution of Jews in Poland during the post-Holocaust period was interpreted as the natural outgrowth of indigenous Polish anti-Semitism, and as the culmination of prewar political policies (boycott, social discrimination, violence, forced emigration) aimed at bringing about the "evacuation" of Polish Jews.[14] Regarding the interwar period, Israel Gutman writes, "The last years of the Polish Republic, from the mid-1930s on, were marked by a grave escalation in the anti-Semitic public mood and of anti-Jewish policies. . . . The goal of decreasing the Jewish population of Poland by immediate mass emigration became something of a national consensus."[15] In a similar vein, in his oft-quoted essay "In Anger and in Sorrow: Toward a Polish-Jewish Dialogue," Rafael Scharf writes:

> Take the vast subject, if now somewhat enveloped in the mist, of Polish-Jewish relations in interwar Poland. If the question were asked whether Poland was a country where anti-Semitism grew and was rampant, the answer for every Polish Jew, an eyewitness, would be so obvious and unequivocal that he would be angered and resentful if anybody doubted it. As soon as Poland regained its independence after World War I, the framework of an anti-Jewish movement began to take shape. It grew in strength and came to be for us an ever-present force, filling the

atmosphere like ether. The fact that the Poles were, and still are, unaware of this—at least this is what many claim—is hard for us to believe and understand. They have either forgotten how it was or they have simply seen life from an altogether different perspective. . . . It behooves us, however, to give due weight to the other side of the picture. Someone asked very pertinently: if it was so bad, why was it so good? Because, despite the fact that the climate was severe, there blossomed on these lands a full, rich, varied and creative Jewish life.[16]

Adam Michnik, the eminent Jewish journalist in Poland, succinctly sums up the current situation as follows:

Relations between Poles and Jews are still burdened by two stereotypes—one Polish and the other Jewish. According to the Polish stereotype there has never been any anti-Semitism in Poland, and the Jews were never so well off as they were there. In this stereotype, each critical voice condemning anti-Semitism is considered an expression of the anti-Polish conspiracy on the part of international forces who are filled with hatred for Poland. There is also a Jewish stereotype, which says that each Pole imbibes anti-Semitism with his mother's milk; that Poles share the responsibility for the Holocaust; that the only thing worth knowing about Poland is just that—that Poles hate Jews.

The Polish stereotype produces among Jews, even Jews well disposed toward Poland, an instinctive dislike of Poles. This stereotype makes any calm and clarifying debate on the history of Polish anti-Semitism impossible. On the other hand, the Jewish stereotype immediately arouses a sort of "secondary anti-Semitism" among Poles, because people who are completely free of anti-Semitic phobias feel accused of sins they've never committed. And having been accused of being natural anti-Semites, they feel hurt and perceive ill will on the part of Jews; and such feelings tend to preclude an honest dialogue with Jews about the past and the future. . . .

Among my friends one thing was always clear: anti-Semitism is the name of hatred. But it was also clear to us that the stubborn categorization of Poland as an anti-Semitic nation was used in Europe and America as an alibi for the betrayal of Poland at Yalta. The nation so categorized was seen as unworthy of sympathy, or of help, or of compassion. That is why, for years and decades, we have stubbornly explained that anti-Semitic pathology doesn't define Poland, just as Le Pen doesn't define France, the John Birch Society doesn't define America, the Black Hundreds don't define Russia, and extreme Israeli chauvinism doesn't define the state of Israel. . . .

Whoever says that all Poles are anti-Semites helps us to justify actual anti-Semitism. It is well known, after all, that whenever everyone is guilty, no one is guilty.[17]

It seems not to occur to many Poles that some of their misfortunes may be self-inflicted rather than caused by the Jews. Similarly, it does not seem to occur to some Jews that manifestations of Polish anti-Semitism might be reactions to Jewish clannishness and parochialism. As a character in Isaac Bashevis Singer's novel *The Manor* puts it, "How can anyone move into someone else's home, live there in total isolation, and expect not to suffer by it? When you despise your host's god as a tin image, shun his wine as forbidden, condemn his daughter as unclean, aren't you asking to be treated as an unwelcome outsider? It's as simple as that."[18] Poles and Jews unfortunately often behave in a similar manner that ironically only serves to reinforce negative stereotypes. As Lech Walesa said in his May 20, 1991, address to the Israeli Parliament, "How alike we are in our mix of good and bad characteristics. . . . We are alike in our quarrelsomeness and solidarity, in our generosity and our petty envy. How much aggression our similarities arouse in each other."

What, then, of the future of Polish-Jewish relations? What, then, of the Poland of today and tomorrow? To get anywhere, stereotypes must be overcome but not ignored. Both the longstanding "official" view of the Polish government that "there is no anti-Semitism in Poland" and the prevailing Jewish view that "all Poles are anti-Semites" must be exposed and discarded as fictions driven by self-serving ideological positions. There was and is anti-Semitism in Poland. Poles are anti-Semitic, philo-Semitic, and neutral. For example, sociological studies of Poles living in rural areas of Poland in the 1970s and in the 1980s found that the same respondents who denigrated Jews as dishonest, lazy, greedy, sly, and dirty also praised them as being industrious, neighborly, intelligent, and pious. Meanwhile, American Jewish folk culture depicts Poles as fools, idlers, alcoholics, wife-beaters, pseudo-aristocrats, and incorrigible anti-Semites. At the same time, most of the rural Poles surveyed have never met a Jew and most American Jews have neither been to Poland nor ever met a Pole. The perspectives of both groups are dominated by selective stereotyping.[19]

While history is not an exact science, neither is it a collection of folktales like the *Arabian Nights*. The popular perception among Jews that the Poles played a crucial role in the mass murder of Jews during the Holocaust must be unmasked as a fiction, as a revisionist history of the Holocaust, and should be discredited. As Israel Gutman of Yad Va-Shem and the Hebrew University has written and said on many occasions, the thesis that portrays Poles as playing a part in initiating and implementing the Holocaust must be summarily dismissed. The claim that the Nazi death camps were built in Poland because of the intensity of Polish anti-Semitism is baseless and is not supported by any documentary evidence. At the same time, Gutman insists, the claim that anti-Semitism either waned or ceased to exist in Poland during the Holocaust cannot be substantiated. Indeed, Polish anti-Semitism did have an adverse effect on the possibilities of Jewish rescue and self-defense during those years.[20]

Jan Karski, the courageous Polish courier who personally brought news of the Nazi death camps and their genocidal activities against the Jews to President Roosevelt and others, wrote in a 1940 report that the Polish people widely sympathized with the German objective to "solve" the "Jewish problem" in the occupied territories. Karski reported that despite the Polish hate of the Germans, the Nazis' activities against the Jews served more to increase than to decrease anti-Semitism among the Poles. By November 1942 Karski was able to report that German actions against the Jews had aroused some sympathies among the Polish populace, but that Poles still demanded for after the war what they had advocated before the war—the voluntary or forced emigration of the Jews from Poland. The Holocaust made this wish easier to enforce. Polish anti-Semitism in the post–World War II era virtually brought it about.[21] The extraordinary hospitality and receptivity granted the Jews by Poland in the late medieval period had no equivalent in the modern period.

The tendency among Jews to stereotype Poles as the perpetuators of the Holocaust not only distorts but obscures the enormous suffering of Poles during the Nazi occupation and their subsequent domination by the Soviet Union. About three million Polish Jews, representing about 90 percent of the pre-war Jewish population of Poland, were murdered by the Germans. Yet an equal number of non-Jewish Poles, representing a much smaller percentage of that population, were also murdered by the Germans. A total of six million Jewish and non-Jewish Poles were killed. In addition, millions more Poles were subjected to slave labor and other forms of Nazi brutality. Most of the Polish intelligentsia and much of the Polish clergy were slaughtered by the Nazis. Poland suffered a physical as well as a cultural genocide.[22] It should be noted that the very word "genocide" was coined in 1944 by Raphael Lemkin, a Jewish lawyer from Poland.

While the "competitive martyrology" of Jews and Poles results in nothing except the amplification of tensions, few Jews have acknowledged the devastating impact that the Nazi occupation had upon the non-Jewish population of Poland. While many Poles sympathized with the Nazis' Final Solution, while others were apathetic or too absorbed with their own concerns at the time, and while some Poles realized financial gains from the expropriated Jewish property, the reality of the enormous destruction of Polish property, culture, and life brought about by the German occupation should not be obfuscated nor ignored. As Jews and non-Jews lived side by side (though not together) in Poland throughout the centuries, during the six horrible years of World War II they suffered and died side by side, but not together. However, while both groups were brutally victimized, they were, in the words of Israel Gutman and Shmuel Krakowski, "unequal victims."[23]

Only since the collapse of communism have Poles begun to confront the experience of Jews in Poland during the Holocaust years. The attempts of Polish scholars to document hitherto unknown efforts of Poles to help Jews during those years have aided in demonstrating that all Poles were not apathetic to the plight of Jews. The efforts of some Polish apologists to give the impression that such efforts were typical or more widespread than they actually were, however, has backfired in that its one-sided view evokes suspicion rather than receptivity among many Jews. Happily, a more balanced view has begun to emerge in Poland.

Pope John Paul II has played a major role in the attempt to bring about a reconciliation between Poles and Jews. John Paul II is a symbol of many things to many people. With special reference to Polish-Jewish relations, he is a forceful exception to the claim that "all Poles are anti-Semites." Throughout his papacy, John Paul II has taken bold and dramatic initiatives in improving Catholic-Jewish relations.[24] Being a Polish patriot who lived through the German occupation of Poland, John Paul II inevitably influences not only the Polish Catholic church, but the Polish people as well, both in Poland and in the Polish diaspora. His moral authority carries substantial weight among Poles.

John Paul II has stated unequivocally that anti-Semitism is a sin. In *Crossing the Threshold of Hope* he writes that the Nazi occupation "was also a personal experience I carry with me today. Auschwitz, perhaps the most meaningful symbol of the *Holocaust of the Jewish people*, shows to what lengths a system constructed on principles of racial hatred and greed for power can go. To this day, Auschwitz does not cease to admonish, reminding us that *anti-Semitism is a great sin against humanity*."[25]

Undoubtedly, the pope's attitudes served as a major force in stimulating the Polish episcopate to issue its pastoral letter on relationship with Jews and Judaism. The document, signed by all cardinals, archbishops, and bishops present at the presentation of the document on November 30, 1990, was mandated to be read in all twenty thousand Polish churches on January 20, 1991.[26] The pastoral letter acknowledged Polish anti-Semitism, condemned it as a sin requiring contrition, rejected the claim that the Poles perpetrated the Holocaust, emphasized the Jewishness of Jesus, and stated that during the Holocaust thousands of Poles helped Jews at great personal risk. In a reconciliatory tone, the document stated that the Nazi oppression of Jews and Poles ought to be a uniting rather than a dividing force between Poles and Jews. In view of the long history of Christian anti-Semitism, and especially in view of the strong anti-Jewish attitudes of the Catholic church in Poland during the interwar period, this document is both groundbreaking and bold.[27] Of additional significance is the fact that the Jesuits in Poland, particularly in Cracow, have been at the vanguard of the attempt to ease tensions between Poles and Jews. In the seventeenth century the Jesuits often had been the instigators of strong anti-Jewish agitation.

Just as Vatican documents and papal pronouncements since Vatican II have stressed the special and unique relationship between Judaism and Catholicism, the pastoral letter of the Polish episcopate underscored the unique relationship between Poles and Jews: "With no other religion does the Church remain in such a close relationship, nor does the [Polish] Church find itself bound so intimately with any other nation. . . . Poland became a second fatherland to Jews. The majority of Jews living in the world today are descended from areas of the old and present-day Republic [of Poland]. Unfortunately, this very land became in our century a tomb for several million Jews; but not by our will nor by our hand."

Like all aspects of Polish-Jewish relations, Polish attempts in the past few decades to improve relations with Jews must be seen in their complexity rather than in their simplicity. Motivations vary and they are not mutually exclusive. To be sure, there are Polish philo-Semites, especially within the church and the intelligentsia. They have taken courageous actions in denouncing anti-Semitism and in encouraging the improvement of Polish relations with Jews. Within the ever shifting Polish political arena, there are also those who are sincerely committed to improving relations. While the "Jewish issue" continually emerges as a factor in Polish national elections, and while anti-Semitic motifs are always present, anti-Semitic political parties have consistently failed to garner enough votes to seat their representatives in the Polish parliament.

During the oppressive Jaruzelski regime of the late 1970s and early 1980s, the Polish government, as a means of achieving international respectability, made substantial efforts to develop good relations with world Jewry, particularly in the United States. These efforts stimulated many projects aimed at evoking Polish interest in the Jews and Judaism—an interest that has continued and expanded since then. This policy, like a similar one advanced by the Polish government during the interwar period, was based largely on stereotypic views of Jews as controlling the media and of having inordinate influence on the political and economic policies of the Western democracies. Nonetheless, this policy of the Jaruzelski regime served as a means of spurring the Polish intelligentsia toward a painful reconsideration of Polish-Jewish relations as a test of their own commitments to democratic values, historical truth, and Catholic morality. The Walesa regime seems to have done its best to effect Polish-Jewish reconciliation, despite the inevitable bumblings of its inefficient bureaucracy.

Some Poles have finally begun to see beyond their own suffering during the Nazi and Stalinist eras. In so doing, they have begun to confront the Jewish plight in Poland during those times. While justifiably shocked and dismayed over the popular Jewish perception of Poles as perpetrators of the Holocaust and as Nazi collaborators, many in Poland are equally agitated by a growing awareness of the "Jewish" Holocaust and of the anti-Semitism prevalent in Poland both during and after World War II. However, to be sure, the pervasive Jewish stereotype of all Poles as anti-Semites may well encourage young Poles initially devoid of anti-Jewish sentiments to become anti-Semites.[28]

The growing awareness of the lives and deaths of Jews in Poland marks a considerable reversal of past attitudes. It is ironic that now, when few Jews remain in Poland, there is an escalation of Polish interest in the Jewish experience in Poland. While Jews have been depicted both positively and negatively in Polish belles lettres, the actual social and religious dimensions of Jewish life in Poland have long been unknown to Poles. Prominent Polish poets and novelists are more likely than not to portray Polish Jews in situations with non-Jewish Poles, and not as Jews living within their own Jewish milieu.[29] Even the powerfully positive portrait of the Jew Jankiel in the classic *Pan Tadeusz* by Adam Mickiewicz, Poland's most acclaimed poet, does not include the Jewish dimension of Jankiel's daily existence. The great Jewish writer Y. L. Peretz observed that whereas Jews in modern Poland knew something of Polish language, literature, social existence, culture, and religion, that is, the inner life of non-Jewish Poles, the inner life of Polish Jewry nevertheless remained terra incognita to the Poles among whom the Jews had lived for centuries. In Aaron Zeitlin's Yiddish play *Esterka*, about Casimir and Esterka, Zeitlin has the character of Peretz say to the character of Mickiewicz, "I know who you are, but who I am, you do not know."[30]

Polish ignorance of Jewish life, and particularly of Jewish religious life, helped to reinforce anti-Jewish stereotypes, particularly the twentieth-century characterization of the Jew as the *zydokomuna* (the "commie Jew"). Without any awareness of the nature of Jewish religion, the *zydokomuna*, the Jew as an atheistic communist, as a tool of Russian oppression, as a "fifth column" in Poland, served as a convenient stereotype to explain Poland's misfortunes.[31] The Polish episcopate's pastoral letter addresses this issue:

> We are aware that there survives among our fellow countrymen a memory of the hurts and injustices inflicted by the postwar Communist regime in which persons of Jewish descent participated. We admit, however, that the source inspiring their conduct was certainly neither their descent nor their religion, but the Communist ideology, from which Jews themselves suffered much injustice.

Here the Church refutes the identification of Jews with communism, and distances those Jews who served communism from the beliefs and values of Judaism. This opened the door to an awareness of a Jewish identity drawn from Jewish religious tradition, and not from communism. The bishops were undoubtedly aware that for most Poles, the more recent memories of communist oppression and their deep historical animosity toward the Russians outweighs their memories of the German occupation and their antipathy toward the German people. The bishops well understood that for Poles to seek to improve their relationships with Jews, the issue of the *zydokomuna* had to be addressed. In this regard, it must be admitted that both for idealistic and self-serving reasons, proportionately more Jews than non-Jews were involved with the communist powers. But the popular Polish perception that Jews outnumbered non-Jews in the party or the state apparatus is patently false. Thus by distancing communist ideology from Judaism, the bishops opened a path for Polish-Jewish dialogue. Building upon the documents of Vatican II, the guidelines for the implementation of those documents, and the many statements of John Paul II on Catholic-Jewish relations, the Polish episcopate focused Polish-Jewish relations as a dialogue between Polish-Catholicism and Judaism, upon spiritual and cultural commonalities between Poles and Jews.

A growing number of Poles, especially among the younger generation, has expressed interest, sometimes bordering on an obsession, with all things Jewish. They are aware that Jews were a part of the Polish landscape for centuries, and that now an important piece of the Polish historical experience is missing. Some young Poles hold a romanticized view of Jews, much like some Americans imagine that Indians enjoyed an idyllic existence in the centuries prior to European settlement of the Americas. Poles are hungry to fill in the "blank spots" of their history and of their national identity. Indeed, the prominence of the Jewish issue in a country virtually devoid of Jews seems to have more to do with the reconceptualization of Polish identity in the postcommunist era than it has to do with an attempt by Poles to recover the lost heritage of Polish Jews.

Like most Europeans, Poles look to history to find a model for the future and to confront the problems of the present. No viable model can be found in the Poland of the communist period or of the Nazi occupation. Nor do the periods of the partitions of Poland that account for most of modern Polish history offer any viable options. The "Jagiellonian concept," however, introduced in the early nineteenth century and adapted during the interwar years by the Pilsudski regime, hearkened back to the times of the Jagiellonian dynasty when Poland was a comparatively powerful, large, politically stable, economically sound, and ethnically diverse realm characterized by religious and ethnic tolerance, various forms of cultural expressions, and a regime as democratic as one could expect during that period. During this time Jews played a visible and vital role.

The Piast concept of the late nineteenth and early twentieth centuries, on the other hand, hearkens back to the vision of creating a modern version of the early Piast dynasty when Poland was ethnically pure—for Poles only. The "Piast concept" coupled nationalism with racism and rejected all foreign influence both from within Poland and from without. This was the approach of Roman Dmowski, the parent of modern Polish nationalism, whose rabid anti-Semitism expressed itself in his support of anti-Jewish economic boycotts and in his advocacy of a policy that called for the expulsion of the Jews from Poland in the 1930s.[32] Among other things, Dmowski sabotaged the efforts of Ignace Jan Paderewski and others to improve Polish-Jewish relations at home and abroad, particularly in the United States.[33]

The current struggle to establish a postcommunist-era Polish national identity also relates to the extremes of the Piast and Jagiellonian concepts, and to the many hues and shades in between. As is usually the case, there is little that is clear-cut and consistent. For example, some of the same churchmen who champion dialogue with

Jews advocate "one nation, one church," and demand that Polish social and political policy reflect the agenda of the church (e.g., the criminalization of abortion and
the inclusion of Catholic catechism instruction in the public school curriculum).
As Antony Polonsky has written, "What is clear is that the conflict between the two
sets of views about the Jewish role in Poland is really an argument over the future of
the country. Attitudes towards the Jews are a touchstone for more fundamental views.
What is really at issue here is whether the Poland of the future will be inward-looking,
chauvinist and prey to conspiracy theories of politics, or pluralistic, tolerant and
western-oriented."[34] Similarly, as Adam Michnik, has written, "Today Poland is a
country without Jews; and when anti-Semitic opinions are expressed in Poland, Jews
are not the issue, whatever the authors of the opinions themselves may think. The
question is whether there will or will not be a Polish democracy." [35]

In sum, the knowledge attained, and the attitudes expressed toward Jews and
Judaism by Poles, both in Poland and abroad, relate in the final analysis to the formu-
lation of a reconceptualized Polish national, religious, and ethnic identity. Consequently, coming to grips with the historical experience and the spiritual heritage of
Polish Jewry is not a marginal affair for Poles; it is a vital issue that strikes at the heart
of Polish self-identity. Those who avoid it risk impeding the emergence of a new Poland.

For Jews, Polish-Jewish dialogue is related to their own quest for self-identity in
the post-Holocaust world. Poles and Poland are a physical link to—and the only
available custodians of—the arena in which the spiritual heritage of Polish Jewry
developed. Without the establishment of viable relationships with Poles committed
to maintaining the places of significance to Jews and Judaism that remain and the
memories that persist, the final obliteration of Polish Jewry will be assured.

In Jerusalem there is a wall that is the only remaining remnant of the Temple.
It is the most sacred spot on earth for Jews. In Poland are the only remaining geographical and physical portals to the spiritual heritage of Polish Jewry. Without these
reminders, without these witnesses to history, the experience of Polish Jewry might
enter the realm of myth and fantasy, to be viewed by succeeding generations as a
place that never was. Reflecting on a visit to Poland, Paul Fenton wrote:

> The Jewish pilgrim to Poland comes not as an entire stranger to an unknown land.
> Something here, left behind, belongs to us. Every landscape is a rediscovery, the
> placing of a face to long familiar names. So rooted is the Jewish past in every inch
> of Polish soil, that every sign of city, village and hamlet conjures up some signifi-
> cant page of Jewish history. Here perhaps more than anywhere else, the Jewish
> past is so present, even in its very absence. . . . Pre-war Poland had been the great-
> est citadel of Jewish spirituality.[36]

In one of his last stories, the Yiddish novelist Joseph Opatoshu tells of a town
once teeming with Jews. Now its Jews have all disappeared. An old Jewish man lives
in the town who remembers when other Jews had lived there. The young people of
the town ask the old man to tell them of the people whose presence haunts the town,
of the people who once laughed and cried in the homes that they now inhabit. By
telling of these Jewish inhabitants, the old man provides them with a life after death.
His young listeners, however, wonder whether the old man is telling the truth or is
merely fabricating a tale.[37]

In Peretz's play *At Night in the Old Market Place* he refers to the legend of Casimir and Esterka with these words:

> Once there was a story
> About you and a king
> The story is not over—
> It is the story of two upon one soil.[38]

In 1943 the American Federation for Polish Jews published *The Black Book of Polish Jewry: An Account of the Martyrdom of Polish Jewry Under the Nazi Occupation*. Even while the destruction of Polish Jewry was underway, and even in this chronicle of that process of annihilation, the editors acknowledged what Jews today often overlook. They wrote, "A thousand threads bind the Jews of Poland to Polish soil. In the course of the nine long centuries which have gone by since the Jews first entered Poland towards the end of the eleventh century, strong links have been forged which bind the Jews to Polish soil with iron bonds; the common earth which nourished both Poles and Jews has been saturated with the sighs and tears of both peoples."[39]

On May 12, 1943, Arthur Zygielbaum was in London from Warsaw on a mission to help save Polish Jewry from extermination. On that date he learned that the last Jews of the Warsaw Ghetto had been massacred. As a statement of solidarity with them, and as a protest against the apathy of the Allies, Zygielbaum committed suicide; he was 48. He left a note that looked forward to a new and better world, and a new and better Poland. In the depths of suicidal despair over the present, Zygielbaum still had hope for the future. He wrote:

> I cannot be silent—I cannot live—while remnants of the Jewish people in Poland, of whom I am a representative, are perishing. . . . By my death, I wish to express my strongest protest against the inactivity with which the world is looking on and permitting the extermination of my people. . . . I know how little human life is worth today, but as I was unable to do anything during my life, perhaps by my death I shall contribute to breaking down the indifference of those who may now—at the last moment—rescue the few Polish Jews still alive, from certain annihilation. My life belongs to the Jewish people of Poland and I therefore give it to them. I wish that this remaining handful of the original several millions of Polish Jews could live to see the liberation of a new world of freedom. . . . I believe that such a Poland will arise and that such a world will come.[40]

Notes

Chapter 1

1. See *Avot d'Rabbi Natan*, ed. Solomon Schechter (New York: Feldheim, 1967), 2nd ed., p. 12b. See also the translation by Judah Goldin, *The Fathers According to Rabbi Nathan* (New Haven: Yale University Press, 1955), p. 37.

2. The historic lands of Poland generally refers to the expansive domain of the Polish-Lithuanian republic in the seventeenth century. On the problem of defining the "Polish lands," see Norman Davies, *God's Playground: A History of Poland* (New York: Columbia University Press, 1982), vol. 1, pp. 23–60.

3. This story is derived from the Yiddish poem by Jakow Frydman, "Der Chelmer Melamed," in his collected poems *Pastekher in Yisroel* (Tel Aviv: Poalim Press, 1953), pp. 427–428.

4. Quoted in David Roskies, ed., *The Literature of Destruction: Jewish Responses to Catastrophe* (Philadelphia: Jewish Publication Society, 1988), pp. 539, 542, 532, 547.

5. On Jewish population figures for Polish cities in the early twentieth century, see Jacob Lestchinsky, "The Jews in the Cities of the Republic of Poland," in Deborah Dash Moore, ed., *East European Jews in Two World Wars* (Evanston, Ill.: Northwestern University Press, 1990), pp. 103–124.

6. Abraham Joshua Heschel, *Man Is Not Alone* (Philadelphia: Jewish Publication Society, 1951), p. 162.

7. The view of nostalgia taken here is similar to that of the American historian Christopher Lasch. Lasch considers nostalgia a betrayal of history that denies the influence of the past in the present and leads to discontinuity and escapism. For a review of Lasch's and other views of the nature of nostalgia, both positive and negative, see Suzanne Vromen, "The Ambiguity of Nostalgia," *YIVO Annual* 21 (1993): 69–86.

8. See, e.g., Alan Chernoff, "New Polish Chic," *Forward* (August 4, 1995): 1, 12.

9. Israel Berger, *Eser Orot* (Pietrikow: Kleiman, 1907), p. 94.

10. Saadya Gaon, *The Book of Beliefs and Opinions*, trans. Samuel Rosenblatt (New Haven: Yale University Press, 1948), part 3, sec. 7, p. 158.

11. Judah Halevi, *The Kuzari*, trans. Hartwig Hirschfield (New York: Schocken Books, 1964), part 2, sec. 56, p. 117.

12. Viktor Frankl, *Man's Search for Meaning* (New York: Washington Square Press, 1963), p. xiii; emphasis mine.

13. Salo Baron, *A Social and Religious History of the Jews* (New York: Columbia University Press, 1952), vol. 1, p. 4.

14. Salo Baron, *Steeled by Adversity* (Philadelphia: Jewish Publication Society, 1971), p. 530.

15. Oedipus and Alex Haley as quoted in Rollo May, *The Cry for Myth* (New York: Delta, 1991), pp. 47–48.

16. Abraham Joshua Heschel, *The Earth Is the Lord's* (New York: Henry Schuman, 1950), p. 107. The original text of Heschel's speech appears in an English translation in Abraham Joshua Heschel, "The Eastern European Era in Jewish History," *YIVO Annual of Jewish Social Science* 1 (1946): 86–106; it was reprinted as the introduction to Roman Vishniac, *Polish Jews* (New York: Schocken, 1947), pp. 7–17. The original talk was recast and expanded as Heschel's Yiddish book *Der Mizrah-Europischer Yid* (New York: Schocken, 1946) and in English as *The Earth Is the Lord's*.

17. Heschel said this to me, as well as to many others, on numerous occasions. See, e.g., Richard L. Rubenstein, *Power Struggle* (New York: Scribner's, 1974), p. 128.

18. While the idea of redeeming the sparks is found in pre-Hasidic Jewish mysticism, particularly in Lurianic kabbalah, the individualistic dimension of this teaching seems to have been introduced and stressed by Hasidism. On this Hasidic emphasis on the redemption of one's own unique sparks, see Louis Jacobs, "The Uplifting of the Sparks," in Arthur Green, ed., *Jewish Spirituality: From the Sixteenth Century Revival to the Present* (New York: Crossroad, 1987), p. 117; and Elliot R. Wolfson, *Along the Path* (Albany: SUNY Press, 1995), pp. 91–93, 230–232.

19. Levi Yitzhak of Berditchev, "Lekh Lekha," *Kedushat Levi* (New York: Yisrael Ze'ev, 1962), p. 5.

20. Quoted in the name of the Ba'al Shem Tov in Aaron Roth, *Shulhan ha-Tahor* (Jerusalem: n.p., 1989), p. 127.

Chapter 2

1. Abraham Joshua Heschel, *A Passion for Truth* (New York: Farrar, Straus and Giroux, 1973), p. 107.

2. On the mystical meaning of storytelling in Hasidism, see Moshe Idel, *Hasidism* (Albany: SUNY Press, 1995), p. 185.

3. This telling of the exorcism of a dybbuk correlates with most recorded accounts. See, e.g., the texts collected and discussed in Gedaliah Nigal, *Sipurei Dibbuk be-Sifrut Yisrael* (Jerusalem: Reuben Mass, 1983). S. A. Ansky, author of the classic play on the dybbuk, is buried in the Jewish cemetery in Warsaw.

Chapter 3

1. Israel Gutman, "Polish and Jewish Historiography on the Question of Polish-Jewish Relations During World War II," in Chimen Abramsky, Maciej Jachimczyk, and Antony Polonsky, eds., *The Jews in Poland* (Oxford: Basil Blackwell, 1986), p. 177.

2. On Hasidic landmarks in Poland, see Paul M. Fenton, "Hasidic Landmarks in Present-Day Poland," *European Judaism* 23, no. 2 (1990): 19–29.

3. On the history of the Jews in Gora Kalwaria, see Eleanora Bergman, "Gora Kalwaria: The Impact of a Hasidic Cult on the Urban Landscape of a Small Polish Town," *Polin* 5 (1990): 3–23.

4. Alfred Döblin, *Journey to Poland*, trans. Joachim Neugroschel (New York: Paragon House, 1991), pp. 74–81.

5. Yitzhak Zuckerman, second in command during the Warsaw Ghetto uprising, said this to the filmmaker Claude Lanzmann. It is in Lanzmann's film *Shoah*. See Claude Lanzmann, *Shoah: An Oral History of the Holocaust* (New York: Pantheon, 1985), p. 196.

6. Talmud, Abot 6:6.

7. An earlier, less embellished, and probably more authentic version is found in Israel Arten, *Emet ve-Emunah* (Jerusalem: n.p., 1969), p. 9: "Our master said that he could resurrect the dead, but that he preferred to resurrect the living."

Chapter 4

1. Usually called the Council of Four Lands, I prefer the Council of Lands, because the geographical representation of the council shifted throughout its existence. While the council's activities were brought to an end in 1764, less than a decade before the first partition of Poland, the question of when in the early or mid-sixteenth century its activities began is a matter of scholarly debate. On the beginnings of the council, see, e.g., Israel Halpern, *Yehudim ve-Yahadut be-Mizrah Airopa* (Jerusalem: Magnes Press, 1969), pp. 39–46. Halpern spent much of his scholarly career studying the council, and his works provide a goldmine of information on its activities and structure. See in particular Israel Halpern, ed., *Pinkas Arba Aratzot* (Jerusalem: Mosad Bialik, 1945). See also the studies on the council and on Jewish autonomy in Poland in Antony Polonsky, Jakub Basista, and Andrzej Link-Lenczowski, eds., *The Jews in Old Poland, 1000–1795* (London: I. B. Tauris and Co., 1993), sec. 2, pp. 93–198.

2. See Lucjan Dobroszycki, "Re-emergence and Decline of a Community: The Numerical Size of the Jewish Population in Poland, 1944–47," *YIVO Annual* 21 (1993): 4.

3. On Shalom Shakhna, see, e.g., Ben-Zion Katz, *Rabbanut, Hasidut, Haskalah* (Tel Aviv: Dvir, 1956), pp. 9–14; Moses Shulvass, *Jewish Culture in Eastern Europe* (New York: Ktav, 1975), pp. 31–33.

4. See, e.g., Gershon D. Hundert, *The Jews in a Polish Private Town* (Baltimore: Johns Hopkins University Press, 1992), p. xiii. In his responsa, the seventeenth-century rabbi Shabbatai Cohen writes that in the area of Brest-Litovsk, "the custom has become widespread that most of our co-religionists who live in this locality speak the local language"; quoted in Nisson Shulman, *Authority and Community: Polish Jewry in the Sixteenth Century* (New York: Yeshiva University Press, 1986), p. 83. Among leading sixteenth-century Jewish scholars in Poland, Solomon Luria, Meir of Lublin, and others knew Polish; see Shulvass, *Jewish Culture*, p. 151.

5. Nathan Hanover, *Abyss of Despair (Yaven Metzulah)*, trans. Abraham J. Mesch (New Brunswick, N.J.: Transaction Books, 1983), pp. 110–111.

6. On Jacob Pollack, see, e.g., Katz, *Rabbanut*, pp. 3–9; Shulvass, *Jewish Culture*, pp. 23–31; Israel Zinberg, *A History of Jewish Literature*, trans. Bernard Martin (New York: Ktav, 1975), vol. 6, pp. 25–29.

7. Quoted in Isaac Alfasi, *ha-Hozeh mi Lublin* (Jerusalem: Mosad ha-Rav Kook, 1969), p. 241; compare, Elie Wiesel, *Four Hasidic Masters* (Notre Dame, Ind.: University of Notre Dame Press, 1978), p. 66.

8. See the version of this story in Wiesel, *Four Hasidic Masters*, pp. 85–86.

9. Martin Buber, *Tales of the Hasidim: Early Masters*, trans. Olga Marx (New York: Schocken, 1947), p. 303.

10. See Isaac Alfasi, *Ha–Hozeh mi–Lublin* (Jerusalem: Mosad ha–Rav Kook, 1969), pp. 97–104.

11. Buber, *Tales of the Hasidim*, pp. 307, 313.

12. Talmud, Abot 6:6.

13. Quoted in Alfasi, *Ha–Hozeh*, p. 152.

14. On the teachings of the Seer of Lublin, see Rachel Elior, "Between *Yesh* and *Ayin*: The Doctrine of the Zaddik in the Works of Jacob Isaac, the Seer of Lublin," in Ada Rapoport-Albert and Steven J. Zipperstein, eds., *Jewish History: Essays in Honor of Chimen Abramsky* (London: Peter Halban, 1988), pp. 393–455.

15. Alfasi, *Ha–Hozeh*, p. 121.

16. Ibid., pp. 120–121.

17. Quoted in Moshe Idel, *Hasidism* (Albany: SUNY Press, 1995), p. 211.

18. See Alfasi, *Ha–Hozeh*, p. 107.

19. For this story, see Salmon Baruch Nissenbaum, *Le-Korot ha-Yehudim be-Lublin* (Lublin: Feder, 1900), p. 17.

20. On Luria's genealogy, see Abraham Epstein, *Mishpahat Luria* (Vienna: n.p., 1901).

21. On Luria's life and work, see Simha Assaf, "Mah-she-hu Le-Toledot Maharshal," in Saul Lieberman et al., eds., *Sefer ha-Yovel L'Khvod Levi Ginzberg* (New York: American Academy for Jewish Research, 1946), pp. 45–63; Katz, *Rabbanut*, pp. 29–38; Shulvass, *Jewish Culture*, pp. 60–70; Zinberg, *History of Jewish Literature*, pp. 39–44; and Samuel A. Horodetzky, *Shalosh Me'ot Shanah shel Yahadut Polin* (Tel Aviv: Dvir, 1946), pp. 36–51.

22. See, e.g., Simon Hurwitz, *The Responsa of Solomon Luria* (New York: Bloch Publishing Co., 1938), p. 6.

23. This translation of Luria's words is in Hurwitz, *The Responsa*, p. 21. It is actually a summary of Luria's statement in his *Yam Shel Shelomoh* (Stettin: Shrenzel, 1862), Yebamot (Introduction).

24. Heinrich Graetz, *History of the Jews* (Philadelphia: Jewish Publication Society, 1967), vol. 4, p. 634. For general surveys of classical Jewish scholarship in eastern Europe, see, e.g., Katz, *Rabbanut*; Shulvass, *Jewish Culture*; Zinberg, *History of Jewish Literature*; Horodetzky, *Shalosh Me'ot Shanah*; Jacob Elbaum, *Petihot ve-Histagrut* (Jerusalem: Magnes Press, 1990); Moses Shulvass, "Ha-Torah ve-Limudeha be-Polin Ve-Lita," in Israel Halpern, ed., *Beit Yisrael be-Polin* (Jerusalem: Youth Department of the Zionist Organization, 1953), vol. 2, pp. 13–35; Moses Shulvass, *Between the Rhine and the Bosporus* (Chicago: College of Jewish Studies Press, 1964), pp. 70–129; Abraham Menes, "Pattern of Jewish Scholarship in Eastern Europe," in Louis Finkelstein, ed., *The Jews: Their History, Culture and Religion* (Philadelphia: Jewish Publication Society, 1960), pp. 276–427; and Hayyim Hillel Ben-Sasson, *Hagut ve-Hanhagah* (Jerusalem: Mosad Bialik, 1959).

25. Moses Isserles, *Responsa* (Hebrew), ed. Asher Siev (Jerusalem: Feldheim, 1970), no. 6, pp. 23–29. This responsum of Luria is found in the collected responsa of Isserles. Isserles's response to Luria is found in Responsum no. 7.

26. Moses Isserles, *Torat ha-Olah* (Lwow: n.p., 1858), part 3, sec. 4. In observing that philosophy and mysticism say the same things with different words, Isserles was paraphrasing the earlier kabbalist Moses Botarel.

27. On the history of Majdanek, see Jozef Marszalek, *Majdanek* (Warsaw: Interpress, 1986).

28. See, e.g., David A. Mandelbaum, *Yeshivat Hokhmei Lublin* (Bnai Brak, Israel: n.p., 1994).

29. Quoted in the February 1940 *Deutsche Jugendzeitung*, in Earl Vinecour, *Polish Jews: The Final Chapter* (New York: McGraw Hill, 1977), p. 88.

30. Salo Baron, *A Social and Religious History of the Jews* (New York: Columbia University Press, 1976), vol. 16, p. 98. On the Jesuits and Jews in Poland, see pp. 101–102.

Chapter 5

1. On Cracowian Jewry, see, e.g., Arieh L. Bauminger, ed., *Sefer Krako* (Jerusalem: Mosad ha-Rav Kook, 1959).

2. Kosciuszko had a positive view of Jews based upon his high estimation of the military abilities of those Jews with whom he fought during his military career, particularly during the Polish war with Russia in 1794. He perceived there to be a Jewish military tradition, rooted in Hebrew Scriptures and continued by the ancient Jews in their wars against Rome. There was a Jewish corps in his 1794 army led by Berek Joselewicz, perhaps the most famous Jewish military leader in modern Poland. Joselewicz was killed in a battle near Kock in 1809. See, e.g., Isaac Lewin, *The Jewish Community in Poland* (New York: Philosophical Library, 1985), pp. 23–25.

3. Moses Isserles, *Responsa* (Hebrew), ed. Asher Siev (Jerusalem: Feldheim, 1970), no. 67, p. 294.

4. Asher Siev, *Ramo* (New York: Yeshiva University Press, 1972), p. 134.

5. On Joseph Katz, see, e.g., Jehiel M. Zunz, *Ir ha-Zedek* (Lwow: Verfassers, 1874), pp. 23–28.

6. On the life and work of Moses Isserles, see, e.g., Siev, *Ramo*; and Moses Shulvass, *Jewish Culture in Eastern Europe* (New York: Ktav, 1975), pp. 35–60.

7. On *Torat ha-Olah*, see the definitive study, Yonah Ben-Sasson, *Mishnato ha-Iyyunit shel ha-Rama* (Jerusalem: Israel Academy of Sciences and Humanities, 1984).

8. The theory that the Greeks expropriated philosophy from the Jews and subsequently distorted it appears in medieval Jewish writings and in the works of Isserles and other sixteenth-century Jewish thinkers; see, e.g., Harry A. Wolfson, *Philo* (Cambridge: Harvard University Press, 1947), vol. 1, pp. 160–163. For Isserles's view, see his *Torat ha-Olah* (Lwow: n.p., 1858), part 1, sec. 11, p. 13a.

9. See Israel Zinberg, *A History of Jewish Literature*, trans. Bernard Martin (New York: Ktav, 1975), vol. 6, pp. 33–34.

10. Isserles, *Responsa*, no. 7, p. 32. Compare the view of Joseph Ashkenazi, who wrote that "each chapter in Maimonides's *Guide of the Perplexed* contains some heresy"; see Jacob Elbaum, *Petihot ve-Histagrut* (Jerusalem: Magnes Press, 1990), p. 163.

11. Isserles, *Responsa*, no. 6, pp. 23, 25–26.

12. On Numbers 11:17, see Hayyim ben Bezalel, *Be'er Mayyim Hayyim* (London: Honig, 1969), vol. 2, pp. 110–111 On Hayyim ben Bezalel and his attitude toward philosophy, see, e.g., Byron L. Sherwin, "In the Shadows of Greatness: Rabbi Hayyim Ben Betsalel of Friedberg," *Jewish Social Studies* 37:1 (1975): 35–61.

13. See Y. Ben-Sasson, *Mishnato ha-Iyyunit*, pp. 193–208. Because the *Yigdal* prayer is based upon Maimonides's "principles" of Jewish faith, Luria discouraged its recitation in the synagogue.

14. On legends related to Ashkenazi, see, e.g., Shlomo Ben-David, *The Travels of Rabbi Eliezer Ashkenazi*, trans. M. Samsonowitz (Israel: Gefen, 1982).

15. On the conflict between Ashkenazi and Loew, see Byron L. Sherwin, *Mystical Theology and Social Dissent: The Life and Works of Judah Loew of Prague* (Toronto: Associated University Presses, 1982), pp. 58–69. This citation, quoted in Sherwin, *Mystical Theology*, p. 59, is from Judah Loew's *Derekh Hayyim* (New York: Judaica, 1969), p. 234.

16. Eliezer Ashkenazi, *Ma'aseh ha-Shem* (Venice: n.p., 1583), Introduction; chap. 31, "Ma'ase Bereshit"; and chap. 21, "Ma'aseh Avot."

17. See Elbaum, *Petihot ve-Histagrut*, p. 167.

18. See Salo Baron, *A Social and Religious History of the Jews* (New York: Columbia University Press, 1976), vol. 16, p. 91.

19. For an analysis of this text, see Baron, *Social and Religious History*, pp. 64–65, and Hayyim Hillel Ben-Sasson, *The Reformation in Contemporary Jewish Eyes* (Jerusalem: Israel Academy of Sciences and Humanities, 1970), pp. 20–21.

20. On Sirkes, see Elijah J. Schochet, *Bach: Rabbi Joel Sirkes* (New York: Feldheim, 1971). This responsum, in the original Hebrew and with an English translation, is on pp. 248– 253. The responsum was written by Sirkes in Brisk (Brest-Litovsk), and was originally printed in Sirkes's collection of responsa, *Bayit Hadash* (Frankfurt: n.p., 1697), no. 4b.

21. See Schochet, *Bach*, p. 38.

22. On Heller, see, e.g., Zunz, *Ir ha-Zedek*, pp. 93–104; Gutmann Klemperer, "The Rabbis of Prague," *Historica Judaica* 12 (1950): 51–66. On Heller's positive attitude toward philosophy and the sciences, see, e.g., Joseph M. Davis, *Yom Tov Lipman Heller, Joseph ben Isaac Ha-Levi, and Rationalism in Ashkenazic Jewish Culture, 1550–1650* (Ann Arbor, Mich.: University Microfilms, Inc., 1990).

23. See Elbaum, *Petihot ve-Histagrut*, pp. 182–185.

24. On Shapiro, see, e.g., Zunz, *Ir ha-Zedek*, pp. 52–62; and Samuel A. Horodetzky, *Ha-Mistorin be-Yisrael* (Tel Aviv: Union of Hebrew Writers, 1961), pp. 129–141. In his work Horodetzky also deals with other Jewish mystics in Poland and with mystical themes in the writings of Solomon Delacrut, Mordecai Jaffe, Samson of Ostropole, and various commentators to the Talmud and Codes in Poland.

25. On the *Arba'ah Turim* and its commentaries, see, e.g., Chaim Tchernowitz, *Toledot ha-Poskim* (New York: Jubilee Committee, 1947), vol. 2, pp. 199–236.

26. On *Sha'are Dura*, see, e.g., Tchernowitz, *Toledot*, vol. 2, pp. 240–243.

27. See Siev, *Ramo*, pp. 158–159.

28. On Isserles's views regarding the authority of custom and the related views of Hayyim ben Bezalel, see Siev, *Ramo*, pp. 219–226.

29. On the *Shulhan Arukh*, its commentaries, and the debate over the codification of Jewish law that its publication engendered, see, e.g., Hayyim Tchernowitz, *Toledot ha-Poskim* (New York: Jubilee Committee, 1947), vol. 3; and Isadore Twersky, "The *Shulhan Arukh*: Enduring Code of Jewish Law," *Judaism* 16 (1967): 141–159.

30. Solomon Luria, *Yam Shel Shelomo* (Stettin: Shrentzel, 1861), "Baba Kamma," 8:72, 2:5; and Solomon Luria, *Responsa* (in Hebrew) (Lublin: n.p., 1774), no. 16.

31. On Heschel of Cracow, see Zunz, *Ir ha-Zedek*, pp. 104–114.

32. Abraham Joshua Heschel, *A Passion for Truth* (New York: Farrar, Straus and Giroux, 1973), p. 283.

33. See Byron L. Sherwin, "My Master," in Harold Kasimow and Byron L. Sherwin, eds., *No Religion Is an Island* (Maryknoll, N.Y.: Orbis Books, 1991), pp. 42–63.

Chapter 6

1. On *yizkor* books, see, e.g., Jack Kugelmass and Jonathan Boyarin, eds., *From a Ruined Garden: The Memorial Books of Polish Jewry* (New York: Schocken, 1983).

2. Isaac Berat, ed., *Maków-Mazowiecki Yizkor Bukh* (Tel Aviv: Makow-Mazowiecki Organization, 1969), p. 40.

3. Ephraim Fishel Neuman, *Darkhei Hayyim* (New York: Daas ha-Torah Publishing Co., 1948), pp. 51–64.

4. Quoted in Howard Schwartz and Anthony Rudolf, eds., *Voices Within the Ark* (New York: Avon Books, 1980), p. 1066.

5. Scholem Asch, *Three Cities*, trans. Edwin and Willma Muir (New York: G. P. Putnam's Sons, 1933), p. 474.

6. See Lucjan Dobroszycki, "Re-emergence and Decline of a Community: The Numerical Size of the Jewish Population in Poland, 1944–47," *YIVO Annual* 21 (1993): 4.

7. See Alan Adelson and Robert Lapides, eds., *Lodz Ghetto* (New York: Viking, 1989), pp. 328–331. Rumkowski's speech ordering the Jewish inhabitants of the Lodz ghetto to hand over their children below the age of ten was delivered on September 4, 1942.

8. See Gershon D. Hundert, "Some Basic Characteristics of the Jewish Experience in Poland," *Polin* 1 (1986): 29.

9. Gershon D. Hundert, *The Jews in a Polish Private Town* (Baltimore: Johns Hopkins University Press, 1992), pp. 36–39.

10. On the first Jewish settlements in Poland, see Aleksander Gieysztor, "The Beginnings of Jewish Settlement in the Polish Lands," in Chimen Abramsky, Maciej Jachimczyk, and Antony Polonsky, eds., *The Jews in Poland* (Oxford: Basil Blackwell, 1986), pp. 15–22. On Jews in Poland in the Middle Ages, see, e.g., Adam Vetulani, "The Jews in Medieval Poland," *The Journal of Jewish Sociology* 4:2 (1962): 274–294; and Bernard Weinryb, *The Jews of Poland* (Philadelphia: Jewish Publication Society, 1972), pp. 17–107.

11. On population growth, see, e.g., Salo Baron, *A Social and Religious History of the Jews* (New York: Columbia University Press, 1976), vol. 16, pp. 207, 311, 414–415; Weinryb, *Jews of Poland*, Appendix 3, pp. 308–320; and the classic, painstaking study of eighteenth-century figures by Raphael Mahler in his *Toledot ha-Yehudin be-Polin* (Israel: Sifrut Poalim, 1946), especially, pp. 230–245.

12. See, e.g., Ezra Mendelsohn, "Interwar Poland: Good or Bad for the Jews?" in Abramsky et al., *Jews in Poland*, p. 133.

13. On the Statute of Kalisz, see, e.g., Isaac Lewin, *The Jewish Community in Poland* (New York: Philosophical Library, 1985), pp. 38–56. See also Shalom A. Cygielman, "The Basic Privileges of the Jews of Great Poland as Reflected in Polish Historiography," *Polin* 2 (1987): 117–149.

14. Weinryb, *Jews of Poland*, p. 151.

15. See Jacob Elbaum, *Petihot ve-Histagrut* (Jerusalem: Magnes, 1990), p. 377.

16. See Hundert, *Jews in a Polish Private Town*, pp. 36–37.

17. The following section on "Poland Through the Eyes of Polish Jews" rests heavily on a chapter by that title in Weinryb, *Jews of Poland*, pp. 156–176. Citations are drawn usually from Weinryb's discussion.

18. Abraham Joshua Heschel, *The Circle of the Baal Shem Tov*, ed. Samuel H. Dresner (Chicago: University of Chicago Press, 1985), pp. 40, 43.

19. On Jewish attitudes toward wealth in sixteenth- and seventeenth-century Poland, see, e.g., Hayyim Hillel Ben Sasson, *Hagut ve-Hanhaga* (Jerusalem: Mosad Bialik, 1959), pp. 69–120.

20. See, e.g., Lewin, *Jewish Community*, pp. 23–25.

21. Quoted in Weinryb, *Jews of Poland*, p. 155.

22. There are many versions of this legend; see, e.g., Abraham Joshua Heschel, *The Earth is the Lord's* (New York: Henry Schuman, 1950), p. 57.

23. On this conflict between the cardinal and the king, see Majer Balaban, *Historia Zydow w Krakowie i na Kazimierzu 1340–1868* (Cracow: n.p., 1931), vol. 1, pp. 46–65.

24. A photostat of the original Hebrew document may be found in Balaban, *Historia*, vol. 1, between pp. 114 and 115. Discussion of the document is on pp. 59–61.

25. On the Turkish visit, the fire, Buonacorsi's intervention, and other dimensions of this episode, see Balaban, *Historia*, pp. 62–65. Buonacorsi was also known by his pen name, Philip Callimico. For discussion of his role at the Polish court, see, e.g., Baron, *Social and Religious History*, p. 54.

26. The general assumption that the expulsion put an end to the Jewish community in Cracow has been proven false by Bozena Wyrozumska, "Did King Jan Olbracht Banish the Jews from Cracow?" in Andrzej K. Paluch, ed., *The Jews in Poland* (Cracow: Jagiellonian University, 1992), vol. 1, pp. 27–37.

27. William Stein, "Cracow," in *The Universal Jewish Encyclopedia*, vol. 3, p. 303.

28. This reconstruction of the story of the Fishel family, including the role of Pollack in that story, is based upon Majer Balaban, "Jakob Polak, der Baal Chillukim in Krakav, und seine Zeit," *Monatsschrift für Geschichte und Wissenschaft des Judentums* 57 (1913): 59–73, 196–210. See also Balaban, *Historia*, vol. 1, pp. 107–118; Arieh L. Bauminger, ed., *Sefer Krako* (Jerusalem: Mosad ha-Rav Kook, 1959), pp. 12–15, 129–130; and P. Wettstein, *Le-Toledot Yisrael ve-Hokhamav be-Polin* (Cracow: ha-Eshkol, 1908), pp. 1–12.

29. Balaban, *Historia*, vol. 1, p. 69. A text of a royal decree describing Chwalka and Esther as ladies in waiting to the queen, and therefore exempt from certain taxes, is found in Jehiel Zunz, *Ir ha-Zedek* (Lwow: Verfassers, 1874), p. 17 of the appendix.

30. On Meir ben Gedalia, see Judah Rosenthal, *Mehkarim* (Jerusalem: Reuben Mass, 1966), vol. 2, pp. 479–513; Samuel A. Horodetzky, *Shalosh Me'ot Shanah shel Yahadut Polin* (Tel Aviv: Dvir, 1946), pp. 68–72; Ben-Zion Katz, *Rabbanut, Hasidut, Haskalah* (Tel Aviv: Dvir, 1956), pp. 65–70; and Zunz, *Ir ha-Zedek*, pp. 28–42.

31. On Dr. Moses Fishel, see Balaban, *Historia*, vol. 1, pp. 112–116.

32. See, e.g., Jacob Elbaum, "Kishrei Tarbut bein Yehudai Polin ve-Ashkenaz le-vain Yehudai Italia be-Me'ah ha-17," *Gal-Ed* 7/8 (1985): 11–40.

33. On Moses Fishel and the Weigel affair, see Balaban, *Historia*, vol. 1, pp. 124–130. On anti-Trinitarian Anabaptism in Poland in the sixteenth and seventeenth centuries, see, e.g., George H. Williams, *The Radical Reformation* (Philadelphia: Westminster Press, 1975), pp. 639–669.

Chapter 7

1. On the genealogy of the Katzenellenbogen-Wahl family, see Neil Rosenstein, *The Unbroken Chain* (Elizabeth, N.J.: Computer Center for Jewish Genealogy, 1990), vol. 1. For a genealogy of the Katzenellenbogen family, beginning with Samuel Judah Katzenellenbogen, see, e.g., Samuel Wiener, ed., *Da'at Kedoshim* (St. Petersburg: Berman and Co., 1897), pp. 84–135.

2. On the early history and rabbis of Brisk, see Aryeh Loeb Feinstein, *Ir Tehillah* (Warsaw: Halter, 1885). The first rabbi of Brisk was Yehiel Luria, the father of Solomon Luria. Solomon Luria and Abraham Joshua Heschel of Cracow also served there. So did many members of the Shor and Katzenellenbogen families. Solomon Luria's daughter, Valentina, was married to Ephraim Fishel of Brisk, who was the great-great-great-grandson of the first Ephraim Fishel of Cracow, who came to Poland in the fifteenth century.

3. On the historical lands of Poland, see Norman Davies, *God's Playground: A History of Poland* (New York: Columbia University Press, 1982), vol. 1, pp. 23–60.

4. Norman Davies, *Heart of Europe* (New York: Oxford University Press, 1984), p. 342.

5. Ibid., pp. 316–317.

6. Oxford ms. No. 2240.

7. The name Wahl may also have been derived from the Polish word *wol*, meaning "ox," the equivalent of the Hebrew word *shor*. See Salo Baron, *A Social and Religious History of the Jews* (New York: Columbia University Press, 1976), vol. 16, pp. 36, 332–333.

8. On Saul Wahl's economic activities, see Majer Balaban, *Historia Zydow w Krakowie i Na Kazimierzu 1304–1868* (Cracow: n.p., 1931), vol. 1, pp. 159–162.

9. Ephraim Zalmen Shor is buried in Lublin; see Salmon Baruch Nissenbaum, *Le-Korot ha-Yehudim be-Lublin* (Lublin: Feder, 1900), pp. 35–36.

10. On the Shor family, see Hayyim D. Friedberg, *Toledot Mishpahat Shor* (Frankfurt: Kaufmann, 1901). On their relationship with the Heschel and Katzenellenbogen family, see pp. 9–12.

11. On Judah Loew Klausner, see Jehiel Zunz, *Ir ha-Zedek* (Lwow: Verfassers, 1874), pp. 114–117; and Arieh L. Bauminger, *Sefer Krako* (Jerusalem: Mosad ha-Rav Kook, 1959), p. 24. It seems that Klausner had a short flirtation with the Sabbatean movement while he was chief rabbi of Cracow. In 1667 the royal court granted him the title "servant of the king." Before coming to Cracow he served in Przemysl and in Vienna. On Saul Heschel, see Zunz, pp. 154–159. Zunz makes no reference to any familial relationship between Heschel and Klausner. Saul served in Breslau and later in Cracow as chief rabbi. Zunz recorded the inscriptions on many tombstones in the old Jewish cemetery of Cracow, including that of Klausner (p. 180), whose tombstone is now gone. In a lengthy discussion of Heschel of Cracow, Chaim Nathan Dembitzer establishes the link between Heschel and Klausner through marriage. See Dembitzer, *Kelilat Yofi* (Cracow: Fischer, 1888), pp. 69–71. On the genealogical intertwinings of the Klausner, Fishel, Heschel, Luria, Shor, Shrenzel, and other families, see Jacob L. Shapiro, *Mishpahot Atikot Be-Yisrael* (Tel Aviv: Holiot, 1981).

12. On Vallentina, see Abraham Epstein, *Mishpahat Luria* (Vienna: n.p., 1901), p. 20.

13. On the rabbis of Lukow, see B. Heller, ed., *Sefer Lukow* (Tel Aviv: Former Residents of Lukow, 1968), pp. 47–53.

14. For example, in 1589 Isaac Nachmanowicz paid the taxes for the Jewish community of the entire Polish-Lithuanian commonwealth. Eventually the family went bankrupt. See Baron, *Social and Religious History*, p. 292.

15. On the rabbis of Lwow during the fifteenth and sixteenth centuries, see Dembitzer, *Kelilat Yofi*; and Jecheskiel Caro, *Geschichte der Juden in Lemberg* (Cracow: Fischer, 1894).

16. See, e.g., *Pinkas Ludmir* (Tel Aviv: Former Residents of Wladimir in Israel, 1962), pp. 31, 290–291.

17. On the shared genealogy of Rabbi Loew of Cracow and Rabbi Loew of Prague, from their generation back to biblical times, see Moses Jair Weinstock, *Tiferet Beit David* (Jerusalem: n.p., 1968), pp. 37–120. On the familial relationship between the two, see Meir Perles, *Megilat Yohasin* (Prague: n.p., 1864), p. 17, notes.

18. On Loew's influence on Hasidism, see, e.g., Byron L. Sherwin, *Mystical Theology and Social Dissent* (Toronto: Associated University Presses, 1982), pp. 52–54; and Bezalel Safran, ed., *Hasidism: Continuity or Innovation?* (Cambridge: Harvard University Press, 1988), pp. xii-xiv, 47–144.

19. On the early history of the Jews of Poznan, see J. Perles, "Geschichte der Juden in Posen," *Monatsschrift für Geschichte und Wissenschaft des Judenthums* 13 (1864): 281–295, 321–334, 361–373, 408–420, 449–461.

20. See, e.g., Abraham G. Duker, "Polish Frankism's Duration," *Jewish Social Studies* 25 (1963): 287–333.

21. Arnold Zable, *Jewels and Ashes* (New York: Harcourt Brace, 1991), p. 42.

22. Lucjan Dobroszycki, "Re-emergence and Decline of a Community: The Numerical Size of the Jewish Population in Poland, 1944–47," *YIVO Annual* 21 (1993): 4.

23. Zable, *Jewels*, p. 162.

Chapter 8

1. See, e.g., Elie Wiesel, *Souls On Fire* (New York: Random House, 1972), pp. 117–118. The Hebrew name of the town of Oswiecim, or Auschwitz, is Ushpizin. Ushpizin is a custom, developed by the Jewish mystics, of inviting mystical guests to one's sukkah (booth) on the Feast of Booths (Hebrew: *Sukkot*). It is tragically ironic that the Hebrew name of the town that proved to be the most inhospitable in Jewish history denotes hospitality and divine providence.

2. The title of Sutzkever's Yiddish poem is "A Vogn Shikh" ("A Cartload of Shoes"). See Frieda Aaron, *Bearing the Unbearable* (Albany: SUNY Press, 1990), pp. 54–55.

3. Primo Levi, *Survival in Auschwitz*, trans. Stuart Woolf (New York: Collier, 1961), p. 22.

4. Arnošt Lustig, *A Prayer for Katerina Horovitzova*, trans. Jeanne Nemcova (New York: Harper and Row, 1973), pp. 50–51.

5. See, e.g., Jonathan Webber, "The Future of Auschwitz," *Religion, State and Society* 20:1 (1992): 81–100.

6. On this line of argument, see, e.g., Jacob Neusner, *Stranger at Home* (Chicago: University of Chicago Press, 1981), p. 88; and Hillel Halkin, *Letters to an American Friend: A Zionistic Polemic* (Philadelphia: Jewish Publication Society, 1977), p. 247.

7. In the words of Yizhak Arad, former chairman of Yad Va-Shem, "The lesson we have learned from the Holocaust is what it means to be on the margins of mankind, to be vulnerable, to be dependent on the good will of other people." Quoted in Leonard Fein, *Where Are We? The Inner Life of America's Jews* (New York: Harper and Row, 1988), p. 61.

8. Quoting Ella Gutman of Yad Va-Shem, Carl Schrag reports in *The Jewish Week* (April 27, 1990) that three themes that should be applied to any trip by Israelis to Poland are: "up-close study of the Holocaust; grasping the fact that Poland was the center of Jewish life and learning until World War II; and developing an understanding of the Polish people and their role in the murder of Jews."

9. See, e.g., Martin Marty, *Righteous Empire* (New York: Dial, 1970); and Winthrop S. Hudson, ed., *Nationalism and Religion in America* (New York: Harper and Row, 1970).

10. On the perception of the American Jewish experience as being essentially different from other Jewish historical experience, see, e.g., Daniel Elazar, *Community and Polity: The Organizational Dynamics of American Jewry* (Philadelphia: Jewish Publication Society, 1976), pp. 14–30.

11. A study of the historiography of the Holocaust by Israeli and American Jewish historians, particularly of works written since the 1967 war, would demonstrate this. A more complete analysis is beyond the scope of discussion here. It is significant that the official name of the day commemorating victims of the Holocaust is "Yom ha-Shoah ve-ha-Gevurah," "The Day of [Remembering] Holocaust and Heroism." As Amos Elon writes in *The Israelis* (New York: Holt, Rinehart and Winston, 1971), p. 206, ". . . the purpose of Yad Va-Shem is not only to commemorate the six million dead but also the heroism and selfless courage of those who fought back in the ghettoes and forests in order to 'save the honor of their people.' In a corner of the mind, many Israelis know there was less resistance in the ghettoes and in the forests than would appear from the voluminous speeches delivered on the subject—primarily because under the circumstances resistance was nearly impossible. But, being human, they hold onto an exaggeration that seems essential to their dignity as a group." In teaching the Holocaust to Israeli youth, instructors "are admonished first to dismiss the vicious allegation leveled against the masses of our people in the Nazi-occupied countries that they 'went like sheep to the slaughter'" (Elon, p. 208).

12. David Ben Gurion articulated an example of this revisionary history of the Jewish past. In a 1944 address he said, "The Jews are the only example of a small, exiled, and forever hated people that stood fast and never surrendered from the time of their revolt against persecution by Hadrian to the recent uprisings in the ghettos of Warsaw, Lublin, and Bialystok. Resistance by a small people for so many centuries to so many powerful enemies—to refuse to surrender to historic density—this, in short, is the essential significance of Jewish history of the Galut [Diaspora]. . . . In the Galut the Jewish people knew the courage of non-surrender. . . . [But] resisting fate is not enough. We must master our fate; we must take destiny into our hands! This is the doctrine of Jewish revolution—not non-surrender to the Galut, but making an end of it." Quoted in Arthur Hertzberg, ed., *The Zionist Idea* (Philadelphia: Jewish Publication Society, 1959), p. 609.

In Israeli literature, the Warsaw Ghetto is often called the "Masada of European Jewry." In his important study of modern Jewry, Israeli historian S. Ettinger writes, "The heroism of the [Warsaw] ghetto fighters proved to be profoundly symbolic for the remnant of Polish Jewry and for the Jewish people as a whole as the courage of the defenders of Masada had been in an earlier generation." S. Ettinger, "The Modern Period," in Hayyim Hillel Ben-Sasson, ed., *A History of the Jewish People* (Cambridge: Harvard University Press, 1976), pp. 1029–1030.

In his account of the Warsaw Ghetto uprising, American journalist Dan Kurzman writes, "[The uprising] signaled the beginning of an iron militancy rooted in the will to survive, a militancy that was to be given form and direction by the creation of the State of Israel." Dan Kurzman, *The Bravest Battle* (New York: Putnam, 1976), p. 17.

The Israeli kibbutz Yad Mordecai is named after Mordecai Anielewicz, the leader of the Warsaw Ghetto uprising. As Elon writes, "Yad Mordecai . . . commemorates Mordecai Anielewicz and the Warsaw Ghetto uprising of 1943. Yad Mordecai also played a crucial role in the [Israeli] War of Independence. The combination of both produces an essential key to an understanding of the modern Israeli temper" (*The Israelis*, p. 191).

13. On Hanukkah in Israeli civil religion, see Charles Liebman and Eliezer Don-Yehiya, *Civil Religion in Israel* (Berkeley: University of California Press, 1983), pp. 51–52.

14. Quoted in Charles S. Liebman and Steven M. Cohen, *Two Worlds of Judaism* (New Haven: Yale University Press, 1990), p. 31.

15. Soon after the Holocaust, the State of Israel entered into negotiations with West Germany for war reparations. This led to a "normalization" of relations between Israel and West Germany. As a consequence, the Poles came to be viewed in the popular Israeli imagination as the major perpetrators of the Holocaust. As one Israeli student put it, "We have to hate someone, and we've already made up with the Germans." See Tom Segev, *The Seventh Million: Israelis and the Holocaust*, trans. Haim Watzman (New York: Hill and Wang, 1993), pp. 491–492.

16. On the civil religion of America, see the groundbreaking article by Robert Bellah, "Civil Religion in America," *Daedalus* 96 (Winter 1967): 1–21. On the "civil religion" of American Jewry, see Jonathan S. Woocher, *Sacred Survival: The Civil Religion of American Jews* (Bloomington, Ind.: Indiana University Press, 1986). On Masada in the civil religion of Israel, see Liebman and Don-Yehiya, *Civil Religion*, pp. 41–44, 148–151; on the Holocaust, see pp. 137–138, 145–148, 151–153, 235–236, summarized on p. 218: "The survival of Israel is a necessary condition to the continued survival of the Jewish people."

17. Quoted in Liebman and Don-Yehiya, *Civil Religion*, p. 39.

18. From an undated letter to a "Friend of Israel," received in September 1995 and signed by Neal M. Sher, executive director of AIPAC.

19. Arthur Hertzberg, *Being Jewish in America* (New York: Schocken, 1979), p. 223.

20. Fein, *Where Are We?* p. 19.

21. Hertzberg, *Being Jewish*, p. 223.

22. Louis Jacobs, *A Jewish Theology* (New York: Behrman House, 1973), p. 281.

23. Fein, *Where Are We?* pp. 134, 142–143. See also Stephen Schwarzschild, "On the Theology of Jewish Survival," in his *The Pursuit of the Ideal* (Albany: SUNY Press, 1990), pp. 83–98.

24. Abraham Joshua Heschel, *Moral Grandeur and Spiritual Audacity* (New York: Farrar, Straus, Giroux, 1996), p. 30.

25. On the findings and implications of the study, see, e.g., Sidney Goldstein, "Profile of American Jewry: Insights from the 1990 National Jewish Population Survey," *American Jewish Yearbook* 92 (1992): 77–177.

26. See Yaffa Eliach, *Hasidic Tales of the Holocaust* (New York: Avon, 1982), pp. 3–4.

Chapter 9

1. On the synagogue built in 1644 by Isaac Yekels (i.e., Isaac ben Jacob), see, e.g., Bernhard D. Friedberg, *Luchot Sikaron* (Frankfurt: J. Kauffmann, 1904), p. 62. Isaac, far from being a poor rabbi, actually was a prosperous merchant and part of a wealthy Cracow family. Both he and his brother married into the fabulously wealthy Shrenzel-Rapoport family, also known as the Nachmanowicz family of Lwow. Isaac was the lay leader of Cracow Jewry for almost forty years, 1608–1647. He died in 1653. See Arieh L. Bauminger, ed., *Sefer Krako* (Jerusalem: Mosad ha-Rav Kook, 1959), p. 20.

2. Israel Friedlaender, *Past and Present* (Cincinnati: Ark Publishing Co. 1919), pp. 261–262. On Friedlaender's life and work, see Baila R. Shargel, *Practical Dreamer* (New York: Jewish Theological Seminary of America, 1985).

3. Friedlaender, *Past and Present*, p. 256.

4. Abraham Joshua Heschel, *Moral Grandeur and Spiritual Audacity* (New York: Farrar, Straus, Giroux, 1996), p. 30.

5. Quoted in *Newsweek*, July 22, 1991.

6. Solomon Schechter, *Seminary Addresses and Other Papers* (New York: Burning Bush Press, 1959), p. 97.

7. Quoted in Arthur Hertzberg, *The Jews in America* (New York: Simon and Schuster, 1989), p. 157.

8. Abraham Cahan, *The Rise of David Levinsky* (New York: Harper and Row, 1966), pp. 86, 87, 513.

9. Amos Elon, *The Israelis: Founders and Sons* (New York: Holt, Rinehart and Winston, 1971), p. 38.

10. Quoted in Arthur Hertzberg, ed., *The Zionist Idea* (Philadelphia: Jewish Publication Society, 1959), p. 615.

11. In a letter from Solomon to his uncle dated July 10, 1783, quoted from manuscript in Jacob Rader Marcus, *Early American Jewry* (Philadelphia: Jewish Publication Society, 1953), vol. 2, p. 153.

12. Jonathan S. Woocher, *Sacred Survival* (Bloomington: Indiana University Press, 1986), p. 132.

13. Haim Hazaz, "The Sermon," trans. Ben Halpern, in Joel Blocker, ed., *Israeli Stories* (New York: Schocken, 1962), pp. 69, 70, 71, 73. For the Hebrew original, see Haim Hazaz, *Kol Kitvei Hayyim Hazaz* (Tel Aviv: Am Oveid, 1968), vol. 1, pp. 219–238.

14. Salo Baron, *A Social and Religious History of the Jews* (New York: Columbia University Press, 1976), vol. 16, p. 35. See also Cecil Roth, "Dr. Solomon Ashkenazi and the Election to the Throne of Poland, 1574–5," *Oxford Slavonic Papers* 9 (1960): 8–20.

15. Salo Baron, *History and Jewish Historians* (Philadelphia: Jewish Publication Society, 1964), p. 96.

16. Salo Baron, *A Social and Religious History of the Jews* (New York: Columbia University Press, 1952), vol. 1 (rev. ed.), p. 297.

17. Hazaz, "The Sermon," pp. 83–84.

18. See, e.g., Joseph Nedava, "Herzl and Messianism," *Herzl Year Book* 7 (1971): 9–26.

19. See Lionel Kochan, *Jews, Idols and Messiahs* (Oxford: Basil Blackwell, 1990), pp. 184–186.

20. Schechter, *Seminary Addresses*, p. xxiv.

21. Woocher, *Sacred Survival*, p. 91.

22. Simon Dubnow, ed., *Pinkas ha-Medinah* (Berlin: Einot, 1925), p. xi.

23. See, e.g., Isaac Bashevis Singer, *Love and Exile* (New York: Farrar, Straus and Giroux, 1986), p. 55.

24. Leonard Fein, *Where Are We? The Inner Life of America's Jews* (New York: Harper and Row, 1988), p. 224.

25. Charles Liebman, *The Ambivalent American Jew* (Philadelphia: Jewish Publication Society, 1973), p. 96.

26. Ibid., p. 141.

27. Abraham Joshua Heschel, *Man Is Not Alone* (Philadelphia: Jewish Publication Society, 1951), p. 260. This story has been attributed to Rabbi Jacob Kranz, known as the Preacher of Dubnow; see Herman A. Glatt, *He Spoke in Parables: The Life and Works of the Dubno Maggid* (New York: Jay Bithmar, 1957), p. 61.

Chapter 10

1. Quoted in Moses Hayyim Efraim of Sudlikow, *Degel Mahane Efraim* (Jerusalem: n.p., 1962), "Tzav," p. 122.

2. Nahum Glatzer, ed., *Franz Rosenzweig: His Life and Thought* (New York: Schocken, 1953), p. 20.

3. Moses Hayyim Efraim of Sudlikow, *Degel Mahane Efriam*, "Bereshit," p. 6.

4. See, e.g., Aaron Wertheim, *Law and Custom in Hasidism*, trans. Shmuel Himelstein (Hoboken, N.J.: Ktav, 1992), p. 297.

5. Talmud, Abot 2:5.

6. Moses Maimonides, *Mishnah in Peirush Rabbenu Moshe ben Maimon*, trans. Joseph Kapah (Jerusalem: Mosad ha-Rav Kook, 1965), "Introduction to *Abot*," chap. 4, p. 253; Abot 2:5, pp. 286–287.

7. Quoted from *Teshuot Hein* in Gershom Scholem, *The Messianic Idea in Judaism* (New York: Schocken, 1971), pp. 195–196. *Teshuot Hein* was written by Gedalyahu ben Yitzhak (Jerusalem: n.p., 1965). On the idea of exile as a mission and as an opportunity for *tikkun* in Jewish thought in sixteenth-century Poland, see Shalom Rosenberg, "Exile and Redemption," in Bernard Dov Cooperman, ed. *Jewish Thought in the Sixteenth Century* (Cambridge: Harvard University Press, 1983), pp. 399–431.

8. Menahem Nahum of Chernobyl, *Me'or Einayim* (Jerusalem: Me'or Einayim, 1966), "Tzav," pp. 130–131.

9. Quoted by Scholem, *Messianic Idea*, p. 190.

10. See ibid., pp. 190–196.

11. Nathan Nata Shapiro of Cracow, *Sefer Megaleh Amukot* (Lwow: n.p., 1882), pp. 71b–72a, on Genesis 49:10.

12. See, e.g., Ben Zion Dinur, *Be-Mifne ha-Dorot* (Jerusalem: Bialik, 1955), pp. 181–227.

13. Menahem Nahum of Chernobyl, *Me'or Einayim*, "Ve-Ethanan," p. 195.

14. See Bernard Weinryb, *The Jews of Poland* (Philadelphia: Jewish Publication Society, 1973), p. 326.

15. That this allegorical understanding of the Land of Israel has very deep roots in Jewish thought has been demonstrated by Moshe Idel, "The Land of Israel in Medieval Kabbalah," in Lawrence A. Hoffman, ed., *The Land of Israel* (Notre Dame, Ind.: University of Notre Dame Press, 1986), pp. 170–187.

16. See Rivka Schatz Uffenheimer, *Hasidism as Mysticism*, trans. Jonathan Chipman (Princeton: Princeton University Press, 1993), pp. 326–339.

17. On these Hasidic views of being inside or outside the Land, see, e.g., Marc Saperstein, "The Land of Israel in Pre-Modern Jewish Thought," in ed. Hoffman, *The Land of Israel*, pp. 200–204. On the roots of this idea in the thirteenth-century teachings of Abraham Abulafia, see Idel, "The Land of Israel in Medieval Kabbalah," p. 179.

18. Dov Baer of Mezeritch, *Magid Devarav Le-Ya'akov*, ed. Rivka Shatz-Uffenheimer (Jerusalem: Magnes Press, 1990), no. 49, p. 70.

19. See Abraham Joshua Heschel, *Torah min ha-Shamayim* (London: Soncino, 1965), vol. 2, pp. 335–337.

20. Elimelekh of Lizensk, *No'am Elimelekh* (Lwow: n.p., 1787), "Va-Yeshev," p. 21a.

21. Representatives of the *Haskalah* or "Jewish Enlightenment," the *maskilim* made little impact in central Poland. They were, however, very active in Polish Galicia, especially in Lwow. Their long-term influence over the secularization of modern Jewry was greater than their short-term influence in Poland. On the *Haskalah* in Poland, see, e.g., Israel Zinberg, *A History of Jewish Literature*, trans. Bernard Martin (New York: Ktav, 1976), vol. 9; and Raphael Mahler, *Hasidim and the Jewish Enlightenment*, trans. Eugene Orenstein (Philadelphia: Jewish Publication Society, 1985). Hasidism was a major target of the *maskilim*, who saw the Hasidic way of life as corrupt, oppressive, and interfering with Jewish cultural assimilation. Some historians, such as Mahler, see the *Haskalah* in eastern Europe as flowing out of the movement of the *mitnagdim* against Hasidism, but this seems to me too simplified a view.

22. Foremost among the critics of Hasidism was David of Makow. See Mordecai L. Wilensky, "The Polemic of Rabbi David of Makow against Hasidism," *Proceedings of the American Academy for Jewish Research* 25 (1956): 137–156, and Wilensky's comprehensive study of the clash between the Hasidim and their opponents in his *Hasidim ve-Mitnagdim*, 2 vols. (Jerusalem: Mosad Bialik, 1970), especially the references to David of Makow throughout vol. 2.

For a presentation of the view that the points of diversion between the Hasidim and the *mitnagdim* were not as great as often had been supposed, see, e.g., Ya'acov Hasdai, "The Origins of the Conflict Between Hasidim and Mitnagdim," in Bezalel Safran, ed., *Hasidism: Continuity or Innovation?* (Cambridge: Harvard University Press, 1988), pp. 27–45. While it may be an overstatement to claim, as some have, that the Musar wing of the *mitnagdim* formulated a Hasidism for the *mitnagdim*, there are, nonetheless, close parallels between the teachings of various representatives of Hasidism and of Musar, including identical stories attributed to Hasidic and Musar masters.

23. On the Musar movement, see Dov Katz, *Tenuat ha-Musar*, 5 vols. (Tel Aviv: n.p., 1972). On the Musar movement in the twentieth century, see David E. Fishman, "The Musar Movement in Interwar Poland," in Israel Gutman et al., eds., *The Jews of Poland Between Two World Wars* (Hanover, N.H.: University Press of New England, 1989), pp. 247–271.

24. On Israel of Salant, see, e.g., Immanuel Etkes, *Rabbi Israel Salanter and the Mussar Movement*, trans. Jonathan Chipman (Philadelphia: Jewish Publication Society, 1993); Hillel Goldberg, *Israel Salanter: Text, Structure, Idea* (New York: Ktav, 1982); and Louis Ginzberg, *Students, Scholars and Saints* (Philadelphia: Jewish Publication Society, 1928), pp. 145–195.

25. See Goldberg, *Israel Salanter*, pp. 50 and 243. On p. 243 Goldberg offers the original Hebrew text of a sermon of Israel of Salant in which these ideas and terms are explicitly expressed.

Chapter 11

1. Nathan of Nemirow, *Sihot ha-Ran* (Ostrog: n.p., 1816), no. 40.

2. There are many versions of this story. See, e.g., Yoetz of Rakatz, *Siah Sarfei Kodesh* (Lodz: n.p., 1931), part 2, p. 29b; and Abraham Joshua Heschel, *The Earth Is the Lord's* (New York: Henry Schuman, 1950), pp. 106–107.

3. For another version of this prayer, see Elie Wiesel, *Souls on Fire* (New York: Random House, 1972), p. 158.

4. Abraham Joshua Heschel, *Moral Grandeur and Spiritual Audacity* (New York: Farrar, Straus, Giroux, 1996), p. 30.

5. Rakatz, *Siah Sarfei*, part 2, p. 58b.

6. See Abraham Joshua Heschel, *A Passion for Truth* (New York: Farrar, Straus and Giroux, 1973), pp. 156–165.

7. Israel Jacob Arten, *Emet ve-Emunah* (Jerusalem: n.p., 1969), p. 76.

8. Rakatz, *Siah Sarfei*, part 3, p. 5.

9. Quoted in Abraham Menes, "Patterns of Jewish Scholarship in Eastern Europe," in Louis Finkelstein, ed., *The Jews* (Philadelphia: Jewish Publication Society, 1960), p. 417.

10. These aphorisms are cited by Menes, "Patterns," pp. 414–420.

11. See Louis Ginzberg, *Students, Scholars and Saints* (Philadelphia: Jewish Publication Society, 1928), p. 174.

12. See Byron L. Sherwin and Seymour J. Cohen, *How to Be a Jew: Ethical Teachings of Judaism* (Northvale, N.J.: Jason Aronson, 1992), pp. 81–90. On pride in the Hasidic equation of pride with idolatry, see the sources collected in *Leshon Hasidim* (Lwow: n.p., 1876), p. 36.

13. Menahem Nahum of Chernobyl, *Me'or Einayim* (Jerusalem: Me'or Einayim, 1966), pp. 353–354.

14. Ibid., p. 39.

15. See sources quoted in Aryeh Kaplan, *The Light Beyond: Adventures in Hasidic Thought* (New York: Maznaim, 1981), pp. 287–300.

16. See, e.g., Morris M. Faierstein, *All Is in the Hands of Heaven: The Teachings of Rabbi Mordecai Joseph Leiner of Izbica* (New York: Yeshiva University Press, 1989), pp. 69–75.

17. See Immanuel Etkes, "Rabbi Israel Salanter and His Psychology of *Mussar*," in Arthur Green, ed., *Jewish Spirituality: From the Sixteenth Century to the Present* (New York: Crossroad, 1987), pp. 229–236.

18. See Ginzberg, *Students*, p. 434.

19. See Gershom Scholem, *On the Mystical Shape of the Godhead*, trans. Joachim Neugroschel (New York: Schocken, 1991), pp. 252–258.

20. See, e.g., Alexander Altmann, *Studies in Religious Philosophy and Mysticism* (Ithaca, N.Y.: Cornell University Press, 1969), pp. 1–40.

21. Judah Loew, *Nezah Yisrael* (New York: Judaica Press, 1969), chap. 51, p. 195. See also the discussion in Byron L. Sherwin, *Mystical Theology and Social Dissent: The Life and Works of Judah Loew of Prague* (Toronto: Associated University Presses, 1982), p. 137.

22. Elijah di Vidas, *Reshit Hokhmah* (Venice: n.p., 1579) "Sha'ar ha-Ahavah," chap. 3, sec. 7.

23. Shabbtai Sheftel Horowitz, *Shefa Tal* (Frankfurt: n.p., 1719), "Introduction." See the discussion of this motif and of this text in Louis Jacobs, *Religion and the Individual* (New York: Cambridge University Press, 1992), pp. 42–58.

24. Menahem Nahum of Chernobyl, *Me'or Einayim*, "Kedoshim," p. 142.

25. Abraham Joshua Heschel, *Man is Not Alone* (Philadelphia: Jewish Publication Society, 1951), p. 154.

26. On ascetic trends in Hasidism, see, e.g., David Biale, *Eros and the Jews* (New York: Basic Books, 1992), pp. .133–141.

27. *Zohar* II 244a.

28. See Judah Loew, *Tiferet Yisrael* (New York: Judaica Press, 1969), chap. 4, p. 16; and *Netivot Olom* (New York: Judaica Press, 1969), vol. 2, p. 130. Also see, Sherwin, *Mystical Theology*, pp. 107–123; and Yoram Jacobson, "Zelem Elohim u-Ma'amado ke-Makor Ra'ato shel Adam le'fi ha-Maharal me-Prag," *Da'at* 19 (Summer 1987): 103–136.

29. See, e.g., Gershom Scholem, *The Messianic Idea in Judaism* (New York: Schocken, 1971), p. 189.

30. Jacob Joseph of Polonnoye, "Lekh Lekhah," vol. 1 of *Toledot Ya'akov Yoseif* (Jerusalem: n.p., 1967), p. 57.

31. Elimelekh of Lizensk, *No'am Elimelekh* (Lwow: n.p., 1787), "Likkutay Shoshanah," p. 102b.

32. Judah Loew, *Derekh ha-Hayyim* (New York: Judaica Press, 1969), chap. 3, sec. 14, p. 143.

33. Isaiah Horowitz, *Sha'ar ha-Otiot*, in vol. 1 of *Shnei Luhot ha-Brit*, 2 vols. (Amsterdam, n.p., 1649), p. 53b.

34. See Louis Jacobs, "Eating as an Act of Worship in Hasidic Thought," in Siegfried Stein and Raphael Loewe, eds., *Studies in Jewish Religious and Intellectual History* (University, Ala.: University of Alabama Press, 1979), pp. 157–166.

35. See Abraham Joshua Heschel, *God in Search of Man* (Philadelphia: Jewish Publication Society, 1955), p. 99.

36. Zadok ha-Kohein of Lublin, *Tzidkat ha-Tzaddik* (New York: n.p., 1947), p. 46b.

37. Martin Buber, *Tales of the Hasidim: Early Masters*, trans. Olga Marx (New York: Schocken, 1947), p. 289.

38. For another version of this statement, see Israel Arten, p 19.

39. See Simeon Mendel of Gavartchov, *Sefer Ba'al Shem Tov* (Lodz: n.p., 1938), vol. 1, p. 144, n. 45.

40. *Likkutim Yekarim* (Lwow: n.p., 1863), p. 15b.

41. See Jacob Yurah Teshima, *Zen Buddhism and Hasidism* (Lanham, Md.: University Press of America, 1995), pp. 141–154.

42. On the debate over pilpul in sixteenth- and seventeenth-century Poland, see Elhanan Reiner, "Temurot be-Yeshivot Polin ve-Ashkenaz be-Me'ot ha-16–17, ve-ha-vikkuah al ha-pilpul," in Israel Bartal et al., eds., *Ke-Minhag Ashkenaz ve-Polin* (Jerusalem: Merkaz Zalmen Shazar, 1993), pp. 9–81.

43. See, e.g., Shelomoh Yosef Zevin, *Ishim ve-Shitot* (Tel Aviv: Zioni, 1966).

44. On Loew's critique of the contemporary rabbinate, see Sherwin, *Mystical Theology*, pp. 165–169.

45. On Judah Loew's view of *devekut* and its anticipation of and influence upon Hasidic views, see Sherwin, *Mystical Theology*, pp. 124–143; and Scholem, *Messianic Idea*, pp. 203– 227.

46. See Heschel, *Passion for Truth*, pp. 58–65.

47. Heschel, *Earth Is the Lord's*, p. 83.

48. Shneur Zelman of Liadi, *Likutei Amarim [Tanya]* (Brooklyn: Otzar ha-Hasidut, 1965), chap. 5, pp. 18–19.

49. Mordecai of Chernobyl, *Likutei Torah* (New York: Noble Printing Co., 1954), "Le-Rosh ha-Shanah," p. 22b.

50. Moses Hayyim Efraim of Sudlikow, *Degel Mahaneh Ephraim* (Jerusalem: Hadar, 1962), "Aharei," p. 175.

51. Moses Hayyim Efraim, *Degel Mahaneh Ephraim*, "Terumah," p. 119.

52. See Simon Mendel of Gavartchov, *Sefer Ba'al Shem Tov*, p. 122.

53. Moses Hayyim Efraim, *Degel Mananeh Ephraim*, "Bereshit," p. 6.

54. Judah Loew, *Tiferet Yisrael*, chap. 69, p. 216.

55. Judah Loew, *Netivot Olom*, p. 32.

56. Isaiah Horowitz, "Beth David," in vol. 1 of *Shnei Luhot ha-Brit*, pp. 25b-26a.

57. Martin Buber, *Tales of the Hasidim: Later Masters*, trans. Olga Marx (New York: Schocken, 1948), p. 116.

58. See Gershom Scholem, *On the Kabbalah and its Symbolism*, trans. Ralph Manheim (New York: Schocken, 1965), p. 47.

59. On the development of the phrase, "God, Torah, and Israel are one," see Isaiah Tishbi, "Al Mekorei ha-Ma'amar: Kudsha Brikh Hu, Torah ve-Yisrael had Hu," *Kiryat Sefer* 50 (1975): 668–674.

60. Nathan Nata Shapiro, *Megaleh Amukot—V'Ethanan* (Bnai Brak: n.p., 1992), no. 186, p. 155.

61. Judah Loew, *Netivot Olom*, vol. 1, chap. 9, "Netiv ha-Torah," p. 40.

62. See Herman A. Glatt, *He Spoke in Parables: The Life and Works of the Dubno Maggid* (New York: Jay Bithmar, 1957), p. 60.

63. Heschel, *Passion for Truth*, p. 266.

64. See Louis Jacobs, *Hasidic Thought* (New York: Behrman House, 1976), p. 205.

65. Levi Yitzhak of Berditchev, *Kedushat Levi* (Jerusalem: n.p., 1964), "Naso," pp. 206–207.

66. On the idea in Jewish mysticism that human actions affect God, see Moshe Idel, *Kabbalah: New Perspectives* (New Haven: Yale University Press, 1988), chaps. 7 and 8, especially p. 189, where "making God" is discussed. The citation from the rabbi of Apt is quoted by Idel, p. 370, from Zevi Hirsch of Zhidochow, *Ateret Zevi*, part 3, "Aharey Mot," p. 25a.

67. Sherwin, *Mystical Theology*, pp. 131–132.

68. Heschel, *Man Is Not Alone*, p. 93.

69. Ibid., p. 87.

70. See ibid., p. 164.

71. See Edels's commentary to *Baba Kamma* 30a in standard editions of the Talmud with commentaries; also in Abraham Mase-Zahav, ed., *Tokhahat Musar* (Jerusalem: n.p., 1962), pp. 30–31. In Judah Loew, see his *Hiddushei Aggadot* (New York: Judaica Press, 1969), vol. 3, p 4.

72. See, e.g., Buber, *Tales of the Hasidim*, p. 87.

73. For various versions of this story, see Gershom Scholem, *Major Trends in Jewish Mysticism* (New York: Schocken, 1946), pp. 349–350 (Scholem claims that he heard this version of the story from S. Y. Agnon); Wiesel, *Souls on Fire*, pp. 167–168; and Moshe Idel, *Hasidism* (Albany: SUNY Press, 1995), pp. 185–186.

74. Heschel, *Earth Is the Lord's*, p. 99.

75. Aaron ben Zvi Hirsch, ed., *Keter Shem Tov* (Jerusalem: n.p., 1968), p. 24b.

Chapter 12

1. Casimir had at least three legal wives, one bigamous consort, and at least two long-term mistresses. See Norman Davies, *God's Playground: A History of Poland* (New York: Columbia University Press, 1982), vol. 1, p. 102.

2. Earl Vinecour, *Polish Jews: The Final Chapter* (New York: McGraw Hill, 1977), p. 82.

3. David Ganz, *Tzemah David* (Jerusalem: Huminer, 1966), p. 177. Rattel's chronicle was published in Latin in 1523 and in German in 1585–1587.

4. See, e.g., Salo Baron, *A Social and Religious History of the Jews* (New York: Columbia University Press, 1957), vol. 3, p. 217. The name Prochownik denotes gunpowder, apparently showing the anachronistic nature of the legend. However, it may also denote "dust."

5. See, e.g., E. Ashtor, "Ibrahim Ibn Yaqub," in Cecil Roth, ed., *The World History of the Jewish People* (New Brunswick, N.J.: Rutgers University Press, 1966), pp. 305–308.

6. See, e.g., Moshe Boné, "Hebrew Inscriptions on Medieval Polish Official Coins," *Israel Numistic Bulletin* 3/4 (August–December, 1962): 88–98.

7. On Casimir's role in Polish history, see, e.g., Norman Davies, *Heart of Europe* (New York: Oxford University Press, 1984), pp. 286–291.

8. On the legend of Casimir and Esterke and its refraction both in Polish and Jewish literature, see the definitive monograph by Chone Shmeruk from which much of the information in this section has been gleaned, *The Esterke Story in Yiddish and Polish Literature: A Case Study in the Mutual Relations of Two Cultural Traditions* (Jerusalem: Hebrew University of Jerusalem, 1985). This monograph is a translation and an expansion of an earlier Hebrew study, Chone Shmeruk, "Sipur Esterke ve-Kasimir ha-Gadol," *Sifrut Yidish be-Polin* (Jerusalem: Magnes Press, 1981), pp. 206–282.

9. Simon Wiesenthal, *Krystyna*, trans. Eva Dukes, (Riverside, Calif.: Ariadne Press, 1992), p. 243.

10. See, e.g., Nechama Tec, *When Light Pierced the Darkness: Christian Rescue of Jews in Nazi-Occupied Poland* (New York: Oxford University Press, 1986).

11. See Irene Tomaszewski and Tecia Werbowski, *Zegota* (Montreal: Price-Patterson, 1994), p. 43.

12. Quoted by Tec, *When Light Pierced the Darkness*, p. 51.

13. According to some historians serious deterioration of Polish-Jewish relations began in the 1860s, after the failed Polish insurrection against the Russians. This decline gained momentum during the interwar period in the early twentieth century. See, e.g., Magdalena Opalski and Israel Bortal, *Poles and Jews: A Failed Brotherhood* (London: Brandeis University Press, 1992). Others attribute the decline to changing economic conditions in Poland, beginning in the eighteenth century; see, e.g., Hillel Levine, *Economic Origins of Anti-Semitism: Poland and Its Jews in the Early Modern Period* (New Haven: Yale University Press, 1991).

14. See, e.g., Israel Gutman, "Polish Anti-Semitism Between the Wars: An Overview," in Israel Gutman, Ezra Mendelsohn, Judah Reinharz, and Chone Shmeruk, eds., *The Jews of Poland Between Two World Wars* (Hanover, N.H.: University Press of New England, 1989), pp. 97–108.

15. Ibid., p. 105.

16. Rafael Scharf, "In Anger and in Sorrow: Toward a Polish-Jewish Dialogue," *Polin* 1 (1986): 271–272.

17. Adam Michnik, "Poland and the Jews," *New York Review of Books* (May 30, 1991): 11–12. Michnik's father is a Jew; his mother is not. Though according to Jewish law he is not a Jew, he nonetheless regards himself as such. See also Jerzy Tomaszewski, "Polish Society Through Jewish Eyes: On the Sources of Anti-Polonism," in Andrzej K. Paluch, ed., *The Jews in Poland* (Cracow: Jagiellonian University Press, 1992), vol. 1, pp. 405–418; and, also in Paluch, Krystyna Daniel and Bozena Traciewicz, "Polish-Jewish Relations in the View of the Jews in Poland," pp. 418–427.

18. Isaac Bashevis Singer, *The Manor* (New York: Dell, 1967), p. 33.

19. Alina Cala, *The Image of the Jew in Polish Folk Culture* (Jerusalem: Magnes Press, 1995).

20. Poles, who themselves were victimized in Nazi camps, strongly resent the term "Polish death camps," which seems to suggest that those camps were created by Poles. The claim that Nazi death camps were placed in Poland because the Germans recognized the strong endemic presence of Polish anti-Semitism has been made for many years. It is found in memoirs of Jewish survivors, in historical works, and in popular discussions of the Holocaust; see, e.g., Alexander Donat, *The Holocaust Kingdom* (New York: Holt, Rinehart and Winston, 1963), p. 229. Gutman writes in *The Jews of Poland*, "I summarily reject the thesis that portrays Poles as playing a part in initiating and implementing the extermination of Jews in the Holocaust. There is no documentary evidence to support the contention that the extermination camps were built in Poland because of the intensity of Polish anti-Semitism. At the same time I do not accept the opposite argument that anti-Semitism ceased to exist,

or at least was significantly weakened, in Nazi-occupied Poland. In my view anti-Semitism was an active factor and to some degree had an adverse effect on the situation of the Jews in Poland, on the possibilities of Jewish defense, and on the extent of rescue of the Jews during this period" (p. 108). The Nazi death camps were placed in Poland for a number of reasons, not the least of which was their proximity to the huge Jewish population center in that country.

21. See David Engel, "An Early Account of Polish Jewry Under Nazi and Soviet Occupation Presented to the Polish Government in Exile," *Jewish Social Studies* 45, no. 1 (Winter 1983): 1–17; and David Engel, *Facing a Holocaust: The Polish Government-in-Exile and the Jews, 1943–1945* (Chapel Hill and London: University of North Carolina Press, 1993), pp. 37–38.

22. See Richard C. Lukas, *Forgotten Holocaust: The Poles Under German Occupation* (New York: Hippocrene, 1986). Lukas writes, "As a result of almost six years of war, Poland lost 6,028,000 of its citizens, or 22 percent of its total population, the highest ratio of losses to population of any country in Europe. About 50 percent of these victims were Polish Christians and 50 percent were Polish Jews" (pp. 38–39).

23. Israel Gutman and Shmuel Krakowski, *Unequal Victims: Poles and Jews During World War Two*, trans. Ted Gorelik and Witold Jedlicki (New York: Holocaust Library, 1986).

24. For John Paul II's views on Jews and Judaism, see his collected statements on this subject in Eugene J. Fisher and Leon Klenicki, eds., *Pope John Paul II on Jews and Judaism, 1979–1986* (Washington: U.S. Catholic Conference, 1987).

25. John Paul II, *Crossing the Threshold of Hope* (New York: Knopf, 1994), p. 97.

26. The English translation of the pastoral letter cited here was privately prepared by Father Joseph Mytych of Chicago. For another translation prepared by Thomas Bird, see Carol Rittner and John K. Roth, *Memory Offended* (New York: Praeger, 1991), pp. 263–266.

27. See, e.g., Ronald Modras, *The Catholic Church and Anti-Semitism in Poland, 1933–1939* (Chur, Switzerland: Harwood Academic Publishers, 1994).

28. See, e.g., Michnik, "Poland and the Jews," p. 11.

29. See Aleksander Hertz, *The Jews in Polish Culture*, trans. Richard Laurie (Evanston, Ill.: Northwestern University Press, 1988), pp. 207–222.

30. Quoted as the motto in Shmeruk, *The Esterke Story*.

31. As David Engel demonstrates, the Polish stereotype of the Jews as communists has its roots in the interwar period, and was especially harmful to Jewish interests during the Holocaust since the Polish Government-in-Exile's policies were motivated by this view. See Engel, *Facing a Holocaust*, pp. 47–78.

32. On the Jagiellonian and Piast concepts, see Davies, *Heart of Europe*, pp. 133, 323–325. It should be noted that Davies's handling of the history of Polish Jewry lacks balance and objectivity. Some of his views are grossly insensitive, especially regarding the plight of Jews in Poland during and after the Holocaust. This is particularly unfortunate in view of the fact that Davies's work has become the definitive history of Poland in English. See Davies, *God's Playground: A History of Poland* (New York: Columbia University Press, 1982), especially vol. 2, pp. 240–267; and Lucy Dawidowicz's critique of Davies in her article, "The Curious Case of Marek Edelman," *Commentary* 83 (March 1987): 66–69.

33. See, e.g., George J. Lerski, "Dmowski, Paderewski and American Jews," *Polin* 2 (1987): 95–116.

34. Antony Polonsky, "Loving and Hating the Dead: Present-Day Polish Attitudes to the Jews," *Religion, State and Society* 20:1 (1992): 74.

35. Michnik, "Poland and the Jews," p. 11.

36. Paul B. Fenton, "Hasidic Landmarks in Present-Day Poland," *European Judaism* 23:2 (1990): 20–21. See also Jack Kugelmass, "The Rites of the Tribe: The Meaning of Poland for American Jewish Tourists," *YIVO Annual* 21 (1993): 395–453.

37. Joseph Opatoshu, *Yidn Legende un Andere Dertzeilungen* (New York: CYCO-Farlag, 1951), pp. 312–317.

38. Quoted in Shmeruk, *The Esterke Story*, p. 102.

39. Jacob Apenszlak, ed., *The Black Book of Polish Jewry: An Account of the Martyrdom of Polish Jewry Under the Nazi Occupation* (New York: American Federation for Polish Jews, 1943), p. 249.

40. Quoted in Aviva Ravel, *Faithful Unto Death: The Story of Arthur Zygielbaum* (Montreal: Workmen's Circle, 1980), pp. 178–179.

Bibliography

Classical Jewish Sources

Aaron ben Zvi Hirsch, ed. *Keter Shem Tov.* 1794. Reprint. Jerusalem: n.p., 1968.

Arten, Israel Jacob. *Emet ve-Emunah.* 1940. Reprint. Jerusalem: n.p., 1969.

Ashkenazi, Eliezer. *Ma'aseh ha-Shem.* Venice: n.p., 1583.

Avot d'Rabbi Natan. Edited by Solomon Schechter. Vienna: n.p., 1887. Reprint. New York: Feldheim, 1967. *The Fathers According to Rabbi Nathan.* Translated by Judah Goldin. New Haven: Yale University Press, 1955.

Ben Asher, Jacob. *Arba'ah Turim.* 1550. Reprint (4 vols.). New York: Grossman, n.d. (with commentaries).

Berger, Israel. *Eser Orot.* Pietrikow: Kleiman, 1907.

Di Vidas, Elijah. *Reshit Hokhmah.* Venice: n.p., 1579.

Dov Baer of Mezeritch. *Maggid Devarav Le-Ya'akov.* Edited by Rivka Shatz-Uffenheimer. Jerusalem: Magnes Press, 1990.

Edels, Samuel. *Hiddushei Aggadot.* In Talmud (with commentaries).

Elimelekh of Lizensk. *No'am Elimelekh.* Lwow: n.p., 1787.

Ganz, David. *Tzemah David.* 1591. Reprint. Jerusalem: Huminer, 1966.

Gedalyahu ben Yitzhak. *Teshuot Hein.* Reprint. Jerusalem: n.p., 1965.

Halevi, Judah. *The Kuzari.* Translated by Hartwig Hirschfeld. New York: Schocken Books, 1964.

Hanover, Nathan. *Abyss of Despair (Yaven Metzulah).* Translated by Abraham J. Mesch. New Brunswick, N.J.: Transaction Books, 1983.

Hayyim ben Bezalel. *Be'er Mayyim Hayyim.* 3 vols. London: Honig, 1969.

Horowitz, Isaiah. *Shnei Luhot ha-Brit.* 2 vols. Amsterdam: n.p., 1649.

Horowitz, Shabbtai Sheftel. *Shefa Tal.* Frankfurt: n.p., 1719.

Isaac of Dureen. *Sha'are Dura.* Cracow: n.p., 1534.

Isserles, Moses. *Responsa* (Hebrew). Edited by Asher Siev. Jerusalem: Feldheim, 1970.

——. *Torat ha-Olah.* Lwow: n.p., 1858.

Jacob Joseph of Polonnoye. *Toledot Ya'akov Yoseif.* 1780. Reprint (2 vols.) Jerusalem: n.p., 1967.

Karo, Joseph. *Shulhan Arukh* (with commentaries). Vilna: Romm, 1911.

Levi Yitzhak of Berditchev. *Kedushat Levi.* 1798. Reprint. Jerusalem: n.p., 1964.

Likkutim Yekarim. Lwow: n.p., 1863.

Loew, Judah. *Derekh Hayyim.* 1589. Reprint. New York: Judaica Press, 1969.

——. *Netivot Olom.* 1595. Reprint (2 vols.). New York: Judaica Press, 1969.

——. *Nezah Yisrael.* 1599. Reprint. New York: Judaica Press, 1969.

——. *Tiferet Yisrael.* 1599. Reprint. New York: Judaica Press, 1969.

Luria, Solomon. *Responsa* (Hebrew). Lublin: n.p., 1774.

——. *Yam Shel Shelomoh.* Stettin: Shrentzel, 1861–62.

Maimonides, Moses. *Mishnah in Peirush Rabbenu Moshe ben Maimon.* 3 vols. Translated by Joseph Kapah. Jerusalem: Mosad ha-Rav Kook, 1965.

Menahem Nahum of Chernobyl. *Me'or Einayim.* 1798. Reprint. Jerusalem: Me'or Einayim, 1966.

Mordecai of Chernobyl. *Likutei Torah.* New York: Noble Printing Co., 1954.

Moses Hayyim Efraim of Sudlikow. *Degel Mahane Efraim.* 1808. Reprint. Jerusalem: n.p., 1962.

Nathan of Nemirow. *Sihot ha-Ran.* Ostrog: n.p., 1816.

Roth, Aaron. *Shulhan ha-Tahor.* 1933. Reprint. Jerusalem: n.p., 1989.

Saadya Gaon. *The Book of Beliefs and Opinions.* Translated by Samuel Rosenblatt. New Haven: Yale University Press, 1948.

Shapiro, Nathan. *Megaleh Amukot–V'Ethanan.* 1637. Reprint. Bnai Brak: n.p., 1992.

——. *Sefer Megaleh Amukot.* Lwow: n.p., 1882.

Shneur Zalman of Liadi. *Likkutei Amarim (Tanya).* 1796. Reprint. Brooklyn: Otzar ha-Hasidut, 1965.

Simeon Mendel of Gavartchov. *Sefer Ba'al Shem Tov.* 2 vols. Lodz: n.p., 1938.

Sirkes, Joel. *Bayit Hadash.* Frankfurt: n.p., 1697.

Talmud. 20 vols. (with commentaries). Vilna: Romm, 1895.

Yoetz of Rakatz. *Siah Sarfei Kodesh.* Lodz: n.p., 1931.

Zadok ha-Kohein of Lublin. *Tzidkat ha-Tzaddik.* 1902. Reprint. New York: n.p., 1947.

Zohar. 3 vols. Vilna: Romm, 1882.

Secondary Sources

Aaron, Frieda. *Bearing the Unbearable.* Albany: SUNY Press, 1990.

Abramsky, Chimen, Maciej Jachimczyk, and Antony Polonsky, eds. *The Jews in Poland.* Oxford: Basil Blackwell, 1986.

Adelson, Alan, and Robert Lapides, eds. *Lodz Ghetto.* New York: Viking, 1989.

Alfasi, Isaac. *Ha-Hozeh mi Lublin.* Jerusalem: Mosad ha-Rav Kook, 1969.

Altmann, Alexander. *Studies in Religious Philosophy and Mysticism.* Ithaca, N.Y.: Cornell University Press. 1969.

Apenszlak, Jacob, ed. *The Black Book of Polish Jewry: An Account of the Martyrdom of Polish Jewry Under the Nazi Occupation.* New York: American Federation for Polish Jews, 1943.

Asch, Scholem. *Three Cities.* Translated by Edwin and Willma Muir. New York: G. P. Putnam's Sons, 1933.

Ashtor, E. "Ibrahim Ibn Yaqub." In Cecil Roth, ed. *The World History of the Jewish People.* New Brunswick, N.J.: Rutgers University Press, 1966. Pp. 305–308.

Assaf, Simha. "Ma-she-hu Le-Toledot Maharshal." In Saul Lieberman et al., eds. *Sefer ha-Yovel L'Khvod Levi Ginzberg.* New York: American Academy for Jewish Research, 1946. Pp. 45–63.

Balaban, Majer. *Historia Zydow w Krakowie i na Kasimierzu 1340–1868.* 2 vols. Cracow: n.p., 1931.

——. "Jacob Polak, der Baal Chillukim in Krakav, und seine Zeit." *Monatsschrift für Geschichte und Wissenschaft des Judentums* 57 (1913): 59–73, 196–210.

Baron, Salo. *History and Jewish Historians.* Philadelphia: Jewish Publication Society, 1964.
——. *A Social and Religious History of the Jews.* 17 vols. New York: Columbia University Press, 1937–76.
——. *Steeled by Adversity.* Philadelphia: Jewish Publication Society, 1971.
Bartal, Israel et al., eds. *Ke-Minhag Ashkenaz ve-Polin.* Jerusalem: Merkaz Zalmen Shazar, 1993.
Bauminger, Arieh L., ed. *Sefer Krako.* Jerusalem: Mosad ha-Rav Kook, 1959.
Bellah, Robert. "Civil Religion in America." *Daedalus* 96 (Winter 1967): 1–21.
Ben-David, Shlomo. *The Travels of Rabbi Eliezer Ashkenazi.* Translated by M. Samsonowitz. Israel: Gefen, 1982.
Ben-Sasson, Hayyim Hillel. *Hagut ve-Hanhagah.* Jerusalem: Mosad Bialik, 1959.
——, ed. *A History of the Jewish People.* Cambridge: Harvard University Press, 1976.
——. *The Reformation in Contemporary Jewish Eyes.* Jerusalem: Israel Academy of Sciences and Humanities, 1970.
Ben-Sasson, Yonah. *Mishnato ha-Iyyunit shel ha-Rama.* Jerusalem: Israel Academy of Sciences and Humanities, 1984.
Berat, Isaac, ed. *Makow-Mazowiecki Yizkor Bukh.* Tel Aviv: Makow-Mazowiecki Organization, 1969.
Bergman, Eleanora. "Gora Kalwaria: The Impact of a Hasidic Cult on the Urban Landscape of a Small Polish Town." *Polin* 5 (1990): 3–23.
Biale, David. *Eros and the Jews.* New York: Basic Books, 1992.
Blocker, Joel, ed. *Israeli Stories.* New York: Schocken, 1962.
Boné, Moshe. "Hebrew Inscriptions on Medieval Polish Official Coins." *Israel Numistic Bulletin* 3/4 (August–December 1962): 88–98.
Buber, Martin. *Tales of the Hasidim: Early Masters.* Translated by Olga Marx. New York: Schocken, 1947.
——. *Tales of the Hasidim: Later Masters.* Translated by Olga Marx. New York: Schocken, 1948.
Cahan, Abraham. *The Rise of David Levitsky.* New York: Harper and Row, 1966.
Cala, Alina. *The Image of the Jew in Polish Folk Culture.* Jerusalem: Magnes Press, 1995.
Caro, Jecheskiel. *Geschichte der Juden in Lemberg.* Cracow: Fischer, 1894.
Cooperman, Bernard Dov, ed. *Jewish Thought in the Sixteenth Century.* Cambridge: Harvard University Press, 1983.
Cygielman, Shalom A. "The Basic Privileges of the Jews of Great Poland as Reflected in Polish Historiography." *Polin* 2 (1987): 117–149.
Daniel, Krystyna, and Bozena Traciewicz. "Polish-Jewish Relations in the View of the Jews of Poland." In Andrzej K. Paluch, ed. *The Jews in Poland,* vol. 1. Cracow: Jagiellonian University, 1992. Pp. 419–427.
Davies, Norman. *God's Playground: A History of Poland.* 2 vols. New York: Columbia University Press, 1982.
——. *Heart of Europe.* New York: Oxford University Press, 1984.
Davis, Joseph M. *Yom Tov Lipman Heller, Joseph ben Isaac Ha-Levi, and Rationalism in Ashkenazic Jewish Culture, 1550–1650.* Ann Arbor, Mich.: University Microfilms, Inc., 1990.
Dawidowicz, Lucy. "The Curious Case of Marek Edelman." *Commentary* 83 (March 1987): 66–69.
Dembitzer, Chaim Nathan. *Kelilat Yofi.* Cracow: Fischer, 1888.
Dinur, Ben Zion. *Be-Mifne ha-Dorot.* Jerusalem: Mosad Bialik, 1955.
Döblin, Alfred. *Journey to Poland.* Translated by Joachim Neugroschel. New York: Paragon House Publishers, 1991.
Dobroszycki, Lucjan. "Re-Emergence and Decline of a Community: The Numerical Size of the Jewish Population in Poland, 1944–47." *YIVO Annual* 21 (1993): 3–33.

Donat, Alexander. *The Holocaust Kingdom*. New York: Holt, Rinehart and Winston, 1963.

Dubnow, Simon, ed. *Pinkas ha-Medinah*. Berlin: Einot, 1925.

Duker, Abraham G. "Polish Frankism's Duration." *Jewish Social Studies* 25 (1963): 287–333.

Elazar, Daniel. *Community and Polity: The Organizational Dynamics of American Jewry*. Philadelphia: Jewish Publication Society, 1976.

Elbaum, Jacob. "Kishrei Tarbut bein Yehudai Polin ve-Ashkenaz le-vain Yehudai Italia be-Me'ah ha-16." *Gal-Ed* 7/8 (1985): 11–40.

———. *Petihot ve-Histagrut*. Jerusalem: Magnes Press, 1990.

Eliach, Yaffa. *Hasidic Tales of the Holocaust*. New York: Avon, 1982.

Elior, Rachel. "Between *Yesh* and *Ayin*: The Doctrine of the Zaddik in the Works of Jacob Isaac, the Seer of Lublin." In Ada Rapoport-Albert and Steven J. Zipperstein, eds. *Jewish History: Essays in Honor of Chimen Abramsky*. London: Peter Halban, 1988. Pp. 393–457.

Elon, Amos. *The Israelis*. New York: Holt, Rinehart and Winston, 1971.

Engel, David. "An Early Account of Polish Jewry Under Nazi and Soviet Occupation Presented to the Polish Government in Exile." *Jewish Social Studies* 45:1 (Winter 1983): 1–17.

———. *Facing a Holocaust: The Polish Government-in-Exile and the Jews, 1943–1945*. Chapel Hill and London: University of North Carolina Press, 1993.

Epstein, Abraham. *Mishpahat Luria*. Vienna: n.p., 1901.

Etkes, Immanuel. "Rabbi Israel Salanter and His Psychology of *Mussar*." In Arthur Green, ed. *Jewish Spirituality: From the Sixteenth-Century Revival to the Present*. New York: Crossroad, 1987. Pp. 206–244.

———. *Rabbi Israel Salanter and the Musar Movement*. Translated by Jonathan Chipman. Philadelphia: Jewish Publication Society, 1993.

Ettinger, S. "The Modern Period." In Hayyim Hillel Ben-Sasson, ed. *A History of the Jewish People*. Cambridge: Harvard University Press, 1976. Pp. 727–1096.

Faierstein, Morris. *All Is in the Hands of Heaven: The Teachings of Rabbi Mordecai Joseph Leiner of Izbica*. New York: Yeshiva University Press, 1989.

Fein, Leonard. *Where Are We? The Inner Life of America's Jews*. New York: Harper and Row, 1988.

Feinstein, Aryeh Loeb. *Ir Tehillah*. Warsaw: Halter, 1885.

Fenton, Paul M. "Hasidic Landmarks in Present-Day Poland." *European Judaism* 23:2 (1990): 19–29.

Finkelstein, Louis, ed. *The Jews: Their History, Culture and Religion*. Philadelphia: Jewish Publication Society, 1960.

Fisher, Eugene J., and Leon Klenicki, eds. *Pope John Paul II on Jews and Judaism, 1979–1986*. Washington: U.S. Catholic Conference, 1987.

Fishman, David E. "The Musar Movement in Interwar Poland." In Israel Gutman et al., eds. *The Jews in Poland Between Two World Wars*. Hanover, N.H.: University Press of New England, 1989. Pp. 247–271.

Frankl, Viktor. *Man's Search for Meaning*. New York: Washington Square Press, 1963.

Friedberg, Bernard D. *Luchot Sikaron*. Frankfurt: J. Kauffman, 1904.

Friedberg, Hayyim D. *Toledot Mishpahat Shor*. Frankfurt: Kaufmann, 1901.

Friedlaender, Israel. *Past and Present*. Cincinnati: Ark Publishing Co., 1919.

Frydman, Jakow. *Pastekher in Yisroel*. Tel Aviv: Poalim Press, 1953.

Gieysztor, Aleksander. "The Beginnings of Jewish Settlement in the Polish Lands." In Antony Polonsky et al., eds. *The Jews in Poland*. Oxford: Basil Blackwell, Inc., 1986. Pp. 15–21.

Ginzberg, Louis. *Students, Scholars and Saints*. Philadelphia: Jewish Publication Society, 1928.

Glatt, Herman A. *He Spoke in Parables: The Life and Works of the Dubno Maggid.* New York: Jay Bithmar, 1957.

Glatzer, Nahum, ed. *Franz Rosenzweig: His Life and Thought.* New York: Schocken, 1953.

Goldberg, Hillel. *Israel Salanter: Text, Structure, Idea.* New York: Ktav, 1982.

Goldstein, Sidney. "Profile of American Jewry: Insights from the 1990 National Jewish Population Survey." *American Jewish Yearbook* 92 (1992): 77–177.

Graetz, Heinrich. *History of the Jews.* 6 vols. Philadelphia: Jewish Publication Society, 1967.

Green, Arthur, ed. *Jewish Spirituality: From the Sixteenth Century Revival to the Present.* New York: Crossroad, 1987.

Gutman, Israel. "Polish and Jewish Historiography on the Question of Polish-Jewish Relations During World War II." In Chimen Abramsky, Maciej Jachimczyk, and Antony Polonsky, eds. *The Jews of Poland.* Oxford: Basil Blackwell, 1986. Pp. 177–189.

Gutman, Israel, and Shmuel Krakowski. *Unequal Victims: Poles and Jews During World War Two.* Translated by Ted Gorelik and Witold Jedlicki. New York: Holocaust Library, 1986.

—— et al., eds. *The Jews in Poland Between Two World Wars.* Hanover, N.H.: University Press of New England, 1989.

Halkin, Hillel. *Letters to an American Friend: A Zionistic Polemic.* Philadelphia: Jewish Publication Society, 1977.

Halpern, Israel, ed. *Beit Yisrael be-Polin.* 2 vols. Jerusalem: Youth Department of the Zionist Organization, 1953.

——, ed. *Pinkas Arba Aratzot.* Jerusalem: Mosad Bialik, 1945.

——. *Yehudim ve-Yahadut be-Mizrah Airopa.* Jerusalem: Magnes Press, 1969.

Hasdai, Ya'acov. "The Origins of the Conflict Between Hasidim and Mitnagdim." In Bezalel Safran, ed. *Hasidism: Continuity or Innovation?* Cambridge: Harvard University Press, 1988. Pp. 27–47.

Hazaz, Haim. *Kol Kitvei Hayyim Hazaz.* 8 vols. Tel Aviv: Am Oveid, 1968.

——. "The Sermon." Translated by Ben Halpern. In Joel Blocker, ed. *Israeli Stories.* New York: Schocken, 1962. Pp. 65–86.

Heller, B., ed. *Sefer Lukow.* Tel Aviv: Former Residents of Lukow, 1968.

Hertz, Aleksander. *The Jews in Polish Culture.* Translated by Richard Laurie. Evanston, Ill.: Northwestern University Press, 1988.

Hertzberg, Arthur. *Being Jewish in America.* New York: Schocken, 1979.

——, ed. *The Zionist Idea.* Philadelphia: Jewish Publication Society, 1959.

Heschel, Abraham Joshua. *The Circle of the Baal Shem Tov.* Edited by Samuel H. Dresner. Chicago: University of Chicago Press, 1985.

——. *Der Mizrah-Europisher Yid.* New York: Schocken, 1946.

——. *The Earth is the Lord's.* New York: Henry Schuman, 1950.

——. "The Eastern European Era in Jewish History." *YIVO Annual of Jewish Social Science* 1 (1946): 86–106.

——. *God in Search of Man.* Philadelphia: Jewish Publication Society, 1955.

——. *Man is Not Alone.* Philadelphia: Jewish Publication Society, 1951.

——. *Moral Grandeur and Spiritual Audacity.* New York: Farrar, Straus, Giroux, 1996.

——. *A Passion for Truth.* New York: Farrar, Straus and Giroux, 1983.

——. *Torah min ha-Shamayim.* 2 vols. London: Soncino, 1962–1965.

Hoffman, Lawrence A., ed. *The Land of Israel.* Notre Dame, Ind.: University of Notre Dame Press, 1986.

Horodetzky, Samuel A. *Ha-Mistorin be-Yisrael.* Tel Aviv: Union of Hebrew Writers, 1961.

——. *Shalosh Me'ot Shanah shel Yahadut Polin.* Tel Aviv: Dvir, 1946.

Hudson, Winthrop S., ed. *Nationalism and Religion in America.* New York: Harper and Row, 1970.

Hundert, Gershon D. *The Jews in a Polish Private Town.* Baltimore: Johns Hopkins University Press, 1992.

——. "Some Basic Characteristics of the Jewish Experience in Poland." *Polin* 1 (1986): 28–35.

Hurwitz, Simon. *The Responsa of Solomon Luria.* New York: Bloch Publishing Co., 1938.

Idel, Moshe. "The Land of Israel in Medieval Kabbalah." In Lawrence A. Hoffman, ed. *The Land of Israel.* Notre Dame, Ind.: University of Notre Dame Press, 1986. Pp. 170–187.

——. *Hasidism.* Albany: SUNY Press, 1995.

——. *Kabbalah: New Perspectives.* New Haven: Yale University Press, 1988.

Jacobs, Louis. "Eating as an Act of Worship in Hasidic Thought." In Siegfried Stein and Raphael Loewe, eds. *Studies in Jewish Religious and Intellectual History.* University: University of Alabama Press, 1979. Pp. 157–166.

——. *Hasidic Thought.* New York: Behrman House, 1976.

——. *A Jewish Theology.* New York: Behrman House, 1973.

——. *Religion and the Individual.* New York: Cambridge University Press, 1992.

——. "The Uplifting of the Sparks." In Arthur Green, ed. *Jewish Spirituality: From the Sixteenth Century to the Present.* New York: Crossroad, 1987. Pp. 99–126.

Jacobson, Yoram. "Zelem Elohim u-Ma'amado ke-Makor Ra'ato shel ha-Adam le'fi ha-Maharal me-Prag." *Da'at* 19 (Summer 1987): 103–136.

John Paul II. *Crossing the Threshold of Hope.* New York: Knopf, 1994.

Kaplan, Aryeh. *The Light Beyond: Adventures in Hasidic Thought.* New York: Maznaim, 1981.

Kasimow, Harold, and Byron L. Sherwin, eds. *No Religion Is an Island.* Maryknoll, N.Y.: Orbis Books, 1991.

Katz, Ben-Zion. *Rabbanut, Hasidut, Haskalah.* Tel Aviv: Dvir, 1956.

Katz, Dov, ed. *Tenuat ha-Musar.* 5 vols. Tel Aviv: n.p., 1972.

Klemperer, Guttman. "The Rabbis of Prague." *Historical Judaica* 12 (1950): 51–66.

Kochan, Lionel. *Jews, Idols and Messiahs.* Oxford: Basil Blackwell, 1990.

Kugelmass, Jack. "The Rites of the Tribe: The Meaning of Poland for American Jewish Tourists." *YIVO Annual* 21 (1993): 395–453.

Kugelmass, Jack, and Jonathan Boyarin, eds. *From a Ruined Garden: The Memorial Books of Polish Jewry.* New York: Schocken, 1983.

Kurzman, Dan. *The Bravest Battle.* New York: Putnam, 1976.

Landman, Isaac, ed. *The Universal Jewish Encyclopedia.* 10 vols. 2nd ed. New York: Ktav, 1969.

Lanzmann, Claude. *Shoah: An Oral History of the Holocaust.* New York: Pantheon, 1985.

Lerski, George J. "Dmowski, Paderewski and American Jews." *Polin* 2 (1987): 95–116.

Lestchinsky, Jacob. "The Jews in the Cities of the Republic of Poland." In Deborah Dash Moore, ed. *East European Jews in Two World Wars.* Evanston, Ill.: Northwestern University Press, 1990. Pp. 103–124.

Levi, Primo. *Survival in Auschwitz.* Translated by Stuart Woolf. New York: Collier, 1961.

Levine, Hillel. *Economic Origins of Anti-Semitism: Poland and its Jews in the Early Modern Period.* New Haven: Yale University Press, 1991.

Lewin, Isaac. *The Jewish Community in Poland.* New York: Philosophical Library, 1985.

Lieberman, Saul, et al., eds. *Sefer ha-Yovel L'Khvod Levi Ginzberg.* New York: American Academy for Jewish Research, 1946.

Liebman, Charles. *The Ambivalent American Jew.* Philadelphia: Jewish Publication Society, 1973.

Liebman, Charles, and Steven M. Cohen. *Two Worlds of Judaism.* New Haven: Yale University Press, 1990.

Liebman, Charles, and Eliezer Don-Yehiya. *Civil Religion in Israel.* Berkeley: University of California Press, 1983.

Lukas, Richard C. *Forgotten Holocaust: The Poles Under German Occupation.* New York: Hippocrene, 1986.

Lustig, Arnošt. *A Prayer for Katerina Horovitzova.* Translated by Jeanne Nemcova. New York: Harper and Row, 1973.

Mahler, Raphael. *Hasidism and the Jewish Enlightenment.* Translated by Eugene Orenstein. Philadelphia: Jewish Publication Society, 1985.

——. *Toledot ha-Yehudim be-Polin.* Israel: Sifrut ha-Poalim, 1946.

Mandelbaum, David A. *Yeshivat Hokhmei Lublin.* 2 vols. Bnai Brak, Israel, 1994.

Marcus, James Rader. *Early American Jewry.* 2 vols. Philadelphia: Jewish Publication Society, 1951–1953.

Marszalek, Jozef. *Majdanek.* Warsaw: Interpress, 1986.

Marty, Martin. *Righteous Empire.* New York: Dial, 1970.

Mase-Zahav, Abraham, ed. *Tokhahat Musar.* Jerusalem: n.p., 1962.

May, Rollo. *The Cry for Myth.* New York: Delta, 1991.

Mendelsohn, Ezra. "Interwar Poland: Good or Bad for the Jews?" In Antony Polonsky et al., eds. *The Jews in Poland.* Oxford: Basil Blackwell, 1986. Pp. 130–139.

Menes, Abraham. "Patterns of Jewish Scholarship in Eastern Europe." In Louis Finkelstein, ed. *The Jews: Their History, Culture and Religion.* Philadelphia: Jewish Publication Society, 1960. Pp. 376–426.

Michnik, Adam. "Poland and the Jews." *New York Review of Books* (May 30, 1991): 11–12.

Modras, Ronald. *The Catholic Church and Anti-Semitism in Poland, 1933–1939.* Chur, Switzerland: Harwood Academic Publishers, 1994.

Moore, Deborah Dash, ed. *East European Jews in Two World Wars.* Evanston, Ill.: Northwestern University Press, 1990.

Nedava, Joseph. "Herzl and Messianism." *Herzl Year Book* 7 (1971): 9–26.

Neuman, Ephraim Fishel. *Darkhei Hayyim.* New York: Daas ha-Torah Publishing Co., 1948.

Neusner, Jacob. *Stranger At Home.* Chicago: University of Chicago Press, 1981.

Nigal, Gedaliah. *Sipurei Dibbuk be-Sifrut Yisrael.* Jerusalem: Reuben Mass, 1983.

Nissenbaum, Salmon Baruch. *Le-Korot ha-Yehudim be-Lublin.* Lublin: Feder, 1900.

Opalski, Magdalena, and Israel Bortal. *Poles and Jews: A Failed Brotherhood.* London: Brandeis University Press, 1992.

Opatoshu, Joseph. *Yidn Legende un Andere Dertzeilungen.* New York: CYCO-Farlag, 1951.

Paluch, Andrzej K., ed. *The Jews in Poland,* vol. 1. Cracow: Jagiellonian University, 1992.

Perles, J. "Geschichte der Juden in Posen." *Monatsschrift für Geschichte und Wissenschaft des Judentums* 13 (1864): 281–295, 321–334, 361–373, 408–420, 449–461.

Perles, Meir. *Megilat Yohasin.* Prague: n.p., 1864.

Pinkas Ludmir. Tel Aviv: Former Residents of Wladimir in Israel, 1962.

Polonsky, Antony. "Loving and Hating the Dead: Present-Day Polish Attitudes to the Jews." *Religion, State and Society* 20:1 (1992): 69–79.

Polonsky, Antony et al., eds. *The Jews in Old Poland, 1000–1795.* London: I. B. Tauris and Co., 1993.

Rapoport-Albert, Ada, and Steven J. Zipperstein, eds. *Jewish History: Essays in Honor of Chimen Abramsky.* London: Peter Halban, 1988.

Ravel, Aviva. *Faithful Unto Death: The Story of Arthur Zygielbaum.* Montreal: Workmen's Circle, 1980.

Reiner, Elhanan. "Temurot be-Yeshivot Polin ve-Ashkenaz be-Me'ot ha-16–17, ve-ha-vikkuah al ha-Pilpul." In Israel Bartal et al., eds. *Ke-Minhag Ashkenaz ve-Polin.* Jerusalem: Merkaz Zalmen Shazar, 1993. Pp. 9–81.

Rosenberg, Shalom. "Exile and Redemption." In Bernard Dov Cooperman, ed. *Jewish Thought in the Sixteenth Century*. Cambridge: Harvard University Press, 1983. Pp. 399–430.

Rosenstein, Neil. *The Unbroken Chain*. 2 vols. Elizabeth, N.J.: Computer Center for Jewish Genealogy, 1990.

Rosenthal, Judah. *Mehkarim*. 2 vols. Jerusalem: Reuben Mass, 1966.

Roskies, David, ed. *The Literature of Destruction: Jewish Responses to Catastrophe*. Philadelphia: Jewish Publication Society, 1988.

Roth, Cecil. "Dr. Solomon Ashkenazi and the Election to the Throne of Poland, 1574–5." *Oxford Slavonic Papers* 9 (1960): 8–20.

——, ed. *The World History of the Jewish People*. New Brunswick, N.J.: Rutgers University Press, 1966.

Roth, John K., and Carol Rittner. *Memory Offended*. New York: Prager, 1991.

Rubenstein, Richard L. *Power Struggle*. New York: Scribner's, 1974.

Safran, Bezalel, ed. *Hasidism: Continuity or Innovation?* Cambridge: Harvard University Press, 1988.

Saperstein, Marc. "The Land of Israel in Pre-Modern Jewish Thought." In Lawrence A. Hoffman, ed., *The Land of Israel*. Notre Dame, Ind.: University of Notre Dame Press, 1986. Pp. 188–209.

Scharf, Rafael. "In Anger and In Sorrow: Toward a Polish-Jewish Dialogue." *Polin* 1 (1986): 270–278.

Schatz-Uffenheimer, Rivka. *Hasidism as Mysticism*. Translated by Jonathan Chipman. Princeton, N.J.: Princeton University Press, 1973.

Schechter, Solomon. *Seminary Addresses and Other Papers*. New York: Burning Bush Press, 1959.

Schochet, Elijah J. *Bach: Rabbi Joel Sirkes*. New York: Feldheim, 1971.

Scholem, Gershom. *Major Trends in Jewish Mysticism*. New York: Schocken, 1946.

——. *The Messianic Idea in Judaism*. New York: Schocken, 1971.

——. *On the Kabbalah and Its Symbolism*. Translated by Ralph Manheim. New York: Schocken, 1965.

——. *On the Mystical Shape of the Godhead*. Translated by Joachim Neugroschel. New York: Schocken, 1991.

Schwartz, Howard, and Anthony Rudolf, eds. *Voices Within the Ark*. New York: Avon Books, 1980.

Schwarzschild, Stephen. *The Pursuit of the Ideal*. Albany: SUNY Press, 1990.

Segev, Tom. *The Seventh Million: Israelis and the Holocaust*. Translated by Haim Watzman. New York: Hill and Wang, 1993.

Shapiro, Jacob L. *Mishpahot Atikot Be-Yisrael*. Tel Aviv: Holiot, 1981.

Shargel, Baila R. *Practical Dreamer*. New York: Jewish Theological Seminary of America, 1985.

Sherwin, Byron L. "In the Shadows of Greatness: Rabbi Hayyim ben Betsalel of Friedberg." *Jewish Social Studies* 37:1 (1975): 35–61.

——. "My Master." In Harold Kasimow and Byron L. Sherwin, eds. *No Religion Is an Island*. Maryknoll, N.Y.: Orbis Books, 1991. Pp. 42–62.

——. *Mystical Theology and Social Dissent: The Life and Works of Judah Loew of Prague*. London: Associated University Presses, 1982.

Sherwin, Byron L., and Seymour J. Cohen. *How to Be a Jew: Ethical Teachings of Judaism*. Northvale, N.J.: Jason Aronson, 1992.

Shmeruk, Chone. *The Esterke Story in Yiddish and Polish Literature: A Case Study in the Mutual Relations of Two Cultural Traditions*. Jerusalem: Hebrew University of Jerusalem, 1985.

———. *Sifrut Yidish be-Polin.* Jerusalem: Magnes Press, 1981.

Shulman, Nisson. *Authority and Community: Polish Jewry in the Sixteenth Century.* New York: Yeshiva University Press, 1986.

Shulvass, Moses. *Between the Rhine and the Bosporus.* Chicago: College of Jewish Studies Press, 1964.

———. "Ha-Torah ve-Limude-ha be-Polin Ve-Lita." In Israel Halpern, ed. *Beit Yisrael be-Polin,* vol. 2. Jerusalem: Youth Department of the Zionist Organization, 1953. Pp. 13–35.

———. *Jewish Culture in Eastern Europe.* New York: Ktav, 1975.

Siev, Asher. *Ramo.* New York: Yeshiva University Press, 1972.

Singer, Isaac Bashevis. *Love and Exile.* New York: Farrar, Straus and Giroux, 1986.

———. *The Manor.* New York: Dell, 1967.

Stein, Siegfried, and Raphael Loewe, eds. *Studies in Jewish Religious and Intellectual History.* University: University of Alabama Press, 1979.

Stein, William. "Cracow." In Isaac Landman, ed. *The Universal Jewish Encyclopedia.* 2nd ed. New York: Ktav, 1969. vol. 3. Pp. 392–394.

Tchernowitz, Chaim. *Toledot ha-Poskim.* 3 vols. New York: Jubilee Committee, 1947.

Tec, Nechama. *When Light Pierced the Darkness: Christian Rescue of Jews in Nazi-Occupied Poland.* New York: Oxford University Press, 1986.

Teshima, Jacob Yuroh. *Zen Buddhism and Hasidism.* Lanham, Md.: University Press of America, 1995.

Tishbi, Isaiah. "Al Mekorei ha-Ma'amar: Kudsha Brikh Hu, Torah, ve-Yisrael had Hu." *Kiryat Sefer* 50 (1975): 668–674.

Tomaszewski, Irene and Tecia Werbowski. *Zegota.* Montreal: Price-Patterson, 1994.

Tomaszewski, Jerzy. "Polish Society Through Jewish Eyes: On Sources of Anti-Polonism." In Andrzej K. Paluch, ed. *The Jews in Poland,* vol. 1. Cracow: Jagiellonian University Press, 1992. Pp. 405–418.

Twersky, Isadore. "The *Shulhan Arukh:* Enduring Code of Jewish Law." *Judaism* 16 (1967): 141–159.

Vetulani, Adam. "The Jews in Medieval Poland." *The Journal of Jewish Sociology* 4:2 (1962): 274–294.

Vinecour, Earl. *Polish Jews: The Final Chapter.* New York: McGraw-Hill, 1977.

Vishniac, Roman. *Polish Jews.* New York: Schocken, 1947.

Vromen, Suzanne. "The Ambiguity of Nostalgia." *YIVO Annual* 21 (1993): 69–86.

Webber, Jonathan. "The Future of Auschwitz." *Religion, State and Society* 20:1 (1992): 81–100.

Weinryb, Bernard. *The Jews of Poland.* Philadelphia: Jewish Publication Society, 1972.

Weinstock, Moses Jair. *Tiferet Beit David.* Jerusalem: n.p., 1968.

Wertheim, Aaron. *Law and Custom in Hasidism.* Translated by Shmuel Himelstein. Hoboken, N.J.: Ktav, 1992.

Wettstein, P. *Le-Toledot Yisrael ve-Hokhamav be-Polin.* Cracow: Ha-Eshkol, 1908.

Wiener, Samuel, ed. *Da'at Kedoshim.* St. Petersburg: Berman and Co., 1897.

Wiesel, Elie. *Four Hasidic Masters.* Notre Dame, Ind.: University of Notre Dame Press, 1978.

———. *Souls on Fire.* New York: Random House, 1972.

Wiesenthal, Simon. *Krystyna.* Translated by Eva Dukes. Riverside, Calif.: Ariadne Press, 1992.

Wilensky, Mordecai L. *Hasidim ve-Mitnagdim.* 2 vols. Jerusalem: Mosad Bialik, 1970.

———. "The Polemic of Rabbi David of Makow Against Hasidism." *Proceedings of the American Academy for Jewish Research* 25 (1956): 137–156.

Williams, George H. *The Radical Reformation.* Philadelphia: Westminster Press, 1975.

Wolfson, Elliot R. *Along the Path.* Albany: SUNY Press, 1995.

Wolfson, Harry A. *Philo.* 2 vols. Cambridge: Harvard University Press, 1947.

Woocher, Jonathan S. *Sacred Survival: The Civil Religion of American Jews*. Bloomington: Indiana University Press, 1986.

Wyrozumska, Bozena. "Did King Jan Olbracht Banish the Jews from Cracow?" In Andrzej Paluch, ed., *The Jews of Poland, Vol. 1*. Cracow: Jagiellonian University, 1992. Pp. 27–37.

Zable, Arnold. *Jewels and Ashes*. New York: Harcourt Brace, 1991.

Zevin, Shelomoh Yosef. *Ishim ve-Shitot*. Tel Aviv: Zioni, 1966.

Zinberg, Israel. *A History of Jewish Literature*. 12 vols. Translated by Bernard Martin. New York: Ktav, 1972–1978.

Zunz, Jehiel M. *Ir ha-Zedek*. Lwow: Verfassers, 1874.